D0065085

The Forming of the
Communist International

James W. Hulse

The Forming of the
Communist International

Stanford University Press, Stanford, California *1964*

Stanford University Press
Stanford, California
© 1964 by the Board of Trustees of the
Leland Stanford Junior University
All rights reserved
Library of Congress Catalog Card Number: 64-12072
Printed in the United States of America
Published with the assistance of the Ford Foundation

Preface

One of the popular clichés of our time is that the struggle between the free world and the Communist bloc is a "battle for men's minds," an ideological contest for the emotional and intellectual endorsement of the so-called uncommitted peoples of the world. The cliché is partly true, but like most catchy phrases it leaves a greater truth unsaid. The struggle is also a test of organizational talent. Communists do not have to win the battle for men's minds in order to seize power. In the countries in which they have set up the Soviet system of government, they did not first convert the citizenry to the principles of Marxism-Leninism. Careful organization was the chief ingredient of Communist success in the past forty-five years.

Although students of Communism have long recognized the importance of the Bolsheviks' organizational weapons, they have given little serious study to the most daring organizational venture Moscow ever undertook. Until recently, neither Western nor Russian writers had produced a balanced, authoritative history of the Third, or Communist, International. Scholars in the West have too frequently judged the entire history of the Third International, which operated from 1919 to 1943, in the light of its record during the Stalin years, when it became a mere pawn of Russian foreign policy. Those who watched the puppet-like conduct of the Communist parties of the world in the 1930's, and who marked Stalin's casual, unilateral abolition of the organization in 1943, tended to assume that it had been founded simply as an instrument of Kremlin conspiracy. Moreover, most Western writers have underemphasized the first fifteen months of the Comintern's operation because the First Congress (March 1919) was obviously staged and artificial, and contact with member parties during the first few months was irregular. They assumed that the real work began at the Second Congress (July–August 1920), with the adoption of the Twenty-one Conditions for member parties, and the plan for splitting the European Socialist movement into Communist and Socialist camps.

This study seeks to show that the period prior to the Second Congress was far more important than has been recognized, and that the aims of the Comintern underwent a substantial change in the first fifteen months of its existence. In spring 1919, the hope and expectation of an immediate revolution inspired the work of the Bolsheviks. The leaders of the First Congress believed that the triumph of Communism was so near in Europe that nothing could prevent it, and that their mission was to prepare the workers for their historically inevitable role. Once the proletariat was aware of its role, it would automatically revolt, create institutions on the soviet model, and join hands with its comrades in Soviet Russia and elsewhere. Propaganda, then, directed toward the working class, was the Comintern's first task.

History, however, did not take the expected course. Bad communications between Soviet Russia and its Western sympathizers, plus a tendency of the Western revolutionaries to approach their problems differently from the Bolsheviks, gave the first member parties of the Comintern a degree of independence that no subsequent parties have ever had. When the revolution did not occur according to the Leninist schedule in 1919 or early 1920, the Bolsheviks shifted their emphasis from propaganda to organization, and from a frank advocacy of their policies to a semiconspiratorial operation. They came to see that they needed a better organizational system and a tighter network of control; revolutionary agitation, they admitted, might have to wait upon institutional decision.

This change in emphasis was indirectly an admission of failure. The Bolsheviks had founded the Comintern on the assumption that they were engaged in a battle for men's minds. It was to be a symbol as well as an instrument of the revolution—a mystical union of the workers, and a banner of the new world order that would bring Marxian justice to the oppressed. This work attempts to show how this founding dream began to degenerate into a clumsy attempt to build a far-flung club of like-minded fanatics, dedicated more to an institution than to a mission—how a messianic idea became transformed, under the pressure of events, into an exercise in political manipulation. The study concentrates on the Bolsheviks' efforts in Europe, since this was the main arena for Comintern activity up to the time of the Second Congress.

I am deeply indebted to Professors Wayne Vucinich, Robert North, and Anatole Mazour for their extensive and patient help in bringing this manuscript to its present state. I also owe special gratitude to the staff of the Hoover Institution on War, Revolution, and Peace, in particular to Irene Hoggan, Marie Benton, Judy Finley, Helga Tyler, Arline Paul, and Witold Sworakowski, for assistance with research problems. Mrs. Olga Hess Gankin and Branko Lazitch gave thoughtful readings to the manuscript and offered valuable critical comments. Further thanks go to Gabor Vermes for help with translations, and to Mr. and Mrs. William James and Mr. and Mrs. Donald Baker for encouragement and technical advice. Above all, I am indebted to my wife, whose patience and endurance have been unlimited. I alone, of course, am responsible for the weaknesses and errors in this work.

J. W. H.

University of Nevada
September 1963

Contents

Abbreviations

AFL	American Federation of Labor
BSP	British Socialist Party
CPGB	Communist Party of Great Britain
ECCI	Executive Committee of the Communist International
ILP	Independent Labour Party
IWW	Industrial Workers of the World
KAPD	Kommunistische Arbeiter-Partei Deutschlands
KPD	Kommunistische Partei Deutschlands
PSF	Parti Socialiste Français
SLP	Socialist Labour Party
SPD	Sozialdemokratische Partei Deutschlands
SWSS	South Wales Socialist Society
USPD	Unabhängige Sozialdemokratische Partei Deutschlands
WSF	Workers' Socialist Federation

The Forming of the
Communist International

Chapter one   Preliminaries to the First Congress

The organizational history of the Communist International begins with a riddle. The radio station of the Soviet government directed a broadcast to revolutionary groups throughout the world on January 24, 1919, inviting them to send representatives to a congress that would create a new Communist International. The invitation asserted that the establishment of a revolutionary International was urgently necessary, but it did not specify a time or place for the delegates to meet.[1] The Bolshevik leaders apparently did not repeat the invitation, and between January 24 and the beginning of the conference on March 2 they made no further efforts to draw attention to their plan. When the conference opened in the Moscow Kremlin, a veil of secrecy surrounded its early sessions, even though the messianic nature of the proposed organization had previously been stressed. These circumstances have never been adequately explained.[2]

Lenin's desire to create a new International, however, was no secret, and there should have been little doubt about the importance he attached to it. He had long dreamed of reviving Marx's International Workingmen's Association (1864–76), and he had been associated with the Second International, which had been founded in 1889 and had regarded itself as the successor to Marx's "first" International. He became active in the Second International in the early 1900's, but disliked its loose organizational form and the moderate, revisionist policies of many of its leaders, who came from the democratically inclined, relatively liberal Socialist parties of Europe. His interest in a Third International dated from the outbreak of World War I, when nearly all the leading Socialists of Europe had violated a pledge made in 1907 to resist international war, and had supported the war efforts of their respective governments. This convinced him that the Second International was led by traitors to the working class; he adopted the position that the Socialists of the Right and Center—with liberal or moderate programs—were enemies of the proletariat because they put national struggles before the class struggle. On November 1, 1914, as he was beginning his wartime exile in Switzerland, he published a manifesto for the Bolsheviks in which he called for a "proletarian International purged of opportunism." He participated in the Socialist Conferences at Zimmerwald (September 1915) and Kienthal (April 1916), and organized the so-called Zimmerwald Left.

The moderate Socialists, who were in a majority at these conferences, hoped to restore the unity of the old International, but Lenin insisted that there could be no reconstruction of the Second International after the war because it had been identified, by the conduct of its leaders, with patriotism to bourgeois governments and with treason to the working class. He demanded a completely new organization, and frequently repeated this message in his writings throughout the war period.[3] However, no effective international organization of Socialists or Communists was possible while the war lasted; and Lenin, who had his hands full governing Russia and defending the Bolsheviks after the October Revolution, made no effort to establish his organization until early in 1919.

The man most closely associated with Lenin in his efforts to found a new International was Gregory Zinoviev. Zinoviev had shared the Swiss exile, the sessions at Zimmerwald and Kienthal, the return to Russia in spring 1917, and the early experiences of the Bolshevik revolution and government. He had prepared some of the documents of the Zimmerwald Left, and in 1915, after the first conference, he declared that a cornerstone of the new International had been laid.[4] A few months later he modified this statement by writing that one could not claim "with a clear conscience" that Zimmerwald had actually provided the "embryo of the Third International," but it had improved the chances for such a body.[5] After his return to Russia and following the October Revolution, he became president of the Petrograd Soviet, and he frequently used that office to publicize the need for the new organization.[6]

At the end of 1918, conditions in Europe convinced Lenin and Zinoviev that the time was at hand to create the International. First, the social and economic chaos of Europe in those post-armistice weeks—and specifically the revolutionary disorders in Central Europe—gave the Bolsheviks hope for an immediate proletarian uprising. Second, the Allies were still intervening in the Russian civil war: they did not seem inclined to withdraw the troops they had sent to Russia in 1918 or to end their blockade of the Soviet-held territory. Had they done so, the Bolsheviks might have been induced to postpone the formation of the International. Third, the sudden appearance of a Communist party in Germany suggested it was time to act. Finally, Lenin feared that the leaders of the Second International would injure the revolutionary movement if their efforts to resuscitate the old organization were successful.

Revolutionary Potential in Europe

These calculations were all based on an awareness of Europe's intense distress at the end of the war; the material and moral dislocations were so extensive and so obvious that even many Westerners felt that a way of life was perishing. John Maynard Keynes, in Europe during the memorable early months of 1919, saw and soon recorded "the fearful convulsions of a dying civilization."[7] In Central Europe, the popularity of Oswald Spengler's *The Decline of the West* reflected the general sense of pessimism. The destruction of the Austro-Hungarian Empire by military defeat and nationalist secession, and the overthrow of the German imperial regime, were only the most obvious manifestations of the death of an era. But whereas many Europeans regarded this change with alarm and regret, the Bolsheviks saw it as a necessary and fortunate development that would end in the creation of a new society ruled by the proletariat.

On the basis of their own revolutionary experience, they anticipated a revolution by German and Austro-Hungarian soviets in the near future. In a speech celebrating the November 3 Austro-Hungarian *coup d'état,* Lenin rejoiced that the Russian soviets now had "millions of allies" among the workers of Central Europe: "We are waging a war not only against Russian capitalism; we are fighting against the capitalism of all countries, against world-wide capitalism, for the freedom of all workers."[8] And a few days later, in a speech commemorating the first anniversary of the October Revolution, he remarked that the countries of Central Europe were experiencing a revolution like the one of 1917 in Russia. "When we took power in October, we represented no more than an isolated spark in Europe. The sparks have multiplied, and they came from us."[9] He regarded the creation of a multinational agency that would coordinate the revolutionary movement as a necessity, and near the end of December he wrote a letter to G. V. Chicherin, the Commissar of Foreign Affairs, suggesting February 1 as an approximate date for a conference of Communists and Left Social Democrats from all countries.[10]

Zinoviev shared the conviction that the unrest in Europe required the early creation of the Communist International. On December 4, he wrote that the revolutions were molding the new organization, "which will finally take shape in an International Congress of Soviets of Workers' and Soldiers' Deputies. The time is not far distant."[11] On December 19, he told an international meeting of revolutionaries who had assembled in Petrograd under the leadership of Maxim Gorky that their gathering was "only a small prelude to a great congress of the real Third International," which Zinoviev expected would meet in the near future.[12]

The Bolsheviks' Quest for Peace

In spite of their eagerness to establish a new International, the Bolsheviks hesitated because they wanted first to end the Allies' intervention in the Russian civil war. The presence of thousands of Allied troops in Archangel, Murmansk, and Siberia was a constant source of worry, not only because of the support they gave to anti-Communist forces but also because of the possibility that their operations would be expanded. Lenin had become convinced during the final phases of the war that capitalist nations would turn on the Soviet regime with all their military power once Germany and Austria-Hungary had been defeated, but the Bolsheviks nevertheless tried to engage in peace negotiations with the victorious governments for several weeks after the armistice of November 11. In his appeals to the West on behalf of the

Soviet government late in 1918, Chicherin frequently asserted that the Socialist and capitalist systems could live at peace. In a typical dispatch, dated December 2, he argued that the "Russian Socialist Soviet Republic has never menaced or tried to invade the Entente countries."[13] On December 24, in an appeal to President Woodrow Wilson, Maxim Litvinov assured the President that the workers of Russia were "aiming at nothing but their own happiness and international brotherhood, constituting no menace to other nations."[14] Although the frequent repetition of this argument was based on considerations of propaganda, the Bolsheviks made a genuine effort to convince the Allies of their good faith, and this effort would not have been served by the creation of an international revolutionary society.

Late in December or early in January, the attitude of the Bolsheviks changed. They abandoned hope for an early settlement with the Allied powers. On January 10, Litvinov and V. V. Vorovsky, who were serving the Soviet regime in Stockholm, wrote a letter in which they expressed the new attitude. After observing that the Western governments had not responded to any Bolshevik peace offer, they concluded that "as long as the Allies continue to show no sign of their willingness to enter into some kind of formal or informal negotiations, no useful purpose would be served by any further peace proposals or declarations on the part of Russia."[15]

This reappraisal may have had an effect on the Bolsheviks' plans for the Third International. If there were no hope for peace, then one reason for delaying the creation of the new revolutionary body was removed. On the other hand, even if the Allies had been willing to negotiate, it is unlikely that the Bolsheviks would have abandoned the goal of a revolutionary International completely; they were too committed to the idea of world revolution. But they might have temporarily muted the phase of their foreign policy that was most objectionable to the West.* Lenin was well aware that the creation of his type of International could anger the Allied leaders; shortly after the Com-

---

* There was precedent for such conduct. For example, after signing the Treaty of Brest-Litovsk, the Soviet leaders had practiced a dual policy of cooperating with the German Imperial government while spreading revolutionary propaganda among its subjects. When the German government objected, the Bolsheviks pretended to restrict their revolutionary activity. See Carr, *History,* III, pp. 75–76.

intern was organized, he remarked that the "jingoes" of England and France would use it as an excuse for further action against the Bolsheviks.[16] He undoubtedly held the same opinion earlier.

In proposing the thesis that the abandonment of the hope for peace was partially responsible for the timing of the decision, one must account for the so-called Prinkipo proposal, which the Allies addressed to the belligerents in the Russian civil war on January 22. The Allied governments proposed that all factions in the Russian war send representatives to Prinkipo Island for consultation on February 15.[17] If it could be proved that the Bolsheviks were aware of this invitation, and then persisted in issuing their invitation for a new International two days later, our thesis would hardly hold.

The Soviet leaders, however, may not have known of the Prinkipo proposal at the time they broadcasted the invitation for the First Congress, and if they were aware of the offer, it had come to their attention so recently and there were so many doubts about its authenticity that it did not immediately alter their existing plans. The invitation to the First Congress had been drafted about January 21, and was first published in *Pravda* on January 24. No treatment of the Prinkipo matter appeared in the newspaper until January 25, and then the Bolsheviks hesitated to treat it as genuine. As received in Moscow, the proposal was only a radio telegram, and the Russians knew only that it had come from the Paris radio; they could not be certain that it came from responsible quarters, for it was unsigned. Since Allied diplomats were "great formalists," it was not yet possible to regard the announcement as a "real proposal."[18] The Bolsheviks waited without result for an official invitation or a more satisfactory approach from the Allies, and on February 4, Chicherin complained that the Soviet government had not yet received any formal notice of the meeting and had relied upon radiogram reviews of the press.[19] Nevertheless, the Bolsheviks responded favorably to the proposal, and their hopes for a negotiated settlement rose.

This may have been why the Soviet radio and press kept quiet about the proposed First Congress during the weeks after January 24; Lenin and his colleagues may have waited to avoid jeopardizing the new possibility of negotiations.

The German Communist Party

Another consideration that retarded the organization of a Third International prior to January 1919 was the absence of strong, independent revolutionary parties in the important industrial nations of Western and Central Europe. The Bolsheviks put considerable emphasis on the need for a separate Communist party in Germany as a prerequisite for a strong International. Until the very end of 1918, those persons whom the Bolsheviks regarded as true revolutionaries in Germany were still affiliated, in most cases, with the despised Social Democrats. Early in January, just as the Bolshevik high command was despairing of a peace settlement with the Allies, they received news that the German Communists had formed a separate party, the Kommunistische Partei Deutschlands (KPD).

Two divisions had occurred within the German Socialist movement between 1914 and 1919 to bring about the creation of a Communist party. In 1914, a single organization, the Sozialdemokratische Partei Deutschlands (SPD), had at least the formal allegiance of all Socialists in the country. With the outbreak of the war, all members of the party in the Reichstag had voted for war credits, to the amazement and disgust of Lenin. As the war continued, a growing number of party members objected to the military policies of the government, and in 1916 a pacifist wing broke away to establish the Unabhängige Sozialdemokratische Partei Deutschlands (USPD), usually known abroad as the Independents. This group contended that the monarchists, militarists, and industrialists had won control of the SPD and were prolonging the war unnecessarily. This view placed the USPD nearer the position of Lenin, but within the new organization there still existed a wide range of opinion. Some members remained liberal and revisionist, while others formed a militant, revolutionary faction known as the Spartakusbund. Rosa Luxemburg and Karl Liebknecht, well-known philosophical revolutionaries, led this group, and they gradually became dissatisfied with the program of the USPD. On December 30, 1918, the Spartakusbund produced another split in the Socialist movement by creating the KPD.

This turn of events alone did not persuade the Bolsheviks to create the Third International, even though they regarded the formation of a German Communist party as a prerequisite for their plan. There had been long-standing disagreements between Luxemburg and Lenin on several theoretical matters, despite their common belief in the necessity for violent revolution. They did not share the same opinions about the relationship between the party and the masses, Luxemburg being much more interested than Lenin in educating the workers and winning their allegiance prior to the revolutionary explosion.[20] She was convinced that premature revolutionary action, or the precipitate creation of an International without adequate participation of the laborers, would injure the revolutionary movement. She felt so strongly about this that she designated one of her supporters, Hugo Eberlein, to leave for Moscow during January to oppose Lenin's plan for a Third International.[21]

Lenin must have anticipated such objections from the German revolutionaries, and it is doubtful whether he would have proceeded to execute his plan for the Comintern if opposition from such respected quarters had been sustained.

Ironically, Luxemburg and Liebknecht were killed in Berlin on January 15 as a result of a premature attempt at revolution that they had neither planned nor endorsed. Their admirers regarded their deaths as a misfortune for the movement, but their removal from the scene made things easier for those who wanted to organize the International. From now on, Lenin and other Bolshevik writers began to mark the foundation of the KPD as the signal of the birth of the Communist International. On January 18, *Pravda* carried a dramatic and emotional account of the murders, and on January 21 (the day the invitation to the First Congress was drafted) Lenin wrote a letter to the West claiming that with the creation of the KPD "the foundation of the truly proletarian, truly international, truly revolutionary Third International—the Communist International—became a fact. Formally, this foundation has not yet been accomplished, but in effect the Third International now already exists." In connection with the KPD, the letter mentioned the martyred German leaders in a manner which implied that they had endorsed the idea of the Third International.[22]

The assertion that the Communist International came into being automatically in 1918 became a standard part of the Bolshevik historical view. After the March Congress of 1919 had performed the formalities of creating the Comintern with a group of so-called delegates who were not actual representatives of the various countries, the Bolsheviks frequently related the creation of the International to the foundation of the KPD, as well as to events earlier than that, in order to deemphasize the role of the questionable March Congress.[23]

The Berne Congress

Although the possibility of peace with the Allies and the developments in Germany helped to shape planning in Moscow, it was the leaders of the Second International who provided the Bolsheviks with the strongest provocation to action. Lenin had long been concerned lest such prominent Socialists as Ramsay MacDonald in Great Britain, Jean Longuet in France, and Karl Kautsky in Germany would trick the workers into abandoning the goal of a violent revolution. These fears multiplied when it became known in December 1918 that leaders of the Second International—including MacDonald, Longuet, and Kautsky—were planning to hold meetings in Lausanne in January to try to rebuild the Socialist unity that had been shattered by the war. Bolshevik propaganda, which had consistently tried to discredit the moderate and quasi-revolutionary Socialists, quickly registered its disapproval, and implored the workers of the West to disregard the meetings.[24] The leaders of the Second International, however, did not alter their plans substantially. Except for being held in Berne rather than in Lausanne, and in February rather than in January, the International Labor and Socialist Congress of Berne, as the meetings were called, took place as arranged.

Socialists in Great Britain, France, Germany, and several smaller countries had been eager to rebuild the old International as soon as possible, because during the war all efforts to convene a major Socialist conference had failed. Even with the hostilities ended, many obstacles confronted those who were attempting to restore Socialist unity. Not only had the Bolsheviks characterized the Right and Center Socialists as class traitors, but also several other Socialist groups had declined to participate, notably the Socialist parties of Italy, Switzerland,

Serbia, and Rumania, the Spartakusbund of Germany, and the "Narrow" Socialists (Tesniaks) of Bulgaria. The Belgian Socialist Party and the American Federation of Labor decided to boycott any congress attended by representatives of parties that had supported the governments of the Central Powers. These tensions kept many party representatives away from Berne, and the question of war guilt caused trouble among those who were there.

Since most of the Left Socialist groups had boycotted the Congress, the reformist wing predominated. The leading participants were Kautsky, Hermann Müller, and Kurt Eisner of Germany; Friedrich Adler of Austria; Arthur Henderson and MacDonald of Great Britain; Longuet, Marcel Cachin, Pierre Renaudel, and Albert Thomas of France; and Paul Axelrod of the Russian Mensheviks. The Bolsheviks had identified all these men as "class traitors," "social chauvinists," or "social patriots." Hjalmar Branting of Sweden became president of the Congress, and in his opening remarks he criticized the Bolsheviks' theory of the dictatorship of the proletariat, and accused the Russians of creating a terrorist regime.[25] Many of the 102 delegates (from twenty-six countries) disagreed with Branting's criticism of the Bolsheviks, but a majority of them demonstrated near the end of the Congress that they agreed with his dedication to liberal principles. The debate on these matters, as reported in garbled form in Moscow over a two-week period, provided the Russians with plenty of propaganda material.

Branting became the foremost proponent of a successful resolution pledging the conference to democracy and liberty as opposed to a system of rule by a single class. This resolution endorsed such principles as freedom of speech and of the press, freedom of assembly, universal suffrage, a parliamentary system based on popular will, and the right of free association. Most of these ideals had been described as bourgeois tricks by the Bolsheviks. The Branting resolution did not specifically condemn Russia's current experiment with Socialism, although it disapproved of the main tactics and goals of Lenin's party and government. It said a dictatorship of a single class would lead to a "dictatorship of reaction."[26] It allowed for future reconciliation by authorizing an investigating committee to assemble information on Soviet Russia for the use of a subsequent congress.

The minority that opposed the Branting resolution supported an alternative statement put forward by Adler and Longuet. The Adler-Longuet group objected to the Branting resolution on the following grounds: first, no stigma should be placed on the Soviet government, since any judgment made at this stage would be based on inadequate evidence; second, the Berne Congress was a preliminary venture, and it should not endorse any statements which might prejudice future relations with parties that were at present opposed to the Second International; and, third, the Branting resolution could be used by the bourgeoisie to damage Socialism.[27] The attitudes of these two blocs foreshadowed the positions to be taken in later years by the Second International and the Two-and-a-Half International.

A third resolution put the Bolshevik arguments before the Congress, but without result. Fernand Loriot, a French delegate associated with the Zimmerwald Left, attended the Berne sessions in order to make a Lenin-like indictment of the Right and Center Socialists for their conduct during the war. Although his statement had no effect on the conference—the delegates did not even vote on it—the Bolsheviks later attached importance to it.

For the founders of the Third International, the Branting resolution seemed to be the essence of the Berne Congress. It confirmed their worst suspicions about the class treason and duplicity of the Right Socialists, and it hardly increased their respect for the Center Socialists—represented by the Adler-Longuet faction—whose attempt to modify the majority resolution had so clearly failed. The Bolsheviks' reaction to the Branting resolution colored their reaction to every resolution adopted at Berne and caused them to minimize the areas of agreement between Bolshevism and other forms of Socialism.

And a few important points of agreement did exist. For instance, the delegates' attitude to territorial annexations was much the same as the Bolsheviks', and a resolution was adopted stating that "the arbitrary and enforced union of people of different nationality in a single state has always been and will always be a cause for international disputes and therefore a danger to peace." Like Lenin's 1916 essay, "Imperialism: The Highest Stage of Capitalism," the resolution said national exploitation and oppression would not be wiped out until the capitalist system was destroyed.[28]

The delegates' attitude, however, to the Paris Peace Conference and the proposed League of Nations contrasted sharply with that of the Bolsheviks. Although many of the Berne Socialists later objected to the decisions made at Versailles, in February they had high hopes for an ideal peace treaty. In a resolution on Wilson's plan for a League of Nations, they agreed that such an organization would be consistent with the aims of international Socialism and necessary for the prevention of future wars; they hoped that Socialists would work closely with the League.[29] The Bolsheviks, on the other hand, regarded the Peace Conference as a bourgeois plot.

The question of war guilt also had different meanings in Berne and Moscow. Early in the conference, French Socialists demanded a partial confession of war guilt from the German Social Democrats who had supported the Kaiser's regime. Many German delegates resisted any such unilateral blame for their country or for the Central Powers. After considerable debate, the conference produced a compromise resolution rather vaguely proclaiming the guilt of the "old system" in Germany, and declaring that the German revolution of November 1918 had cleared this system away. The task of formulating a final judgment on war responsibility was left to a future congress.[30] The Bolsheviks had consistently held that the capitalists of all countries were guilty of the war, and that those Socialists who had supported the war effort, or acquiesced in it, shared the guilt.

The Berne resolution on international labor legislation endorsed the Marxian theory on the exploitation of the working class by capitalism, but it asserted that the evil could be mitigated by the resistance of organized workers and by state intervention on behalf of labor. This conflicted with Lenin's belief that under capitalism any state organization was necessarily the instrument of bourgeois oppression. The resolution proposed an international standard for labor legislation, to be determined by a law of the League of Nations. Such a law would provide for compulsory education, restrictions on the employment of women and children, maximum hours of labor, social and medical care for workers, the right of association, international freedom of movement for workers, minimum wages, unemployment insurance, industrial compensation, an international seamen's code, and an international agency to enforce regulations. The underlying assumption was that such benefits could be instituted by peaceful transition, with the League as the activating agency.[31] The Bolsheviks seized upon this assumption as proof of the treasonable and immoral cooperation between capitalists and moderate Socialists.

The Bolsheviks did not wait until the end of the Berne Congress to arrange their conclusions about it. They analyzed the facts partly in the light of their own preconceptions and partly in the shadow of ignorance imposed by poor communications. Because of the blockade and civil war, no regular or reliable channels of information existed between Russia and the West. The nature and sequence of reports in *Pravda* suggest that Moscow received only occasional information by radio, and most of it came indirectly and several days late in incomplete form. On February 6, with the Congress only three days old and only fragmentary reports available, *Pravda* accused the Berne delegates of being tools of the League, whose chief aim was the "suffocation of the workers' revolution." These "lackeys" and "social obscurantists" who had met to revive the old International had a single goal: "One feeling unites them: a furious hatred for Bolsheviks. One slogan unites them: the slogan of war against the Bolsheviks. The first words of the Yellow International were 'Fight the Bolsheviks!' "[32] Branting's opening speech had left an indelible mark.

By February 15, the Bolsheviks knew that a commission had been appointed to assemble information on Russia, and that some of their ideological opponents—Adler, MacDonald, and Longuet among others—were members.[33] At about the same time, they learned that part of the commission wanted to visit the country, and this caused some concern. The English journalist Arthur Ransome, who was in close contact with the Bolsheviks at that time, described their reactions: "I do not remember the exact date when the proposal of the Berne International Conference to send a Commission of Enquiry to Russia became known in Moscow, but on February 20th everybody who came to see me was talking about it, and from that date the question as to the reception of the delegates was the most urgently debated of all political subjects."[34]

The Bolsheviks were in two minds about whether the visit would help or harm their cause. Chicherin, unaware that the Berne Congress had ended before he acted, sent a reply saying the delegation would be given an opportunity to see what conditions in Russia were like, just as any bourgeois commission would, even though it could not be regarded as a working-class delegation.[35] According to Ransome's account, Litvinov objected to this message, and considered the visit dangerous, since there had been a long period of war between the "two Internationals" and the commission consisted of persons who were certain to condemn Bolshevism. The Soviet leaders finally agreed to receive the delegation without any honors or formal reception, but the Mensheviks hoped to arrange an enthusiastic welcome. Ransome received the impression that the First Congress of the Third International "had its origin in a desire to counter any ill effects that might result from the expected visit of the people of Berne."[36]

This explanation does not account for Chicherin's invitation of January 24; there was no indication then that a commission of inquiry would be appointed by the leaders of the Second International. But if the Bolsheviks decided to act quickly early in January as a result of Allied disregard of their peace proposals and the creation of the KPD, and if they then hesitated after issuing the invitation because of the proposed Prinkipo conference, it is possible that they renewed their decision for an early congress when the Prinkipo idea failed and when the threat from the Second International increased in late February.

The Calling of the Moscow Congress

There is one eyewitness account of the meeting at which the decision to summon the Moscow Congress was presumably made. J. Fineberg, an Englishman who had attached himself to the Bolshevik cause, wrote a description of the gathering ten years after the event, but his statement contains much internal evidence that he had difficulty remembering details. According to Fineberg, the meeting was held in the Kremlin, one evening in January, in the room that had been

Nicholas II's bedchamber; Lenin presented the draft of an invitation
to be sent to parties that opposed the Second International, calling
them to an inaugural meeting of the Third International. Fineberg
said the invitation and a "manifesto" were broadcasted a day or two
later.[37]

Fineberg's account of the meeting becomes more meaningful if it
is correlated with recent Soviet scholarship, which describes a similar
meeting on January 21, with a larger group of participants than Fineberg remembered.[38] A comparison of these accounts tends to support
the theory that the decision to issue the invitation became final after
the deaths of the Spartakusbund leaders and a few days before the
Bolsheviks learned of the Prinkipo proposal.

The invitation was issued over the names of nine men who purported to sign on behalf of Communist parties or left-wing groups
in Russia, Poland, Hungary, German Austria, Latvia, Finland, the
Balkans, and the United States. The only signatories who were in fact
authorized to affix their names on behalf of an actual party were Lenin
and Trotsky, who signed for the Central Committee of the Russian
Communist Party. Those who signed for other parties had no formal
mandate to do so.

Besides announcing the intention to hold an early congress, the invitation summarized the aims and tactics of the new International and
the attitude to be taken toward the Socialist parties. It said that the
capitalist states were banding together in a League of Nations to fight
against the revolution, and that the "social traitors" were once again
helping the bourgeoisie to deceive the working class. The Third International should do everything to counteract such efforts. The statement summarized Bolshevik theory on the imminent decay of capitalism, and on the need for the proletariat to seize power immediately,
so that a nationalized system of industry, commerce, and agriculture
could be created in the place of the bourgeois institutions.

In the paragraphs dealing with the Socialists, the invitation repeated
Lenin's assumptions about the decay of the Second International and
about the necessity of barring the Right and Center Socialists from the
new movement. The Comintern should include those revolutionary
elements that had not formerly belonged to Socialist parties, the invita-

tion asserted; there was a specific indication that the syndicalists of Western Europe—who had traditionally avoided political activity— would be welcome. The invitation listed thirty-nine parties or groups that were eligible to participate. In many instances, the references make it clear that the Bolsheviks had only the briefest information about the organizations mentioned. A key passage near the end of the message outlined the organizational scheme. It advocated a "common fighting organ for the purpose of maintaining permanent coordination and systematic leadership of the movement, a center of the Communist International subordinating the interests of the movement in each country to the common interest of the international revolution." Although the invitation provided that the final form of the organization would be determined by the Congress, the last paragraph repeated the name it must assume and the elements it must exclude.[39]

The document of January 24 was a synopsis of the ideas and problems that guided the Bolsheviks in their earliest efforts to expand their revolution. It also gave a preview of the dogmatism later to be imposed on the organization. It revealed the absence of adequate contacts with allies in the West and the paucity of information about Leftist groups outside Russia. It had no substantial impact on the building of the Comintern, because it was not distributed widely enough to be effective. The views within it, however, carried over into the earliest period of Comintern operations.

The conference that opened in the Kremlin on March 2 had little re-semblance to the pre-war international congresses of the Socialist par-ties.[1] No delegates from Berne had arrived, since most Western gov-ernments denied them permission to visit Russia. The broadcasted invitation of January 24 brought no more than one or two persons from other parts of Europe, although a number of participants claimed to speak as representatives of revolutionary movements abroad. Nearly all the Socialists in Central and Western Europe remained unaware of the Moscow conference until after it had ended.

Of the fifty-two persons who participated, only twelve were legiti-mate spokesmen for active Communist or Socialist groups, and eight of these represented the Soviet Russian Communist Party. This dele-gation consisted of Lenin, Zinoviev, Leon Trotsky, N. I. Bukharin, Chicherin, V. V. Obolensky-Osinsky, V. V. Vorovsky, and possibly Joseph Stalin.[2] The other four delegates who had at least slight con-nections with important Leftist movements were Hugo Eberlein of the KPD, Otto Grimlund of the Left Social Democratic Party of Sweden, Emil Strange of the Norwegian Social Democrats, and Karl Steinhardt (Gruber) of the Austrian Communist Party. Eberlein had a mandate from the late leaders of his party instructing him to oppose the immediate creation of a new International. Grimlund had specific authorization from his party to attend the Moscow conference and to vote for the founding of a Third International.[3] Strange had left Nor-way before his party had learned of the Congress.[4] Steinhardt had participated in a conference of his party in Vienna on February 9 shortly before leaving for Moscow, but the record of this meeting does not mention the Moscow Congress, even though the Austrian Communists had received Chicherin's January 24 invitation.[5]

The status of the other so-called delegates was even more questionable. Henri Guilbeaux, an exiled Frenchman who had lived in Switzerland during most of the war and who had arrived in Moscow while the conference was in session, was allowed to participate as though he were a representative of the French Socialist Party, probably because he had been an associate and supporter of Lenin and Zinoviev at the Zimmerwald conference.[6] Similarly, Fritz Platten, who had been largely responsible for arranging Lenin's 1917 trip from Switzerland to Russia, acted as the delegate for the Swiss Socialists, although he had left his country with Lenin in the spring of 1917 and had not since returned.[7] Boris Reinstein, a Russian-born citizen of the United States, represented himself as a spokesman for the American Socialist Labor Party although he was not in contact with it and had not been in the United States for two years.[8] Andreas Rudniansky, a former Hungarian prisoner of war who had no contact with the Communists or Socialists in Budapest, represented Hungary's Leftists in the absence of any other delegates; and Christian Rakovsky, a Rumanian agitator, was summoned from revolutionary activities to which he had been assigned in the Ukraine in order to speak for the Balkan Socialist Federation, which was then virtually defunct. Angelica Balabanoff, a Russian revolutionary writer and translator who had spent several years in Italy, resisted Lenin's request that she speak on behalf of the Italian Socialist Party, so Italy was not represented.[9] She did, however, attend the Congress.

The conference recognized voting delegates from Communist groups in Poland, Finland, the Ukraine, Latvia, Estonia, Eastern Russia, and the German colonies in Russia, and a group of non-voting "deliberative" delegates were seated as affiliates of Czech, Bulgarian, Yugoslav, English, French, Dutch, American, Swiss, Chinese, and Korean groups. None of them represented bona fide parties in the various countries.[10]

Under the rules of the conference, the representatives of the most important countries—the Russian delegation, Reinstein, Guilbeaux, and Eberlein—had the right to cast five votes each on behalf of their respec-

tive parties, and other delegations were permitted to cast either one or
three votes, depending on their predetermined importance. Thus the
Russian group, with only five votes in a total of fifty-three, superficially avoided the appearance of dominating the meetings, but the fact
that the Bolshevik leaders had selected the representatives and designated their voting strengths gave them almost complete control of the
proceedings. At Lenin's suggestion, Zinoviev became president of the
conference, and this provided another assurance that the Bolsheviks
would be able to guide matters.

In spite of these careful arrangements by the Bolsheviks, the conference nearly failed to achieve its purpose because of Eberlein's objections; Rosa Luxemburg's influence weighed heavily in the first
meetings despite her death and Lenin's efforts to turn her fate to his
own ends. The delegates intended to assemble as an international conference that would quickly transform itself into the First Congress of
the new International; but on March 1—the eve of the first meeting—
Eberlein objected to this scheme so effectively that the Bolsheviks
hesitated. The conference met on March 2 and 3 without taking any
action to constitute itself as a Congress. Eberlein had temporarily convinced the participants that the premature creation of the new International could damage or alienate the working-class movement in
Central Europe, so that during these first two days the delegates and
pseudo-delegates confined themselves to giving reports on the revolutionary situations in their respective countries. Zinoviev announced
that the meetings would be regarded merely as a preliminary conference, not a founding Congress, because of the objections of the representative of the KPD.[11]

Luxemburg's caution—as personified by Eberlein—had won the
battle only momentarily, however. On March 4, Steinhardt arrived in
Moscow after an eventful seventeen-day trip from Vienna through
the war zone, and he made a dramatic appearance before the conference, predicting immediate revolution in the West. "A big, awkward
figure of a typical laborer, in high boots, in shabby clothing, with a
long, unclipped beard," Steinhardt had a decisive impact on the conference and gave the Bolsheviks justification for disregarding Eberlein.[12] One after another, the delegates rose to argue against the

German position, and when a vote was taken, forty-eight of the fifty-three authorized ballots supported the creation of the Third International. Eberlein abstained with his five votes, but he later gave oral endorsement to the decision.

After the conference had thus become the First Congress, there were two more days of meetings, on March 5 and 6. During these days, the delegates approved a number of documents and endorsed an organizational structure that fulfilled the Bolsheviks' objectives. The Congress provided for the creation of an Executive Committee and a central Bureau, but these agencies did not come into existence during the Congress, and the delegates did not select their personnel. The Congress provided only that there should be an Executive Committee of the Communist International (ECCI), with members from Russia, Germany, German Austria, Hungary, the Balkan Federation, Switzerland, and Scandinavia. It was obvious that the persons at the Congress who pretended to represent those countries would become the ECCI members, and considering the orientation of the representatives from five of these units, Russian control was assured. A resolution empowered the ECCI to select a Bureau of five members, but its relationship to the ECCI was not specified. This Bureau eventually included Zinoviev, Lenin, Trotsky, Rakovsky, and Platten. The Russians were authorized to assume the burden of work until representatives from other countries could arrive from abroad.[18] Zinoviev later emerged as chairman of the Executive Committee, and as a result he became head of the Comintern. His appointment was not announced until several days after the Congress had adjourned, perhaps because he was not popular among the delegates.

Plans and Documents of the First Congress

The Bolsheviks had achieved the organizational structure they had sought. The form of the new agency had been outlined not only in the January 24 invitation, but also in a statement made on the opening day of the Congress. On March 2 Zinoviev published an article in *Pravda* in which he predicted that the program of the Russian Communist Party would be acceptable to the parties that would participate in the founding congress of the Third International. The article did not reveal that the conference had been convened on that very day; it was not a news account of a current event but a propaganda statement designed to win support for a Bolshevik scheme. It may have been directed toward the delegates to the conference as well as the reading public. On the question of organizational form and leadership, Zinoviev was explicit: "The organizational form of the Third International must be determined at the First Congress of the Communist Parties. A strong guiding center must be established, which will be able to lead, in ideas and organization, the movements in all countries."[14]

This statement should not be taken to mean that the Bolsheviks were expecting to control all parties of the world; it would have been impossible for them to do so early in 1919. They did not anticipate that the organization would become simply a pawn of Soviet Russia's foreign policy. They assumed that the "strong guiding center" would be established in one of the Central or Western European industrial cities. Nor did they expect that they would soon have altercations with their own supporters in the West. At this stage, the Bolsheviks were more interested in putting their record and example before the world than in creating a rigid control system. The main purpose of the First Congress was propaganda, and the very act of creating the Third International in March 1919 was intended to serve a propaganda end. In this phase of its existence, the Comintern tried to identify Bolshevism with the expected proletarian uprisings of Europe, and the documents issued by the First Congress are an expression of this effort.

Of the six major statements of the First Congress, the Manifesto, probably written by Trotsky, was most explicit on the objectives of the Congress. It accused capitalist countries of causing the war, and directed much of the blame to the Socialists of the Right and Center. It accused capitalist imperialists of creating the threat of a new war, while the Bolsheviks were seeking to assure peace and to build a better world under a proletarian dictatorship, a "new and higher workers' democracy" to replace the bourgeois democracy. It restated the class-war thesis, and repudiated the "reformism" and "opportunist character" of the Second International. Finally, like the statement of the Berne Socialists, it promised peace and prosperity for new national states, for colonial peoples, and for the underprivileged of all kinds once the bourgeois system had been vanquished. The document was obviously intended as a reply to the Berne conference.

The five other important documents of the Congress supplemented the Manifesto. The first, presented by Lenin, was a group of statements on bourgeois democracy; the Congress adopted these without change. They included polemics on such institutions as freedom of the press and freedom of assembly, which Lenin regarded as exclusively bourgeois privileges, harmful to the proletariat. A second document, the Platform, again revealed the extent to which the Communists were reacting to Berne. It reasserted the need for violent revolution, and contained paragraphs against bourgeois democracy, the parliamentary system, and capitalist oppression as interdependent elements. A third resolution was devoted completely to denouncing the Berne Congress and the leaders of the Second International. Hence, the Manifesto and three key documents—or four of the six most important statements—contained much that aimed simply at demolishing Socialism of the Right and Center, in line with Lenin's convictions developed during the war. A fourth document appealed to the workers of the world to bring pressure on their governments to give formal diplomatic recognition to the Bolshevik regime. The fifth statement contained an evaluation of the current international situation and the policy of the Allied powers. It objected to the Allies' efforts to reestablish the old European order and to create a League of Nations; and it assumed that the heads of governments at the Peace Conference were guided exclusively by class considerations. None of these documents of the First Congress contained any new basic theory; they were restatements of previously expressed Leninist ideas in a form and in circumstances which, it was hoped, would appeal to a wider audience than ever before.[15]

A sentence from the first paragraph of the Manifesto can be taken as a summary of the goals the International set itself: "Our task is to consolidate the revolutionary experience of the working class, to cleanse the movement of the destructive elements of opportunism and social patriotism, and to mobilize the forces of all genuinely revolutionary parties of the world proletariat, thereby facilitating and hastening the victory of the Communist revolution throughout the world."[16]

This three-part division of functions was followed by the ECCI in the ensuing months. The Committee tried to consolidate "revolutionary experience" by an ambitious program of research and publication; it tried to purify the movement by the same methods, as well as by the strategic use of sympathizers or trusted representatives abroad; and its mobilization plans involved guidance over the most promising elements in other countries. All these objectives, and the transmittal of the program to the world's proletariat, depended on a good communications system between the organization and the workers whom it sought to arouse. The lack of such a system became the first problem of the Comintern leaders.

It was a simple matter to stimulate expressions of allegiance and revolutionary zeal from the Russian proletariat. On the final day of the Congress, the Bolsheviks summoned a mass rally in Moscow, at which they emphasized the historical importance of the occasion. The sessions of the conference had been held without any press attention for the first three days, despite Zinoviev's article of March 2, and were, for all practical purposes, secret—probably because Eberlein's objections had kept the result in doubt. On March 5, however, *Pravda* announced the formation of the International in a banner headline, and in subsequent editions it compensated for its earlier silence. The concluding rally on March 6, which was held in the Bolshoi Theater, succeeded in attracting an overflow crowd of workers, and was intended to set an example for the proletariat of other countries.[17]

Zinoviev and several other delegates conducted a similar meeting in Petrograd three days later. Trotsky distributed a message of greeting on behalf of the Congress among units of the Red Army and Navy shortly after adjournment,[18] and the acts of the Congress became subjects of discussion and objects of praise at meetings of local soviets throughout Russia.[19] Two weeks after the close of the Congress, both Lenin and Zinoviev elaborated upon the importance of the Comintern at the Eighth Congress of the Russian Communist Party.[20] By the end of March, Soviet Russia had been well introduced to the literature and objectives of the new International, but to extend this information beyond the borders of Russia was a more difficult matter. Lack of staff, the pressures of the civil war, and the Allies' blockade were the chief problems.

Building a Staff

The development of a staff and an organizational procedure became the first responsibility of the ECCI. Lenin and Trotsky had pre-emptive responsibilities in the government, Rakovsky had duties in the Ukraine, and Platten was soon to leave for a mission to the West; so Zinoviev became the main designer of the machinery of the Executive Committee. Angelica Balabanoff, who had served as secretary and translator during the Congress, was designated secretary of the Comintern at the request of Lenin, because he wanted the organization to benefit from her reputation among the Socialist parties of the West. The first few meetings of the ECCI were in Balabanoff's living quarters until the Committee appropriated the former German Embassy building, "one of the few large houses where the furnishings had been kept intact and in perfect order."[21]

From the start there was tension between Zinoviev and Balabanoff, whose divergent political philosophies and mutual distrust had been known to Lenin. He counseled Balabanoff not to cause trouble;[22] but, as she later wrote, this advice had little effect:

I was surprised to find that the topics of discussion at our Executive meetings had so little relation to the work we had been elected to do. (Later, when I discovered that our meetings were mere formalities and that real authority rested with a secret Party Committee, I was to understand the reason for this.) I had decided to dedicate all my energy to the building up of the new International and I had conceived of our work as that of strengthening and solidifying the Left Wing forces throughout the world —not by artificial stimulation or by the wrecking of existing movements, but by propaganda and comradely aid. I knew that their respect could only be won by the quality of our program and the superiority of our leadership. But it soon became obvious that Zinoviev and the rest of the Bolsheviks had other methods in mind—methods which I considered as dangerous to Russia as to the labour movement abroad—the effects of which were to become obvious within the next two years. Why bother to win the loyalty of a party or a union movement when it was so much easier for the Bolsheviks to wreck it and create from its ruins a docile sect, dependent for its very existence upon the Comintern? Why discuss methods, confront honest differences of opinion, when with the resources of the nation behind them, it was so much easier to discredit their more formidable opponents, to buy off the less scrupulous and weaker? I was not fully aware of all this during these early months as secretary of the Comintern. The worst of its abuses developed gradually within the coming year.[23]

She said her name was used on documents without her knowledge, and her quarrels with Zinoviev became frequent. During the summer of 1919, she was asked to go to the Ukraine to aid the revolution there; she regarded the request as a subterfuge to remove her from Comintern activities.

One decision in the organizational period that pleased Balabanoff was the appointment of Vorovsky to the staff of the Comintern's Moscow headquarters. She described him as an intellectual and an honest revolutionary. He gave his full attention to Comintern matters for only two months (he then became manager of the government press), and he seems to have made little effective contribution during this time.[24] According to a recent biographer, Vorovsky's most significant act in this phase of his career was to help prepare an appeal on behalf of Guilbeaux for distribution in France.[25]

Balabanoff's complaints are substantiated by the fact that the International had two headquarters from an early date. While the secretary's office remained in Moscow, Zinoviev created another office and staff in Petrograd, and from there the Comintern issued most of its propaganda and publications. The new office was established at the Smolny Institute, where Zinoviev also had his headquarters for the Petrograd Soviet, and this became the real center of the agency. During the first few weeks, the staff consisted of only two men, Serge (Victor Lvovich Kibalchich) and Mazine (Vladimir O. Lichtenstadt). Serge was the Belgian-born son of a Russian couple who had been expelled from the Tsarist empire for revolutionary conduct. Serge, too, had engaged in revolutionary activities. He had studied journalism, photography, and typography in his early years, had been imprisoned in Belgium in connection with an assassination, and had served eighteen months in a French jail. All these attributes made him appear desirable to the Bolsheviks, and in January 1919 they released a French officer in return for Serge's release and safe passage to Petrograd. He arrived just as plans for the International were developing, and Zinoviev asked him to devote his publishing talents to the new organization, although he was not at the time a member of the Communist Party.[26]

Serge accepted the assignment, and when he asked for an assistant,

Zinoviev provided Mazine. Mazine, too, had a history of illegal activity, which had begun during the 1905 uprising in St. Petersburg. Like Serge, he had served a prison sentence for an assassination plot. He had become a Bolshevik only in recent months. These two young men, who were virtually conscripted for their assignments with the Comintern, found it ironical that they should have been singled out to organize and plan the world revolution. Mazine remained at the headquarters only until August, when he left to join units of the Red Army that were then defending Petrograd from an assault in the civil war. He died in battle against the White Army on October 15.[27] Up to then, Mazine and Serge shared most of the responsibility for handling Comintern business under the general guidance of Zinoviev. As Serge wrote later, they served as "counselors, functionaries, secretaries, editors, translators, printers, organizers, directors, members of the collegium, and many other things."[28] Their most important task was to prepare propaganda material aimed at the proletariat in Russia and abroad, and at the Allied military personnel serving in Russia.

Spreading the Message: The First Phase

The internal and external situation of Soviet Russia did not make the task of the Comintern easy during the first months of its operation. E. H. Carr has described 1919 as "the Year of Isolation" in Soviet history. One of the most effective blockades in modern times sealed off the Bolshevik-held territory from the rest of the world. The presence of British and French fleets in the Baltic and Black Seas, the Allies' control of Murmansk and Archangel during the early months of the year, and the attacks of anti-Bolshevik Russian armies all jeopardized the Communist government. Although by spring the Allies were gradually beginning to withdraw, the threat from the White Russian forces continued for several more months. Admiral Alexander Kolchak's advances from Siberia into the Upper Volga basin in the spring, General Anton Denikin's spectacular successes in the Ukraine during the summer, and the advances of General N. N. Yudenich's Baltic-based forces in June and October were a serious danger to the Communists. This situation made it difficult for the Comintern to export revolutionary propaganda and agents, and demanded most of the resources and energy of the Bolshevik leaders. Although Lenin and his closest associates regarded the Third International as vitally important, they could devote little time to it in 1919.

After the anti-Bolshevik offensive reached its climax in September and October and began to recede, the Comintern's prospects improved. Before the end of 1919, Yudenich had been defeated, and the successful offensive against Denikin had brought much of the Ukraine back under Bolshevik control. The Red Army's advance into Siberia and the capture of Kolchak at Irkutsk in January 1920 relieved the pressure on the Bolsheviks. When the Allied Supreme Council lifted its blockade in the same month, avenues of contact with the West opened immediately, a highly important development for the Comintern. This may be regarded as the end of the first phase of Comintern history, because it gave the Bolshevik brain trust a new perspective on the European revolutionary potential and coincided with important changes in the International's policy.

During the initial period from March 1919 to January 1920, publication was the most important activity of the Comintern's office at Smolny, much of this effort going to the preparation of the magazine *The Communist International*. The first issue of this periodical appeared about two months after the Congress, dated May 1. The ECCI had decided in March to publish a journal in four languages—Russian, German, English, and French—and these foreign-language editions were issued in Petrograd.* The journal was originally planned as a monthly publication, and during 1919 there was in fact an issue for every month from May through October; a single issue appeared for November and December. In 1920, however, publication was much

* The foreign-language editions of the journal present problems for the scholar. In addition to the Petrograd editions (which often reached the West belatedly, and often undated), reprints were occasionally issued by the various branches of the Comintern in Europe. Thus, a French reprint was published in Stockholm, and English ones in London and Paris, apparently on an irregular basis. There were at least two German-language reprints for a time, one prepared by a branch of the Comintern in Berlin, and the other by the Austrian Communist Party in Vienna. In some cases, articles that appeared in the Petrograd editions were omitted in the reprints. Where possible, I have consulted and cited the Petrograd issues, unless there was a special reason for using another edition; I have relied upon the excellent collection of the Hoover Institution. I have referred to the journal by its English title throughout the text, since the Notes make it clear which edition was actually used.

more erratic. Eberlein, who became an enthusiastic supporter and willing functionary of the Comintern after his protest against it failed, wrote a piece for the first issue. The journal was appearing at a time, he wrote, when readers had no patience with broad theoretical discussions. *The Communist International* must be more than an ornament on the workers' bookshelves; it should become a "constant companion" from which to derive guidance.[29] To a large extent, the early issues of the magazine became a compendium of those arguments that the Bolsheviks felt would win the working class to their cause.

Gabriel A. Almond, in his recent study of Communist periodicals, has said that such publications for mass consumption often give little attention to internal party matters or to the actions of the Communist movement. Referring largely to the pro-Bolshevik press in non-Communist countries, he observes that the journalistic works tend to emphasize the evils of the Communists' enemies, and thus seek to convert readers to Bolshevism by first alienating them from the capitalists or whomever the immediate enemy of the party might be. The winning over of new members is regarded as a gradual process, a long-range goal.[30] This procedure is a refinement that came later in Comintern history, since these remarks do not apply to the *Communist International* of 1919 and 1920. Although a high percentage of articles did stress the sins of the capitalists, many articles, too, were devoted to the internal affairs of the various parties and of the International, and long-term programs were explicitly discussed. In its original editorial policy, the *Communist International* did not contemplate the need for gradual conversion of the working class over a period of years; it preached the message of class warfare in the frankest possible manner.

The contents of the magazine during 1919 suggest some general conclusions about Bolshevik propaganda in this era. The journal was a random collection of clippings from the revolutionary press of Russia and Europe, plus a few documents produced by Comintern headquarters and occasional letters or reports from abroad. Its standards of accuracy were not high, and the editorial staff obviously sought desperately at times for favorable reports from the West. Vitriolic and hate-inducing language became routine; Zinoviev, in particular, appears to have liked images of blood and suffering in various forms, and he may have guided the selection of materials on the basis of this preoccupation.

Zinoviev made the most frequent contributions to the *Communist International* in 1919; eleven articles bear his name, besides those which he wrote on behalf of the ECCI. Lenin contributed seven articles, and Serge's name or initials appeared on eight pieces. A large number of other revolutionaries—actual or intended—were represented. Classification of the contents of the seven editions of 1919 is difficult because the editors did not establish any definite method of categorizing their materials, but the general emphasis of the magazine is indicated by the following breakdown:[31]

Manifestoes, resolutions, appeals, letters, etc., from the First Congress or the ECCI	47
Documents on the international movement (mostly dealing with revolutionary activity abroad)	61
Articles on heroes or martyrs of the proletarian revolution	14
Reports from Communist Party movements abroad	37
Reports from delegates to the First Congress	15
Articles on the Young Communist International	6
General articles (many of them taken from Russian and other pro-Bolshevik newspapers)	102

The ambitious propaganda enterprise represented by this organ went awry for one fundamental reason: the journal could not be distributed among the proletariat in the West. As will be shown later, the Communist-inclined movements in Britain, France, and Germany remained unaware of its existence during 1919, owing to poor communications between Russia and the West.

Radio contact with the West proved to be only slightly more helpful to the Comintern's cause. Moscow and Petrograd seldom gained any vital information about the revolutionary movements abroad by monitoring Western stations, and they obviously could not maintain extensive or confidential contact with their allies by means of radio-telegram. Radio communication was in its infancy; transmission and reception were poor. Broadcasts from Russia might be heard in Sweden or Switzerland, reported in the left-wing press, and then gradually relayed to Britain, France, and Germany by means of newspaper, but there was nothing systematic about this. Soviet newspapers carried daily reports summarizing radio messages from the West, but little news of the Communist parties appeared.

To take a few examples. The leading organ of the French Socialists, *L'Humanité,* did not have a report of the First Congress until March 17, eleven days after adjournment, when it indicated receipt of a radiogram from Petrograd dated March 9. Lenin's "Theses on Bourgeois Democracy and Proletarian Dictatorship" from the Congress did not appear in full in the French Socialist press until the last week of July. The leading British Socialist organ, *The Call,* could not offer its readers the "Theses on the International Situation and the Policy of the Entente" until September, about six months after the document had been issued at the Congress. An ECCI appeal to the workers of the world that appeared in the *Communist International* on July 1 reached *The Call* only on October 30. The situation appeared to be worse near the end of the year than it had been in the spring. This failure to transmit even basic documents quickly testifies to the isolation of the self-appointed headquarters from the expected revolution in the West.

Moscow and Petrograd leaders of the International knew that even if radio communications worked well, their enemies might hear conversations intended only for partisans of the revolution. After the Béla Kun regime came to power in Hungary in March 1919 and the first communiqués had been transmitted, Chicherin reportedly cautioned Kun to be more careful about the kind of messages he sent, since the world could listen.[32]

In view of these difficulties, the Russians in the Kremlin and Smolny depended primarily on individual couriers to carry messages and instructions and to bring reports from the West. This procedure, too, had many flaws; travel through the blockade and civil war areas had to be conducted in secret, and the record of failure was high. One of the first persons to conduct a mission abroad specifically for the International was Beatrice Rutgers, a Dutch woman who had traveled to Russia with her husband via America and Japan, arriving in the fall of 1918. Her husband, S. J. Rutgers, became a consultive delegate from Holland and America to the First Congress, but she received an assignment in January to return to the Netherlands to invite Dutch Communists and revolutionaries from other Western European groups to attend the First Congress. She apparently carried a copy of the January 24 invitation. She reached Amsterdam safely but belatedly; the document appeared in the Amsterdam Communist newspaper only on March 4, two days after the Congress opened.[33] After completing her mission in Holland, she attempted to return to Russia, but the police arrested her at the border.[34]

Fritz Platten also encountered trouble as a Comintern courier. He received instructions to return to Switzerland shortly after the Congress. As a long-standing associate of Lenin and Zinoviev and as a member of the Bureau of the Comintern, he probably had extensive plans for agitation in the West. He entered Finland on April 8, and the authorities arrested him, identifying him as an unauthorized immigrant. Soviet authorities managed his return to Russia through an exchange on May 14.[35] During the summer, he made an attempt to get to the West via Rumania, where another arrest put him in prison for several weeks. He finally reached Switzerland in the spring of 1920, only to be jailed again.[36] Even when the messengers managed to get abroad without incident, many betrayed their cause. Some of them carried substantial amounts of money and other valuable items, and simply disappeared with the loot.[37]

Some of the Comintern representatives, however, did achieve their destinations and did accomplish part of their missions, as later chapters will show. Before the Third International had been created, the Soviet government had been training revolutionaries—many of them recruited from prisoners of war—for future service to the Soviet system abroad. The Comintern was thus able to draw upon a corps of agitators trained in the Moscow procedures of propaganda. Magyar, Rumanian, Czech, Serbian, and Turkish groups had been organized and were publishing revolutionary newspapers in their native languages in Moscow in 1918.[38] A few Hungarians who had received this indoctrination had already been sent home in the fall of 1918, and the Comintern was to see the first results of their work when a Soviet government was established in Budapest in March 1919.[39]

There was also a group of French expatriates in Moscow, who published a newspaper called *La IIIme Internationale*. This group named itself "La Section Française du Parti Communiste (Bolchevik) Russe," and its main objective was to dissuade French soldiers in the intervention army from fighting the Bolsheviks. It sought to inoculate the French military personnel with Bolshevism in the hope that they would carry the revolution back to their homes.[40] The most prominent member of the organization was Jacques Sadoul, a former member of a French military mission in Petrograd who had defected to the Bolsheviks shortly after the October Revolution. He was later to have a role in the Comintern's propaganda in France. In such groups the Comintern found much of its talent.

In their preparations for the expected revolution, the Comintern's founders did not reckon with some of the forces and ideas that would compete with Bolshevism in Europe. In the crucial early months of 1919, when revolution was most likely, Bolshevism did not offer the most attractive solution for the unfortunate or the discontented. Woodrow Wilson's program of democracy and national self-determination had more appeal for most Western and Central Europeans than Communism's offer of a Soviet state and international regime. Most Westerners found more reassurance in Wilson's promise of peace and justice than in the Bolshevik proposals that advocated international peace but demanded an immediate era of class war. Much of Europe was hungry for several months after the armistice, and America was the most likely source of food.

The widespread urge for national revenge also ran counter to Bolshevik expectations. Most English, rich and poor, found more satisfaction in Lloyd George's vigorous election promise to punish the Kaiser than in Moscow's invitation to punish the bourgeoisie. Similarly, Clemenceau's demands that Germany should pay for the war had more impact than the Bolsheviks' assertion that capitalism should be destroyed.

All these factors worked against Communism. Besides this, propaganda from Russia was nearly choked off during 1919 and part of 1920. Whereas most of the Communist-oriented media of the West were small and powerless, the Western-style offers of peace, revenge, and a new order had the backing of the most influential periodicals, churches, and politicians in Europe. It is hardly surprising that Moscow's appeal was small; the center of interest was elsewhere. In Churchill's words, "Appetites, passions, hopes, revenge, starvation and anarchy ruled the hour; and from this simultaneous and almost universal welter all eyes were turned to Paris. To this immortal city —gay-tragic, haggard-triumphant, scarred and crowned—more than half mankind now looked for satisfaction or deliverance."[41] Even after the results of the Paris Peace Conference had disappointed many, the desire for stability and order remained stronger than Bolshevism's appeal. A central fact in the story of the Comintern in 1919 and 1920 is that its initial trust in Europe was contrary to the tide of history.

Long-Range Plans

It is doubtful whether the creators of the Third International foresaw the day when they would disband the organization. They do not seem to have felt that its work would be finished when the revolution had become triumphant throughout the world. Many of the early documents claimed that the Comintern was the spiritual and ideological heir of Marx's International Working Men's Association, and the Bolsheviks may have anticipated a function of this kind for the Comintern after the universal victory. There are clues that they may even have regarded the International as a potential organ of world-wide government, sharing responsibility with, or perhaps even superseding, the Soviet government in Moscow.

During 1919 and even into 1920, the Soviet leaders did not bother to make any distinction between the policies of the Comintern and the foreign policy of the Russian Soviet government. The goals of the two institutions were identical, and their leadership was thoroughly meshed. This remained true throughout the twenty-four-year history of the Comintern, but in later years the Soviet government found it expedient to assert that no connection existed. In the 1920's and 1930's it became embarrassing for the government, in its quest for friends on the diplomatic level, to have connections with a revolutionary organ. Before 1921, however, no such disavowal seemed necessary. Chicherin had acted in his capacity as foreign minister when he issued the invitation to the First Congress. Such leading Commissars as

Lenin and Trotsky doubled as delegates, officers, and literary contributors to the Comintern. In May, when the Allies revealed their peace
terms at Versailles, Zinoviev and Chicherin issued statements almost
simultaneously, condemning the proposed treaty and advocating revolution. It was widely accepted that these statements were intended to
be complementary.[42]

A revealing comment on the relationship between the Soviet government and the International appeared in the *Communist International*
in October, written by Chicherin. He explained that in the period of
the proletarian revolution, the new workers' governments must have
a close connection with external revolutionary movements. However,
he said, when the Commissar of Foreign Affairs of a Soviet state is
writing an article for a periodical of the Third International, he must
remember that he is bound by the position of his government to certain types of limited contacts and affiliations with the governments of
capitalist states. His tone is faintly apologetic as he demonstrates the
non-revolutionary aspect of his office; here is an early expression of
the conflicting interests—traditional versus revolutionary—that complicated Soviet foreign policy. Chicherin specified that the external
policies of the Third International and the revolutionary parties of all
countries revolve around the governments of existing Soviet states.[43]

This effort to define the relationship between the Soviet states (the
short-lived Hungarian Soviet regime may have still existed when he
wrote) and the International implies that the latter would become a
kind of connecting agency for the former. Vorovsky, another high
diplomatic official in the Moscow government who participated in the
founding Congress, shared the idea that the Comintern would soon
be more than an instrument for inciting rebellion. He wrote on May 13
that the climax of the current trend would be "a world-wide Soviet
republic with the Communist International at its head."[44]

One of Lenin's earliest comments on the future and the function of
the Comintern was an article entitled "The Third International and
Its Place in History." He saw the organization as a future league of
Soviet republics (obviously a competitive comparison with the League
of Nations). He felt that the leadership of the proletarian revolution
—which in the nineteenth century had passed from the working class
of Britain to that of France and then to that of Germany—had now

passed "for a short time" to the Russian proletariat. The backwardness of the Tsarist regime and the adoption of the Soviet system had enabled the Russians to achieve this position, but the leadership of the world revolution—and by implication the leadership of the Third International—would soon pass to the more highly developed proletariat of the West.[45] In this connection, the Bolsheviks envisaged an early transfer of the headquarters of the Comintern to the West. Shortly after the First Congress, both Trotsky and Zinoviev expressed the hope that such a transfer would soon be made,[46] and even a year and a half later, Zinoviev was still recommending it.[47]

The Bolsheviks created the Comintern for propaganda purposes: to spread the message of their own revolution and to keep the proletariat of the capitalistic states from being duped by the reformist views of the Western Socialists. They had dreams, however, of the day when the organization would evolve beyond this function, when it would become the means by which Soviet states could exchange ideas and work jointly for the establishment of a Communist world order. The Bolsheviks themselves had no idea at this time that the Comintern would eventually be reduced to an unofficial and unacknowledged branch of the Russian government, responsible for the detailed control of Communist organizations abroad.

The fact that the Russian Soviet government was giving extensive financial support to the Comintern in its early months was completely logical in view of the initial concept of the organization. There was no reason to hide the fact, and as late as October of 1920, Zinoviev acknowledged in a speech in Germany that much of the International's money came from the Russian state treasury.[48] The Bolsheviks assumed that future Soviet states would share the responsibility for financing and guiding the organization.* The event that caused the Comintern leaders to begin adjusting their views was the rise and fall of the Hungarian Soviet Republic.

---

* Besides treasury support, funds for the International were raised by means of "Communist Saturdays," a system instituted in autumn 1919. Under this program, Russian laborers worked overtime on Saturday afternoons, and turned over their wages for these periods to the Comintern. *Kommunisticheskii Internatsional,* No. 7/8 (November/December 1919), cols. 1127-28. See also *Workers' Dreadnought* (London), Oct. 18, 1919, 1507: 3.

Chapter three Hungary

Only two weeks elapsed between the close of the First Congress and the establishment of the second Soviet government in Europe. Although no causal relationship existed between the founding of the Comintern and the proclaiming of a pro-Communist regime in Hungary, this triumph for Bolshevism so soon after the formal birth of the International induced a sense of pride and accomplishment at Moscow and Petrograd. Events in Budapest were seen as proof of the revolutionary conditions in Europe. The Hungarian situation provided the International with the first test of its assumptions and of its ability to lead a revolution. The Communist regime lasted from March 21 until August 1, and its failure gave the Comintern one of the most critical defeats of its early history.

Communist Growth in Budapest

The Communists won their opportunity in Hungary under conditions much like those that had helped the Bolsheviks to power in 1917. The old Austro-Hungarian imperial order had collapsed under the pressures of war. On October 31, 1918, a *coup d'état* established a provisional government under the leadership of the liberal-pacifist Count Michael Károlyi. This government had proclaimed a republic on November 16, emphasizing its division from the Hapsburg dynasty and the old Empire. For four and a half months, Károlyi's coalition government teetered precariously, in Kerensky fashion, amid threats from irate monarchists, dissatisfied peasants, reform-minded Socialists, and a generally discontented and exhausted citizenry.

Archibald C. Coolidge, a member of the American Peace Commission who arrived in Budapest in mid-January, described Károlyi's difficulties. Soldiers returning from the front had been sent home without being disarmed, and they were not responding well to discipline; in fact, many were forming councils, or soviets. The Social Democrats were not well-organized, and no strong middle class existed to stabilize the government. Inflation and foreign intervention had wrecked the economy, and a shortage of coal and clothing troubled the country.[1]

The most trying of Károlyi's problems originated abroad. In the immediate post-armistice period, the Yugoslavs, Czechoslovaks, and Rumanians were seeking the best territorial arrangements possible to improve their respective positions at the pending peace negotiations. In those awkward months, when the status of all former Austro-Hungarian lands was in doubt, Hungary's neighbors found it relatively easy to win permission to occupy some of the rich lands traditionally subject to the Hungarian crown. Károlyi protested in vain to the Allied leaders as, little by little, Hungary's lands were seized, and finally, on March 20, his government suffered its final humiliation. The Allied military representative in Hungary delivered an ultimatum insisting upon immediate withdrawal of Hungarian forces from an additional strip of territory on the eastern frontier. This included some distinctively Magyar-populated communities, and it seemed in Budapest to be conclusive evidence that Károlyi's pleas were having no effect in Paris. The conservative parties found it politically impossible to accede to the ultimatum and militarily impossible to resist it. Because of the unwillingness or inability of the conservatives or the liberals to form a government in the crisis, a power vacuum existed. Into this void stepped a group of left-wing Social Democrats and the only other party willing to assume power, the Communists. Thus the Communists won the chance to share the government of Hungary by default, because of the despair of other parties at the critical moment, and not by virtue of a Leninist revolution.

The Hungarian Social Democrats and Communists resembled their counterparts in other European countries. The Social Democrats frequently advocated violent revolution, but in practice they were reformist. When the republic had been proclaimed in November 1918, the party's journal, *Népszava,* had printed a statement endorsing the political revolution and asserting that a social one must follow. Party leaders pledged themselves to use "all the weapons of agitation, mass organization, mass enlightenment and persuasion" to realize these ends, and proclaimed Communism as the "glorious, ultimate goal."[2] Many of them, however, hoped for a reconciliation between the Bolsheviks and the Socialists of the Right and Center, and disapproved of the radical stand the Bolshevik propaganda took.

Shortly after the political transitions of October and November, the Communists began to advocate and practice the kind of revolutionary program that most Social Democrats were willing to endorse only in theory. They encouraged violence and a complete social upheaval. The men responsible for this new direction were Béla Kun, Tibor Szamuely, and a few of their associates who, like Kun and Szamuely, had been prisoners of war in Russia, and had been converted and trained by the Bolsheviks. Both Kun and Szamuely had been active in Russia in 1918, when they had assisted in the publication of a journal, *Szociális Forrodalom* (Social Revolution), for distribution to Magyars. As early as April 1918, Szamuely had looked forward to the formation of a Third International.[3] They arrived in Hungary at about the time the republic was proclaimed and generated trouble immediately. The Communist Party was founded on November 21,[4] and publication of a party newspaper, *Vörös Ujság* (Red Journal), began on December 7. The militancy of the paper and its frequent attacks on the moderate wing of the Social Democrats soon created animosity and seemed temporarily to make chances for a reconciliation impossible. From its first numbers, *Vörös Ujság* carried a column called "The Third International," which described the activities and hopes of revolutionary parties in other countries.

Serious mutinies in the army, disorders in the factories, and sporadic acts of violence began to occur within a few days after the first issue of the paper appeared, and they continued throughout the winter. As a result, the Károlyi government arrested Kun and several other Communist leaders about February 21, but this backfired for the government when police allegedly gave Kun a severe beating and thus made him the object of popular sympathy.[5] Kun's imprisonment was accordingly modified, to the extent that he was able to make radio contacts with Moscow and to continue writing for his paper, although he remained in jail.[6] While in prison, he heard about the First Congress of the International. The first report apparently reached Budapest by wireless several days after the Congress had ended; the initial article appeared in *Vörös Ujság* on March 13. The Hungarian Communists appear to have assumed the Congress was still in session, and the article erroneously recorded that 245 comrades had been present.[7] The Hungarians had little accurate information about the events of the First Congress for several weeks after it met.

Compromise with the Social Democrats

Kun and his followers had no hesitations about embracing the Third International, and when the leaders of the Social Democrats visited Kun in jail on March 21 to discuss the sharing of power, one of his conditions was affiliation with the Comintern. The Social Democrats yielded to this and most of Kun's other demands. One provision of the reconciliation was the merger of the two parties into a single organization, which would call itself the Socialist Party of Hungary until the International established a final name for it.[8] Two days later an official message went from Budapest to Petrograd, asking the International for instructions on this point.[9] The Hungarians did not know that the Comintern wanted all affiliated units to adopt titles containing the term "Communist" rather than "Socialist." This question of a name, trivial enough in itself, became a source of trouble between the Communists and the Social Democrats during the period of Soviet rule in Hungary. The Social Democrats resisted efforts to change the title, and the controversy achieved a historical importance later for the Bolsheviks.

Kun, now Commissar of Foreign Affairs in the new government as well as leader of the Bolshevik wing of the Socialist Party, made early radio contact with Lenin, and there is evidence that Lenin sought communication without recourse to the staff of the International. One of his first messages to the new Budapest government instructed Kun to state whether he could guarantee that the regime would be Communist, rather than Social Democratic. He requested a report on whether the Communists were in a majority in the government and when a party Congress would be held.[10] Kun's answer apparently quieted Lenin's doubts, and in spite of the difficulties of radio communication, Lenin rapidly became satisfied that the Kun regime was progressing along Communist lines.[11]

News of the Hungarian developments stirred Zinoviev to action in the Smolny headquarters at about the same time that it had roused Lenin's interest in Moscow. Although Lenin had not employed Zinoviev's staff and apparently had not consulted the ECCI in his initial communications with Budapest, the new organization was now getting into business. In response to the request for instructions, Zinoviev radioed that the ECCI expected the Hungarians to unite the Communist party, to give it a "clearly formulated Communist program," and to name it the "Communist Party." The message praised the wisdom of the initial actions of the Soviet government, but insisted that the Communists must maintain their organizational distinctiveness, that membership in their movement must be well disciplined, and that it must have a definitive program.[12] There were redundancies in the message and also an element of equivocation; Zinoviev endorsed by implication the action of the Communists in working with the Social Democrats, but he also insisted on a purity of program and organization that would have made any effective compromise impossible.

Although there do not appear to have been any additional messages from the Comintern instructing the party to call itself "Communist," there may have been some informal prompting from Lenin. Late in May, Szamuely flew to Moscow and consulted with Lenin. The formal greeting that he carried back to Budapest on May 31 contained no mention of the party's title, but shortly after his return a debate on the question broke out between the Social Democrats and the Communists. Kun and Szamuely advocated the change, but Sigismund Kunfi and other Social Democrats questioned whether this was necessary and whether the Russians even desired it. At a party conference in mid-June, the debate reached a climax, with Kunfi arguing for the preservation of the party's original title approved on March 21 and with Szamuely presenting a copy of the first issue of the *Communist International* to prove the nature of the instructions of the First Congress. Some Social Democrats challenged the authenticity of the documents that Szamuely presented and the accuracy of the translations. In the end, the coalition decided to call itself "The Party of the Socialist-Communist Workers of Hungary."[13]

This question appears to have been the only procedural matter of the Hungarian Soviet regime on which the International exercised a direct influence. Poor communications accounted for this, information being particularly meager (according to a Comintern official) in the two months before the Budapest government fell.[14] Therefore, relations between the Comintern and the Hungarian Communists must be viewed from two perspectives—from the point of view of Budapest and from that of the International's leaders in Petrograd and Moscow.

Béla Kun, the Comintern, and Austria

Béla Kun needed no instructions on the general objectives or operational method of the International beyond those he had brought from Moscow. He regarded the International as a higher sovereignty than his government. During April, his regime and party became involved in theoretical and procedural disputes with the Socialist government of Austria, and he tried to persuade Otto Bauer, the Austrian Foreign Minister, to submit these matters to the International for decision. When Bauer replied that the International was only a Russian instrument, the Hungarian Communists asserted that it was a legitimate multinational agency with broad influence in Hungary, Germany, Italy, Holland, and elsewhere.[15] Like the Russian Communists, the Hungarians saw the Comintern as a force or an ideal that antedated the formal creation of an organization. At one point, *Vörös Ujság* remarked that the Third International differed from the Second in that the former was more than a mere office or bureau; it was a manifestation of proletarian internationalism and the active union of the masses in revolution.[16]

The Hungarian Soviet regime undertook its responsibilities on behalf of the International with dispatch. It created a Red Army, which it regarded as an international unit, and it made immediate efforts to spread the revolution abroad. Within a few days after March 21, there were indications that revolutionary agents had been sent to Bulgaria, had been placed among Rumanian troops, and had begun operating from the Hungarian legation in Vienna.[17]

The Magyar Communists made their most forceful effort in Austria, where conditions seemed to be particularly favorable. The existence of an active proletariat in industrialized Vienna and the rise to power of such Left Socialists as Adler and Bauer at the end of the war opened the possibility that Austria would move toward, or perhaps into, a league of Soviet states. But the country's new government—a coalition of the Social Democrats and the Christian Social Party—had more pressing concerns in the spring and summer of 1919. A struggle with the new Czechoslovakian state over the Sudetenland and a strong desire for unification with Socialist Germany influenced the Austrian leaders more than the importunings of the Communists. The government had to keep the capital city fed, and for this it depended on the non-Socialist countryside and food shipments from the Allies. Under the circumstances, good relations with the peasantry and with the Allies were crucial. Since the Austrian government looked westward rather than eastward for answers to its problems, Kun tried to prepare the small Austrian Communist Party for a *coup* against the existing regime.

The beginnings of the Communist Party in Austria, as in Hungary, had been closely related to the return of war prisoners from Russia. The Austrian counterpart of Kun was Karl Tomann, who had served in the Austro-Hungarian army, had been captured by the Russians during the war, and had worked among the Hapsburg troops on behalf of the Bolsheviks. While in Russia, he helped to publish two propaganda newspapers, *Die Weltrevolution* and *Die Nachrichten,* and in December 1918 he returned to Vienna just as the Austrian Communist Party was being established.[18] At the party's first congress on February 9, he presented the program and the organizational statute that the new party adopted.[19] The first point of the statute provided that the Communist Party of German Austria was part of the "International Communist League."[20] Like other students of Bolshevism, Tomann had learned well the commandment to preach the message of international union.

The Austrian Communists decided to abstain from the elections of

February 1919, at which the country would select members of a constituent assembly. Like many of the new Communist movements of
that period, the Austrian group felt that it should not try to elect representatives to what appeared to be a bourgeois and Social Democratic
institution. They decided to rely instead on capturing the workers'
councils or soviets, which were also then being formed, and to await
the proper time for seizing power by force. The Social Democrats won
an impressive victory and became the principal party in the new government, at the same time retaining control of the soviets. The leading
figure in this accomplishment was Friedrich Adler, the highly popular moderate Socialist who had advocated a mild attitude toward Bolshevism during the Berne conference. By following a policy of encouragement and sympathy toward the Communists in Russia and Hungary, and one of firm restraint toward them in Austria, he managed
to give the appearance of revolutionary attitudes and at the same time
to save moderate Socialism.[21]

Against this background, Kun tried to export his revolution to Austria. Even while negotiating with Bauer and trying to induce him to
accept the Third International as arbiter, Kun was directing the conspiracy in the Hungarian legation to put Tomann into power. A demonstration in front of the parliament building in Vienna was called by
the Communists on April 17, but was dispersed rather easily by the
Volkswehr, a popular army under the control of officers sympathetic
to the Socialists.[22] Kun's agents, however, resumed their plotting, until on May 2 a group of counterrevolutionaries from Hungary forced
their way into the legation. They won control of the building, captured some of Kun's agents who were carrying money and conspiracy
plans, and turned the evidence over to the Austrian government.[23]

The Communists continued their planning undaunted, while the
Socialists, aware of the danger, prepared for the test. It came on June
14; the Communists issued a call for a mass demonstration for the following day and summoned members of the Volkswehr to join with
the workers in creating a Soviet dictatorship. The Socialist government and militia leaders acted efficiently to confine the dangerous elements of the Volkswehr, to arrest Communist Party officials, and to
protect vital points in the city. The plot collapsed almost immedi-

ately.[24] The Communists made still another attempt on July 21, in connection with an effort to provoke a Continent-wide demonstration on behalf of the Russian and Hungarian governments, but this also failed.

The Hungarians tried to emulate their teachers not only in exporting revolution, but also in publishing activities. They established a French-language newspaper similar to the one the French émigrés had published in Moscow in the winter of 1918–19. Like its Moscow predecessor, the Budapest journal was called *La Troisième Internationale,* and it was directed primarily toward members of the French military missions in Central Europe.[25] The government and party press also produced a quantity of theoretical and provocative tracts in German.[26] The regime thus tried to spread its message beyond the national borders before it had consolidated its position domestically, and this procedure corresponded with Kun's estimate of his duties toward the International.

It is possible, however, to overemphasize the extent to which Kun's foreign policy was subordinated to the ends of the Comintern. Like the Russian Soviet leaders earlier, he admitted that his regime was willing to enter into conventional relations with capitalistic governments for the sake of achieving peace. Similarly, he denied government responsibility for revolutionary propaganda.[27] It is also possible to give too much stress to the degree of control that Moscow exercised over such peace gestures. When an Allied peace mission, headed by Jan Christian Smuts, visited Budapest for negotiations on April 4 and 5, its members generally assumed that Kun was consulting the Russians on every point, but this is extremely doubtful in view of the state of communications.[28] During a period of frequent telegram exchanges between Kun and Clemenceau in June and July when both sides were seeking the basis for a truce on Hungary's borders, no intimate guidance from Moscow or Petrograd existed. When the Hungarian government dispatched Wilhelm Boehm to Vienna in the middle of July to negotiate with Allied diplomats, the action seems to have been taken without specific instructions from Moscow.

In other words, though Kun applied the general procedures that he had learned in Moscow to foreign affairs, he acted with relative freedom in his day-to-day foreign policy decisions. In view of the Bolsheviks' practice of finding errors in unsuccessful decisions that have not had the benefit of Moscow's participation, one might expect Communist literature to stress the administrative flaws in the Hungarians' execution of their Comintern mission. Although some such criticism exists, the real lesson the Bolsheviks drew from the Hungarian experience was the "error" of association with the Social Democrats.[29]

The Comintern and the Hungarian "Error"

The Bolsheviks later claimed to have perceived the "error" soon after they had learned of the agreement of March 21. They cited the previously mentioned messages of Lenin and Zinoviev as evidence of early recognition of the dangers of affiliation with the Social Democrats. But an examination of Comintern literature for the period indicates that they abandoned these misgivings when the Hungarian regime seemed to be successful. Not only had the initial messages from Russia contained a degree of approval for the arrangement with the Social Democrats, but later messages broadened and deepened this endorsement, and the International headquarters sanctioned the very conditions of union that it had originally questioned and was later to condemn.

One of the most explicit messages of approval for the Hungarian alliance came from Lenin in May. In a greeting that appeared in the *Communist International,* Lenin said the Hungarian situation "fills us with joy and triumph." He had only recently made his observation that the more cultured and better-developed nations would eventually bypass Russia in advancing the cause of the proletarian revolution, and he remarked that in the matter of organization, "it seems the Hungarian proletariat has overtaken us already." He added: "Comrade Hungarian workers, you have given the world an even better example than Soviet Russia in that you have immediately been able to unite all Socialists on a platform of true proletarian dictatorship."[30]

Zinoviev shared this enthusiasm for the work of the Hungarians. He did not reprove them for failing to heed his admonition about maintaining a separate party and identifying themselves as Communists. He called them by the name they had adopted rather than the one he had imposed, and he applauded the "enormous and beneficial influence" their work was giving to the Communist movements of the whole world.[31] A recurring theme of Comintern literature in this period was that the Social Democrats had capitulated and accepted the Bolshevik position. Eugene Varga, a commissar in the Kun regime, explained in an article sent to Petrograd that it had been possible to achieve complete harmony because the Hungarian Social Democrats had been much more radical than their counterparts in other European countries.[32]

The Communist-Social Democratic regime in Hungary fell on August 1 because of an invading Rumanian army, a note from Clemenceau indicating unwillingness to make peace with Kun, and internal chaos. It immediately became necessary for Communist spokesmen to explain this failure, and the development of their explanation is illuminating. Kun's initial evaluation, made on the day of his government's collapse, was that the proletariat had left its leaders and itself in the lurch; the regime had lacked class-conscious revolutionary masses to support it, and this had made the chaos and the defeat by the counterrevolutionaries possible.[33]

Such an explanation obviously could not be reconciled with the Comintern's statements about the basic revolutionary nature of all the proletariat, and this line was gradually eliminated. The attitude that Moscow-Petrograd adopted immediately on learning of the defeat eventually became the standard line: it was a tactical error for the Communists to have affiliated with the Social Democrats, because this allowed the Social Democrats to betray the regime and the working class by secret agreements with Hungarian and foreign bourgeoisie. *Pravda*'s main headline on August 6, the day the capitulation was announced in Moscow, read, "Proletarian Hungary Falls Under the Attack of Imperialist and Menshevik Traitors," and another banner line said, "No Agreements with the Traitors."[34] This, in essence, was the lesson that the international Communist movement was to derive from the Hungarian episode, although it took some time to impose it on all affiliated parties and members.[35] The Russian leaders tacitly overlooked the extent to which they had endorsed the merger, and in this way they avoided the responsibility for the "error."

The Comintern's first official announcements on the subject asserted that the Social Democrats had helped create the disaster by making "secret treaties" with the "Versailles murderers."[36] The state of communications at the time was so erratic that Moscow could not have had evidence to support this accusation, and the Bolsheviks did not offer any that can be corroborated satisfactorily. And although the explanation was given widespread publicity by *Pravda, The Communist International,* and similar journals, conflicting theories still made their way into the Communist press.

For instance, Andreas Rudniansky, who had remained in Russia after the First Congress and had become one of the Comintern's experts on Hungary, wrote an early detailed study of the regime in which he concluded that the trade unions had helped to destroy the proletarian dictatorship. Professional and middle-class elements as well as the opportunist Social Democrats had filled the unions with "middle-class spirit," thereby destroying the influence of the Communists and undermining the revolution.[37] This argument had two edges. It employed the thesis that the Social Democrats were treacherous allies, but if the trade unions were imbued with "middle-class spirit," did this mean that Bolshevik ideas had not been accepted by the Hungarian proletariat? Zinoviev recognized the possibility of such a deduction from the Rudniansky article; he published it nevertheless, but appended an editorial note explaining that this did not imply trade unions were generally unreliable.

Kun, who fled to Vienna immediately after his government fell, modified his initial explanation within a few weeks after the collapse. His new theory was that the bureaucrats and the leaders of the trade union movement had demoralized the workers, with the aid of the Social Democrats. He wrote a pamphlet in November in which he expanded this statement into an accusation that the Social Democrats had committed treason against the proletarian dictatorship by making first a secret alliance and then an open one with the imperialist international counterrevolution. He pointed out that the Social Democrats were traditionally anti-revolutionary and anti-proletarian. He offered little evidence of the "treason," except to assert that the Social Democrats Kunfi and Boehm were traitors.[38] Kunfi had been a commissar in the government, and Boehm had commanded the armed forces until July, when he was sent as ambassador to negotiate with representatives of the Allied powers.

The adoption of the "treason" line by Kun represents a substantial change from his initial assertion that the regime had failed because the proletariat had deserted it. It is impossible to determine the extent to which Kun's later version was influenced by Moscow. Probably he adopted the new explanation mainly because the Hungarian Communists and the Social Democrats who had reached Austrian exile had become involved in a controversy about responsibility for the failure, and he found it advantageous to accuse his former allies of duplicity as a means of diverting blame from himself.[39] Boehm and Kunfi, both of whom also went into exile, had become two of his harshest critics, so it became practical to apply to them the epithet which, perhaps incidentally, Moscow-Petrograd had chosen. Kun seems to have used the explanation of Social Democratic treason with much more vigor when he was quarreling with his ex-colleagues than he did otherwise.

At times, the treason theme disappeared altogether from the argument. The Hungarian Communists' frequent failure to mention the alleged betrayal to foreign powers and the Comintern's insistence that this was the basic reason for the defeat indicates the role the International was assuming for itself. It was becoming the final authority for explaining what had happened in each revolutionary situation, regardless even of what those who had participated might claim.

One reason for the inconsistencies of the Magyar Communists was the need to justify the initial alliance with the Social Democrats. Béla Szántó, one of the Communist commissars who went into exile with Kun, wrote an essay saying that complete fusion of the two parties had not been intended, only the unity of the working class.[40] In November, a "member of the Hungarian Socialist Republic" published an article in a Communist paper in England indirectly accusing Kun of sowing the seeds of failure when he allowed the party to assume the title "Socialist." "Only a few of us could foresee then the calamitous meaning of this coalition," the writer claimed. He named a number of causes for the defeat, including such dishonorable ones as corruption, dilettante financial policies, and the lack of adequate preparation. It is notable, however, that he did not accuse the Social Democrats of making secret and treasonable treaties with the bourgeoisie, as the Comintern had reported.[41]

Writing for the same paper early in 1920, Kun denied that it had been a tactical error to associate with the Social Democrats, although he admitted it had been a mistake to allow them to attain positions of authority. Somewhat inconsistently, he said the Social Democrats had obtained "absolution" by their temporary residence under the dictatorship of the proletariat and the Third International, but had lost it by their subsequent repudiation of the revolution.[42] This hardly tallied with the assertion of consistent betrayal of the regime. Kun here neglected to mention the international treason of the Social Democrats, but he did comment on their unrevolutionary agreements since August 1.

On January 29, the leading pro-Bolshevik newspaper in Britain printed two letters from the Central Committee of the Hungarian Communist Party, which was then operating from Vienna. One of these letters said the downfall of the regime in Hungary had been "due entirely to the military pressure of the Entente."[43] Hungarian appraisals of the cause of the collapse thus seem to have varied according to the propaganda objectives and the personal motives of the individual writers.

There was no such wavering at the Petrograd headquarters. The Comintern leaders assumed their duty to be a definitive analysis that could be used as a lesson for the whole world. Having decided that widespread treason accounted for the defeat, they sought to inject this reasoning into future writings. The first extensive study of the Hungarian collapse in the *Communist International* appeared over the name of M. Gabor, and Zinoviev identified it as a work of importance. It elaborated on the assertion that direct negotiations had occurred between the Social Democrats and the Allies, and it cited Boehm's trip to Vienna as evidence; this ignored the fact that Boehm had been sent to Austria on behalf of the revolutionary government. Gabor also claimed that the majority of the Hungarian Communist Party had opposed the merger of March 21.[44]

Lenin lent his authority to the doctrine of clandestine international

negotiations by the Social Democrats. Several times in the months following the collapse, he used the Hungarian experience as proof that
affiliation with the Socialists in a position of power would encourage
treason against the revolution. In February 1920, he warned French
Communists against cooperation with the Second International, and
cited the history of the Hungarian Soviet Republic as an example of
failure to heed this caution.[45] In his famous essay *"Left-wing" Communism: An Infantile Disorder,* written in May, he again observed
that Social Democrats would become Communists temporarily in
some cases but would shortly appeal to the Allies, as they had done
in Hungary.[46] The climax of his propaganda on this point came at the
Second Congress of the International in July and August. In his opening statements, Lenin invoked Hungary as an example of how the
Social Democrats had identified themselves with revolution and the
Third International in order to betray them.[47] The Twenty-One Conditions for prospective member parties, adopted by the Second Congress, had a number of references to this thesis; according to the pre-
amble, "No Communist should forget the lessons of the Hungarian
revolution. The Hungarian proletariat paid a high price for the fusion of the Hungarian Communists with the so-called 'Left' Social
Democrats."[48] Over half of the Conditions had direct references to the
need for avoiding the kind of Socialist alliances or associations that
could hurt the revolutionary movement. Mátyás Rákosi, the most important Hungarian participant at the Second Congress, delivered a
report in which he, too, employed the Comintern interpretation, and
this served to standardize the explanation for the future.[49]

  The Comintern headquarters used Hungary as more than an object
lesson on alliances. It made use of the Hungarian exiles in Austria as
the nucleus for a Central European Bureau of the International, and
it also spread accusations of a "White Terror" in Hungary in an effort
to generate hatred for the bourgeoisie and the Allies. Kun, Rákosi,
and several other leading Bolsheviks fled Budapest immediately after
they lost power, and most of them spent the next several months in
Austria. Szamuely was killed at the border, and his death gave the
International another martyr.

  The Hungarians who escaped received kind but cautious treatment from the Austrian government. The Socialist leaders in Austria were half sympathetic toward the Hungarian exiles and half concerned about the potential menace of the Bolsheviks. Kun and his entourage were placed in protective custody in a castle of Karlstein, and from there they wrote their works on the revolution, received and sent messengers, and carried on their quarrels with the Social Democrats. Kun went to a provincial hospital briefly in the early part of 1920, and from there he was moved to the Steinhof lunatic asylum near Vienna—apparently not because of any mental disorder but for his own protection. He tended to describe his confinement as being more oppressive than it was, thus increasing his prestige abroad. At one point, he went on a hunger strike.[50] The new Hungarian government continuously sought to extradite him for trial, and the Moscow government wanted him for its own purposes. During June and July, he managed to get through Germany to the Baltic Sea and then to Russia in a contingent of war prisoners. He arrived in Moscow in August, shortly after the Second Congress ended.[51]

In addition to writing articles on the Hungarian revolution, Kun and his confederates worked closely with the Austrian Communist Party. For a time in 1920, the Austrian party's newspaper, *Die Rote Fahne,* published *Vörös Ujság* as a supplement. Kun's activities in the affairs of other West European Communist parties will be examined later.

Shortly before the Hungarian Soviet Republic fell, its leaders tried to encourage a one-day general strike among all the workers of Europe as a demonstration of sympathy for the Russian and Hungarian Soviet Republics. The idea was rapidly endorsed by many small revolutionary parties in Western Europe, and July 21 was chosen as the date. Such newspapers as *De Tribune* in Amsterdam, *The Call* and *The Workers' Dreadnought* in London, and *La Vie Ouvrière* in Paris —all organs of pro-Communist factions—tried to persuade the workers to engage in this demonstration of class solidarity, but the Socialists of the Right and Center opposed the plan, and no significant demonstrations or strikes occurred in the major countries of Europe. Owing to poor communications, Moscow and Petrograd were not well enough informed about either the planning or the results of the general strike to exert much influence. It soon became evident, however, that there had been something less than a massive proletarian demonstration. The fact that the workers had failed to rise to save the Hungarian Soviet Republic must have increased the Bolsheviks' disappointment when the Republic fell on August 1. Here was evidence that the laborers of Europe might not be as enthusiastic about Communism as had been assumed, although Zinoviev and his colleagues could not believe it at this time.

The initial success of the Communists in Hungary strengthened the belief of the Comintern leaders in immediate and inevitable revolution, and neither the failure of the Kun regime within five months nor the events of July 21 caused them to change their minds. They ignored or eliminated reports that the proletariat was not ready for revolution, and they accepted those accounts that confirmed their sentiments about the unreliability of the Socialists. Comintern headquarters came to regard the question of party name as crucial and to identify party exclusiveness as a great virtue, as if some kind of organizational perfection and purity would preclude future failures.

The Hungarian revolution was not the only episode on which the Comintern drew as it sought to "consolidate" the revolutionary experiences of Europe in 1919. In some instances, the lessons were at least partially, perhaps completely, contradictory to the one that had come from Budapest.

Chapter four Southern Europe and Scandinavia

The impact of the Hungarian revolution on Moscow-Petrograd went beyond the issue of affiliation with the Social Democrats. The temporary victory by revolutionary Communists in Hungary—primarily an agrarian country—helped to remove the distinctions Lenin and Zinoviev had previously made about the types and categories of revolution. It has recently been demonstrated that Zinoviev's concept of the international revolution was changing in the 1918–20 period.[1] In 1914–17, he had spoken in terms of "socialist" revolutions in highly industrialized states, "bourgeois democratic" revolutions in less industrialized ones, and revolutions of "national liberation" in countries financially and economically subservient to the capitalistic powers. In about January 1918, however, Zinoviev began to merge these categories, and to identify all revolutions as "socialist" even though they had not occurred in highly industrialized societies.

The October Revolution in underindustrialized Russia helped to bring about this change in attitude. By 1919, Zinoviev was referring less often to the three kinds of revolution; by 1920, he believed virtually all uprisings were "proletarian" revolutions that could occur with equal probability in any kind of society.[2] Undoubtedly, the establishment of a proletarian dictatorship in Hungary less than five months after the country's "national liberation" and "bourgeois democratic" revolution helped to destroy the old theory about different stages. And the collapse of this proletarian dictatorship did not cause Zinoviev or his colleagues to revive the former classifications, although developments might have suggested that Hungary had not been ready for a proletarian revolution. Some of the early statements of the Hungarian

Communists implied that the proletariat had not given adequate support to the revolution, but the adoption of the treason theme by Moscow-Petrograd precluded such ideas in official Comintern circles.

Another factor operated in favor of keeping the new single classification: the Hungarian revolution was not an isolated incident. Although it was the most important event in the Comintern's first year, it was only one of a number of apparently revolutionary manifestations in Europe. By the time the Hungarian dictatorship fell, several moderate successes had been recorded in other countries, and these helped to sustain the theory of the universal adherence of the masses to the ideal of proletarian revolt.

The Comintern leaders placed their greatest hopes for quick results in the three most powerful and most heavily industrialized countries —Germany, Britain, and France. In the first few months of its life, the Comintern received only mild satisfaction from events in those countries, as the next three chapters will show. Nonetheless, Bolshevik expectations remained high. From the standpoint of organizational accomplishment and the attracting of mass parties, the International fared much better at first in some of the less industrialized states, especially Italy, Bulgaria, and Norway. The Comintern also believed it saw favorable signs in several other countries in 1919, and all this served to crystallize the idea of the one-purpose, one-phase revolution.

Italy

Only one party from abroad responded more quickly than the Hungarian Communists did: the Italian Socialist Party, which claimed a membership of 300,000,[3] announced its affiliation to the Third International on March 19. The party's executive committee voted ten to three to leave the Second International and to enter a new organization based on the principles outlined in the Russians' January invitation.[4] The committee obviously knew little about the Moscow Congress; only the briefest reports of it had reached Western Europe at that time. The Italians' rapid and unquestioning support was a product of widespread sympathy for the Russian Revolution and for the Communists' expressed pacifism.

The Italian Socialist Party had been the only major Leftist party of Western Europe to oppose its country's entry into the war. For this reason its leaders were praised by Lenin, while he described the leaders of most other Socialist parties as class traitors. The majority of the party's leaders preached pacifism, and those like Mussolini who broke from the party to support nationalism when Italy entered the war were exceptions.[5] Like the Bolsheviks, most Italian Socialists wanted nothing to do with the elements of the Second International who had aided their respective governments in waging war. They boycotted the Berne Conference on the same grounds that the Bolsheviks did.

These shared viewpoints temporarily hid the differences between the Italian Socialist Party and the Bolsheviks, and enabled each to rejoice in the other's association for the time being. Balabanoff, who had worked closely with the Italian Socialists before and during the war, wrote that "feelings of joy, gratification, pride, and approval" were evoked in Russia by the decision of the Italians to affiliate.[6] The Comintern leaders were not in close enough touch with the Italian scene to know that the party's leadership had no intention of expelling the few members who had preferred to support the government's war efforts. The Comintern became more insistent about expelling moderate Socialists after the fall of the Hungarian Soviet Republic.

Giacinto Serrati, the editor of the party's daily newspaper, *Avanti!*, led the majority bloc of the party and gave it direction. The official formulation of a policy for the post-war period occurred at a national party congress at Bologna on October 5–8, 1919, at which the central committee submitted for ratification its endorsement of the Third International. The Bologna Congress also rewrote the traditional party platform.

In 1892, when the Italian Socialist Party had been formed, the original statement of objectives had called merely for an immediate "professional struggle" to improve conditions of work, and a long-range "wider struggle" to win control of the organs of government for the benefit of the working class.[7] Serrati and his followers now replaced this relatively mild language with a declaration that workers' and peasants' councils (soviets) must be established, and that they must function as "instruments of the violent struggle for liberation, and later as organs of social and economic transformation and of reconstruction in the communist new order."[8] Bolshevik influence was obvious here, but that influence had important limitations. The Serrati group had not adopted Moscow's beliefs about the need for purging the party of the moderate Socialists, and it did not feel compelled to assume the name "Communist Party," as the Comintern doctrine required.

One of the minority groups within the party did propose such action. An extreme Left wing, led by a Neopolitan engineer named Amadeo Bordiga, wanted to expel the Right wing of the party, to adopt the name imposed by the Comintern, and to withdraw from all types of participation in civil government, including parliamentary action. Serrati's program called for continued participation in parliament as a means of advancing the class struggle. The Bordiga group was more radical on this point than even the Comintern headquarters.[9]

Two other minority factions existed on the party's Right. One, led by the party secretary, Constantino Lazzari, wanted to retain the 1892 platform and favored a non-violent approach, although it basically endorsed the Bolshevik revolution. The other, identified with Filippo Turati, was a small reformist wing that sought gradual evolution and cooperation with the bourgeois parties. The Bordiga group would have expelled this faction from the party had the opportunity existed, but the overwhelming majority favored toleration. When conflicting proposals were offered to the Bologna Congress, the Serrati section won 48,411 votes, compared with 14,880 for Lazzari and 3,417 for Bordiga.[10] The Third International thus had unambiguous support; no significant resistance to the endorsement developed, and the Soviet system was hailed as the instrument of the future. Superficially, the Comintern had safely captured the Socialist movement in Italy. Lenin wrote a letter to Serrati describing the Bologna Congress as a great victory for the cause of Socialism.[11] He praised the decision of the party to continue its participation in elections and in parliamentary affairs in order to propagandize, and he thus repudiated the position of the Bordiga group.

On October 10, following the Bologna Congress, a few of the Italian delegates, as well as some foreigners who had attended the Congress, traveled to Imola, a town not far from Bologna, for another brief and informal meeting. This spontaneous gathering produced a decision to call a conference of all parties then adhering to the Comintern to study means of increasing revolutionary propaganda. This was the first effort of Western supporters of the Comintern to assemble a meeting outside Russia. The Imola participants apparently did not manage to establish a date for the conference, but they did pass several resolutions along the lines of earlier Comintern statements, chastizing the Second International and the "social patriots."[12]

In the 1919 Italian election, the Socialist Party fared well; it elected its candidates to 156 of the 508 positions in parliament, so that it controlled more than 30 per cent of the seats. The hammer and sickle had proved to be a popular political emblem.[13] Socialist newspapers throughout Europe took note of this victory, and the prestige of both the Italian party and the Comintern increased. The party's success seemed to be related to its adoption of a Bolshevik-style program. Once again, the superficial evidence implied complete agreement, but the election victory had depended on a degree of toleration within the party that the Bolsheviks would not have approved. According to Borkenau, "there was hardly a single man who agreed with the Bolsheviks" in the Italian Socialist Party. "The majority . . . rejected absolutely the idea of purging the party of reformists and 'traitors.' "[14] But this fact did not become evident until the spring and summer of 1920, when a delegation from Italy traveled to Russia and stayed on to participate in the Second Congress of the Comintern.

Switzerland

In Switzerland, as in Italy, the cause of the Third International won a quick victory, and although it turned into a defeat within a few months, it contributed to the impression that the Comintern was winning in all parts of Europe. The Swiss Socialists (the Social Democratic Party) had a wartime record much like that of the Italians; the two parties had shared a pacifist viewpoint, and they had jointly sought to re-establish Socialist unity on an anti-war basis. They had formed the so-called Italo-Swiss Committee that organized the Zimmerwald Conference in 1915. Such collaboration was still typical in 1919, when both parties refused to participate in the Berne Conference.[15]

The exile of Lenin and Zinoviev in Switzerland during the early part of the war had done little to convert the Swiss Socialist movement to Bolshevism. In fact, the contacts between Robert Grimm, the most influential of the Swiss Left Socialists, and Lenin had been unsatisfactory to both. Grimm disliked Bolshevism both for its leaders and for its ideology. The man whom Lenin and Zinoviev regarded as their most reliable agent was Fritz Platten, who had acted as a Swiss delegate to the First Congress although he had no mandate. He could not get back to Switzerland in time to guide the organizational work there for the Comintern, and the cause remained in the hands of less thoroughly trained comrades during 1919.

In spite of the reservations of Grimm and some of his associates about Bolshevism, disgust with the Second International and the example of the Italian party induced the Swiss Socialists to endorse the new International temporarily. On July 12, 1919, the executive committee issued a recommendation that the party adhere to the Third International; it cast a vote of twenty to ten in favor of affiliation, and thereby placed the question before an extraordinary party conference that had been summoned to meet in Basel on August 16 and 17.[16] The situation resembled that at the Bologna Congress. Most of the delegates arrived ready to accept affiliation, but few if any of them knew the extent to which Moscow-Petrograd would require a surrender of party sovereignty. As in Italy, there were no strong feelings about the need for expelling the Center and Right Socialists.

At the opening of the Basel Congress, a number of local party organizations submitted alternative proposals regarding the Comintern; some members sought to place conditions on the affiliation, and others wanted to suspend a decision until a new, post-war party program could be written.[17] After a long debate, the delegates voted 459 to one for withdrawal from the Second International, eliminated the modifying alternatives by decisive votes, and then, by a margin of 318 to 147, accepted the executive committee's recommendation for unqualified affiliation with the Third International.[18] Superficially, therefore, it appeared that more than two-thirds of the delegates accepted the Comintern without reservation, and when this became known abroad, another major victory for the Third International seemed to have taken place. Another less sensational vote followed, however, which received less attention but was much more indicative of the mood of the Basel conference. On the question of whether the affiliation should be submitted to party members at large for ratification by referendum, the delegates cast 224 affirmative votes and 232 negative votes. Although those who opposed the party-wide ballot had a slight majority, the rules required a referendum whenever one-third of the delegates at a congress desired one.[19]

Local units of the Social Democratic Party conducted their balloting during September. Of about 52,000 party members, fewer than half expressed a preference, and the proposal for affiliation with the Comintern was defeated by 14,612 votes to 8,722.[20] The Swiss party now found itself outside both the Second International and the Third. In subsequent months, parties in France, Germany, and the United Kingdom were also to leave the Second International without immediately joining the Third, but for the time being, the Swiss party stood alone in this position. The Comintern had suffered a defeat; but as in the case of Hungary, it eventually developed an explanation attributing the failure to the evils of the Social Democrats rather than to any weakness on the part of the Comintern or its supporters. In most public announcements after September, the Comintern minimized the importance of the referendum.

Two men shared responsibility for directing the Comintern program in Switzerland during 1919 and 1920. One was Jules Humbert-Droz, a leader of the French-speaking radicals and a man who had won notoriety during the war by his conscientious objections to defense preparations. As early as July 1919, he and some other young Leftists had recommended affiliation.[21] Humbert-Droz represented the *romand* supporters of the Third International at the Basel Congress. His counterpart for the German-speaking Swiss was Dr. Franz Welti, a Marxist who led a well-organized group in Basel. By Bolshevik standards, the arguments of these two men were relatively moderate during the Basel meetings, although they represented Bolshevik theory faithfully enough.[22] They made less use of hate-provoking slogans and vitriolic accusations than the Russians normally did, relying more on rational persuasion. Their arguments were tailored to the situation: they anticipated a victory and did not press for any division of the party. They assured the delegates that affiliation would not deprive the party of its freedom to devise its own tactics for Swiss conditions.

The unfavorable results of the referendum did not immediately cause the pro-Communist groups of Humbert-Droz and Welti to break with the party, but they did begin to discuss the possibility soon after their defeat became a fact. On September 20, *La Nouvelle Internationale,* a journal for the young French-speaking Left Socialists, said that the victory of the right-wing Socialists created the possibility of a split in the party, since the Social Democrats were even fiercer enemies of the revolution than the bourgeoisie.[23] Welti and Humbert-Droz, nevertheless, seem to have retained the hope that the whole of the party could be won over to the Comintern, or that the majority could be converted to the Left's position before a division occurred. This kept the Leftists within the party through 1920.

The most active and important factions for the Third International developed in the French-speaking cantons. In addition to *La Nouvelle Internationale,* which was published weekly, the *romand* Socialists issued a monthly theoretical journal called *Le Phare,* under the editorship of Humbert-Droz. This publication served the function of a news collection and distribution service for revolutionary parties and newspapers of Western Europe. It appeared for the first time on September 1, 1919, and its editors intended it for the same kind of role as that of the *Communist International,* except that *Le Phare* was published in only one language. It supplemented and reproduced the work of the Petrograd organ for several months. In addition, the presses of *La Nouvelle Internationale* and *Le Phare* produced dozens of brochures, leaflets, and other propaganda items.

The German-speaking Left Socialists were less effective in their propaganda enterprises. The strongest units existed at Zurich and Basel. Although a tiny group that called itself the Communist Party operated in the Zurich region, it had no general appeal or membership. It was headed by Jakob Herzog, and it had been expelled from the

Zurich Socialist organization in 1918 because of its ultra-Leftist, anarchistic point of view.[24]

Grimm, in spite of his dislike for Lenin and Bolshevism, constantly tried to rebuild an all-inclusive International to accommodate every shade of Socialism. He worked closely with elements of the French Socialist Party, the German Independent Social Democratic Party, and the British Independent Labour Party, the leaders of which had the same objective. He also tried to avoid a split within the Swiss party when the danger of one increased after the referendum. He represented himself and his faction as being in favor of affiliation with the Third International at the same time that he was trying to create a more moderate organization in Western Europe.

At a meeting of the party's central committee on April 17, 1920, Grimm proposed a motion again calling for affiliation with the Communist International. His proposal won by a vote of twenty to eighteen over a motion put forward by Paul Graber, who wanted to reconstruct an organization on the lines of the Second International but with the assurance that it would act as a unit against war credits and declarations of war in all countries.[25] The Left wing of the party, far from applauding Grimm's stand, described it as "opportunistic." According to Humbert-Droz, Grimm was simply making a gesture toward Moscow for the sake of Socialist unity without really endorsing the Comintern ideals. The central committee further aroused Humbert-Droz's suspicions by deciding to send a delegation to Russia for a conference. The German Independents, the French Socialist Party, and the British Independents had likewise by this time decided to send representatives to Moscow, and the Swiss Left Socialists read into this fact evidence of a "reconstructionist" plot.[26]

This turn of events, plus the announcement that the Second Congress of the Comintern was scheduled for July, prompted the Left wing of the party to take independent action. The Comintern headquarters, hoping to accelerate the division of the party, sent an invitation to the "Left wing" rather than to the entire party, and on June 26 and 27, the Left held a conference at Olten. This meeting selected two delegates to the Congress and adopted a resolution announcing its intention to adhere to the Third International, regardless of the decision of the party as a whole.[27] By mid-year the Swiss Socialists seemed to be near the point of decision or division.

Bulgaria

The Bolsheviks' theory that "proletarian" revolutions were possible in all kinds of societies received encouragement from Bulgaria, where one of the most active and pure parties of the Bolshevik type had a large following.[28] As we have seen, the Comintern tried to use Hungary as a base for spreading its doctrine into the Balkans; it also hoped the Bulgarian Tesniaks or "Narrow" Social Democrats would soon take power and share this work. Bulgaria did not have a well-developed proletariat, but this did not diminish the possibility of an early "socialist" revolution, according to Zinoviev's new view. The Tesniaks had pointedly repudiated the gradualist and patriotic policy of the Right wing or "Broad" Socialists. This division within the Bulgarian Social Democratic Party was recognized as early as 1903—the same year that the Bolshevik-Menshevik factions became formalized. The leader of the Tesniaks, Dimitur Blagoev, who had received some of his revolutionary training by working in Russia with the Narodnaia Volia group, developed a party hierarchy on Bolshevik lines. The Tesniaks shared the Bolsheviks' attitudes on class war, opposition to nationalistic wars, and international organization.

The Tesniaks had protested vehemently against the Balkan Wars and World War I, and each time had urged the implementation of a "Balkan Federated Republic." Their party had gained strength during the World War because of its pacifism, particularly after Bulgaria's position became serious and the war became unpopular among the people. Early in the war, Blagoev disassociated himself and the party from the Second International, and discussed the possibility of a new International that would be composed only of elements faithful to revolutionary Socialism.[29] The Tesniaks constantly attacked the right-wing Broad Socialists for their support of the war. When the Broad Socialists became associated with the defeat, the Tesniaks profited at their expense, and made significant gains in membership. The party had only 2,500 members in 1912 and 3,400 in 1915; it had 21,000 members in the spring of 1919.[30]

In one vital respect, the Tesniaks had less imagination and success than the Bolsheviks. They did not try hard enough to enlist peasant support, and they did not win it. The strong Agrarian Party, under the leadership of Alexander Stambuliski, had also opposed the war and had increased its political strength as a result. At the end of the war, it was the only party with more supporters than the Tesniaks. A mutual distrust kept the two parties apart. When a coalition government of Radicals, Agrarians, and Broad Socialists took power in September 1918, and when Stambuliski later tried to form Agrarian-Socialist governments, the Tesniaks consistently declined to participate. They regarded the peasant parties as rivals, and refused to consider the peasantry as a potential revolutionary element, although a few peasants did join the party.[31] This attitude prevailed in the Bulgarian Communist Party for many years.

The Tesniaks, like the Italian Socialists, formed a large party eager to associate with a Third International, but again like the Italians, they did not have the opportunity to participate in its creation. A Bulgarian group did exist in Petrograd at the end of 1918, much like the Hungarian group that produced Kun and Szamuely. At the meeting in Petrograd on December 19, 1918, that was regarded as a preliminary to the founding Congress, a Comrade Antonov spoke briefly and predicted that Bulgaria would not long tolerate Allied occupation. The Bulgarian group dispatched a message to their comrades in Bulgaria at this time, advocating the principles the future International was to adopt.[32] At the First Congress, the Rumanian Rakovsky represented himself as spokesman for the Balkan Federation, which presumably included the Communist groups of Rumania and Bulgaria. He had no mandate from the party in either country, and he could only claim to speak for the Bulgarians because he had once been engaged in revolutionary activity among them. He made a brief report on Bulgaria, which betrayed his lack of information on the situation there.[33]

In Bulgaria, meanwhile, the Tesniaks had prepared better than Rakovsky knew. On January 15, 1919, the party had published a declaration of principles that stated its willingness to join a new International.[34] Georgi Dimitrov, who was then a leader both in the party and in the trade union movement, and who became president of the Comintern a decade later, adopted the cause immediately. He helped to guide the party and the unions toward endorsement of the Comintern when they held congresses in May.[35]

When the Tesniaks held their meetings on May 25, 26, and 27, they adopted all the important programs the Comintern had urged, and overwhelmingly voted to affiliate. The party's official statement revealed some reluctance to abandon the title "Social Democratic," but the name "Bulgarian Communist Party" was nevertheless adopted.[36] One feature of the Congress's basic declaration was the fact that the peasants and their problems were virtually ignored. The only important reference to them came in a section calling for the abolition of private property. It said the land would become the property of all the "workers and toiling masses." It promised to expropriate large estates, but this typical Communist provision had little meaning in Bulgaria, where few large tracts remained in 1919. For the small, privately owned plots, the platform proposed collectivization and mechanization, but it also promised not to deprive peasants of their land. In other words, the Communists had relatively little to offer the peasants in Bulgaria, and the standard proposals for collectivization were a possible cause for suspicion. In the initial basic documents of the party, there were a few references to the "workers and the poor" or to the "workers and soldiers," but no mention of the peasants.[37] The Comintern headquarters later tried to correct this omission.

The Congress also became involved in a controversy over the question of parliamentary action. One group of delegates, including the editor of the party newspaper, *Rabotnicheski Vestnik* (Workers' News), opposed election campaigns and participation by Communists in the parliament; they wanted "spontaneous action in the streets" instead of political work. The Congress rejected this view and voted to offer a ticket of candidates for the summer election.[38] This debate proved to be a forerunner of the quarrels that were soon to be waged in nearly every Communist group in Europe.

The decision to place candidates in the parliamentary races brought quick rewards; in the election of August 1919, the Communists received about 120,000 votes, or 20 per cent of the total, and they won

47 of the 236 seats in the Sobranie, or parliament. Their chief competitors, the Agrarians, had about half again as many votes and 85
seats.[39] The Agrarians once more formed a coalition government without the Tesniaks (now the Communists). The Communists, however,
had considerably improved their position; they had won about twice
as many votes and four times as many seats as in the previous election.
This victory, yet another triumph for the Comintern, encouraged
Communists throughout the Continent as the news filtered north and
west.[40] But it also became obvious that if the Bulgarian Communists
could tap the political force of the peasantry, they could nearly domi-
nate the political order. The Comintern was quick to learn its lesson.
In the months that followed, propaganda from Moscow and Petrograd put special emphasis on the need for revolutionizing the peasants, not only in the Bulgarian context, but in general.[41]

On December 24, a railroad union not under Communist control
went on strike, and four days later a general strike was proclaimed
with the Communists taking the lead. Stambuliski acted vigorously
against the strikers, and by using troops and arresting several Communist leaders, he broke the general strike in eight days, although the
transportation strike lasted another month and a half.[42] The Commu-
nist-led trade unions capitulated early, but the International represented the entire fifty-four days of the railroad strike as a Communist
project and as proof of Communist-inspired revolutionary efforts.[43]
The strike failed, but the Comintern associated itself with the heroes
and victims of this proletarian unrest.

In another parliamentary election in March, the Communists made
more gains; their popular vote increased to about 180,000, and their
representation in the Sobranie rose to fifty.[44] Party membership continued to increase, reaching 35,478 in 1920.[45] The Comintern had reason to be pleased with the Bulgarian party; it was one of the most
effective and one of the largest parties in the International's network,
free of "social traitors" and "social patriots," and correct in all important theoretical matters except its peasant policy.

During the spring of 1920, the Bulgarian Communists decided to
send a delegation to Moscow for the Second Congress. Dimitrov and
Vasil Kolarov, who had managed to avoid arrest after the general

strike by going into hiding, set out by ship across the Black Sea, but the ship struck a storm and was blown onto the Rumanian coast, where they were arrested. The Rumanians surrendered the two Communist leaders to Bulgarian governmental authorities. Khristian Kabakchiev, traveling in a different ship, arrived safely in Russia and led the Bulgarian delegation to the Congress.[46]

Other Balkan States

The course of events in the new kingdom of Yugoslavia resembled that in Bulgaria in several particulars. The Serbian Social Democratic Party, like the Tesniaks, had opposed the Balkan Wars. In 1914, the party's two deputies in the Skupshtina had voted against war credits.[47] Of all the European Socialists who were required to decide between patriotism and pacifism, the Serbian Social Democrats were the only ones to vote their anti-war convictions in a parliament at the outbreak of hostilities. After the war, they benefited from the discontent and radicalism that were affecting Yugoslavia along with the rest of Europe. The party also sought to achieve unity with similar political groups in Croatia, Slovenia, Montenegro, and Bosnia-Hercegovina, which were now merging with Serbia in the new kingdom.

The Serbian party took the lead both in endorsing the concept of the Third International and in rallying the Socialists of other regions to it. The party replied to Chicherin's invitation of January 24 with an enthusiastic message that arrived in Russia about three weeks after the First Congress had closed. The communiqué expressed regrets that representatives could not be sent to the Congress, but endorsed the "Communist platform" and claimed that the workers of Serbia, Croatia, and Slovenia shared the belief in the dictatorship of the proletariat.[48]

The fact that the Serbian Social Democrats had not been able to send a delegate to Moscow did not prevent the leaders of the Congress from providing one. Il'ia Milkich, a Serb living in Moscow who had been connected with pre-war Socialism in a minor way, acted as an advisory delegate and delivered a report on the situation in his country.[49] His statements were largely confined to a description of the party's anti-chauvinist and anti-patriotic activities.[50] Milkich remained the leading spokesman for the Comintern on Yugoslav affairs until the end of the Second Congress.[51]

The Serbian Social Democrats issued an invitation on February 20 to all potentially sympathetic organizations to attend a unification conference, and the groups assembled in Belgrade on April 20–23.[52] They jointly created the Socialist Workers' (Communist) Party of Yugoslavia, uniting on principles that generally corresponded with those of the Bolsheviks. The conference endorsed the Third International, but it is questionable whether this should be regarded as formal affiliation, since the party did not officially vote to join until its second congress in June 1920.[53] This technicality, however, did not trouble the Petrograd propagandists, who wrote as if the party had affiliated.[54]

At the Belgrade Congress, the Serbian and Bosnian participants were the most eager to associate with the Comintern, while some of the Socialists from Croatia and Slovenia preferred to remain in contact with the Second International and to support the existing government temporarily.[55] The majority faction did not expel or exclude these moderates, as strict compliance with Comintern principles would have required. The desire for unity was too strong. The Comintern took note of this fact, and in one of its rare comments on the Yugoslav situation in 1919, it predicted that these "last remnants" of the Second International's ideology would soon be eliminated.[56]

Circumstances did not allow the young party the luxury of theoretical and organizational problems. The new Yugoslav government, still uncertain of itself and worried about the influence of neighboring Soviet Hungary, arrested the entire central committee within a few days of the Belgrade Congress. It banned all May Day demonstrations and hindered party operations for several weeks.[57] The party could make little contribution to the work of the Comintern, since most of the newspapers that its constituent groups controlled were also suppressed; for a short time, only *Radničke Novine,* the main organ of the Serbian Communists, remained in operation. By early 1920, most of the restrictions had been relaxed, and according to reports reaching Moscow, about sixteen newspapers were in action.[58] The Comintern, however, still had no direct contact with the Yugoslav party.

At the party's second congress, which met in Vukovar on June 20–

25, 1920, the disciples of the Third International excluded all supporters of the Second International, not from the party itself, but from positions of leadership, and elected a slate of officers completely devoted
to Moscow.[59] Hence, by the time of the Second Congress of the Comintern, the party had come closer to satisfying Bolshevik standards.
They did not manage to send any delegates to the Second Congress,
and once more Milkich spoke on their behalf.[60]

Greece likewise remained on the fringe of the Comintern's European affairs, but its Socialists, like those of Yugoslavia, contributed to
the appearance of a Comintern landslide. The Greek Socialist Workers' Party was only slightly older than the unified party of the same
name in the South Slav kingdom. It had been founded at a conference
in Piraeus in November 1918, at which time reformist Socialists predominated in the party, and they endorsed a program calling for parliamentary democracy.[61]

By spring 1919, the revolutionary faction had gathered strength; on
June 8, at a meeting of the party's national council, the Left, under the
leadership of Ligdopoulos, repealed the reformist policy of the Piraeus
meetings, denounced the Second International, and instructed the executive to affiliate with the Comintern. This action was proposed by
the Salonika section of the party, which was one of the most radical
sections but had not had much voice at Piraeus because Salonika was
in a region newly annexed to Greece. The council agreed to maintain
contact with those member parties of the Second International that
had remained faithful to the revolutionary tradition, pending the com-
pletion of arrangements for joining the Comintern.[62]

The party's second congress, meeting in Athens on April 18–25,
1920, confirmed this decision and inserted the word "Communist" in
the party's name. As in the Yugoslav party, the triumphant Left wing
allowed a minority group of moderates to remain within the organization.[63] The Greek party was smaller and weaker than the Yugoslav
one, and the *Communist International* paid little attention to the
Greek situation or the Greek party between the First and Second Congresses; in a major message from the ECCI to the Balkans on March
5, 1920, Greece was hardly mentioned.[64] It may be that the Executive

Committee made a geographical distinction for the purposes of this message, but it may also be that its members saw little support in Greece.

The Comintern found even less cause for celebration in Rumania, where the Left Socialist movement was so weak that no formal announcement of affiliation was made until May 1921.[65] Nationalism and fear of Russian aggression were too strong among the Rumanian working classes to give Bolshevism much opportunity to spread, and the post-war annexation of Bessarabia from Russia stimulated these sentiments. It was unpopular to advocate friendship with a Russian government or any kind of federation that might eliminate the country's newly won provinces.

Reformist elements retained control of the Rumanian Workers' Social Democratic Party through 1920; in the spring of 1919, as the Left wings of the Greek and Yugoslav Socialist movements were gaining control in their respective parties, the Rumanian Socialist leaders held a conference and advocated a Rightist, evolutionary approach toward a Socialist society.[66] In a national election held in November, the party received 148,000 votes and won seven seats—a comparatively good showing at that time. It ran on a platform advocating demobilization, anti-militarism, and adjustments in the social and economic order, but without the revolutionary slogans that seemed to help the Left Socialist parties in Yugoslavia and Bulgaria.

At a meeting of the party's national council in spring 1920, party leaders discussed "reconstructionist" efforts to revive the Second International as opposed to the attractions of the Comintern, but they postponed making a choice until the meeting of a party congress scheduled for August.[67] By the time of the Second Congress of the Comintern in July, Moscow-Petrograd had no reason for optimism about Rumania, except to the extent that the country was in turmoil owing to the recent war and the annexations. Rakovsky and other pro-Comintern writers produced the standard articles and slogans deducing imminent revolution from the serious economic disorder. But these same documents admitted that the workers did not want to break away from their Social Democratic leaders, that much "opportunism" existed within the party, and that the Left wing had no printing establishment or newspaper.[68]

The Balkan Communist Federation

There was some confusion among Communist leaders at this time about whether or not an affiliate of the Comintern existed in Rumania. The confusion was partly due to the creation of the Balkan Communist Federation, which had been founded in January 1920 in Sofia and had joined the Third International. According to some reports, the Rumanians were members of the Federation.

The Socialist parties in the Balkans had been interested in some kind of regional federation for many years. At the beginning of 1910, representatives of the Socialist units in Turkey, Serbia, Macedonia, Bulgaria, Rumania, Montenegro, and the South Slavic provinces under the control of Austria-Hungary met in Belgrade. They created a rather loose association called the Balkan Socialist Federation and passed a series of resolutions denouncing the reactionary Turkish and Austro-Hungarian empires and the governments of the young kingdoms of Serbia, Rumania, and Bulgaria. At that time the Socialists called for the creation of federal unity among the Balkan nations. Most of the groups represented at Belgrade subsequently opposed the Balkan Wars of 1912 and 1913.[69] During World War I, representatives of the Greek, Rumanian, Bulgarian, and Serbian Socialist parties held a second conference in Bucharest in July 1915. They rebuked the governments that were involved in or preparing for the "imperialist war," and once again advocated a Socialist federation of the states of Southeastern Europe.[70] Late in 1919, the Tesniaks decided to exploit this desire for Balkan Socialist unity on behalf of the Third International.

Little is known of the conference that assembled in Sofia on January 15, 1920, since it had to be conducted in secret.[71] This was the time of the acute labor trouble in Bulgaria; the general strike had only recently collapsed, and some of the Bulgarian Communist leaders were in hiding. The documents produced by the conference tell nothing about the participants except their attitude. It is impossible to make out whether the parties mentioned were legitimately represented. The resolutions issued by the conference implied that they had been endorsed by the "Communist and Socialist parties of Bulgaria, Serbia, Greece, and Rumania," but this cannot be definitely ascertained. According to the introduction to the resolutions, the decisions had been made with the participation of the Bulgarian Communists and the Yugoslav, Rumanian, and Greek Socialist parties, but details of the approval are not given. The introduction indicates only that the "Balkan Socialist Federation" approved the resolutions, and the reader is left to assume that the participating parties also approved.[72] In view of the Communists' willingness to find pseudo-delegates for their conferences when no legitimate ones had been appointed, suspicion is warranted. Skepticism is also invited by the fact that some of the earliest accounts of the conference reaching Petrograd and Western Europe said the Rumanians were not represented.[73] Other accounts, however, reported the participation and approval of the Rumanian party.[74]

The resolutions of the conference were unremarkable. They contained the usual accusations against nationalistic wars, imperialism, and the bankers and bourgeoisie of the great powers. They presented Communism and a Balkan Communist federation as the only cure for the region's troubles. They offered no new theories or programs. The terms "Balkan Socialist Federation" and "Balkan Communist Federation" appeared interchangeably, and in the final paragraph it was announced that the latter name had replaced the former.[75] Just as the Bolsheviks at the First Congress of the Comintern had identified themselves with the Zimmerwald movement and then announced they were replacing it with the Third International, so the anonymous organizers of the Sofia conference posed as the legitimate successors of the Balkan conferences of 1910 and 1915. Perhaps they were, but the evidence is not complete.

The Balkan Communist Federation proclaimed itself the "Balkan section" of the Third International. It is possible that Petrograd encouraged such a step, since at that time efforts were being made to establish several sections or branches—in Amsterdam, Berlin, and Copenhagen—for propaganda purposes. In addition, the Russian leaders liked the federation idea because they felt it encouraged class-consciousness and might stop the worker-soldiers of one country from marching against another country where a proletarian revolution was under way. In a commentary on the Balkan Communist Federation written early in March, Zinoviev stated that the Hungarian experience—in which the Soviet government did not receive support from the workers of Yugoslavia, Czechoslovakia, and Rumania—should have provided a lesson in the need for federation. He concluded that without close association among all Balkan revolutionary parties, victory would be impossible.[76]

Zinoviev also saw another fundamental condition for Communist success in the Balkans: "The triumph and consolidation of Soviet power in Rumania, Bulgaria, Serbia, Greece, Turkey, in all the Balkan countries, will depend on the ability of the Communists to extend the influence of their party to the *peasant masses*."[77] So two indispensable conditions—in addition to an aroused proletariat—were needed for the "inevitable" revolution. First, the Comintern leaders seem to have regarded the Federation as an instrument for preventing the kind of intervention that Rumanian troops made in the Hungarian civil war in the previous summer. Second, they obviously hoped the combined parties could avoid the error of neglecting the possibility of alliance with the peasants. Meanwhile, the Federation was supposed to convey the impression of a growing, multinational class movement.

Later in the 1920's, the Balkan Communist Federation became an active organization, but during its first year only an office for issuing proclamations existed, and it is doubtful whether any kind of formal organization operated. Certainly no bureau could function openly in Sofia at that time. A manifesto of the Federation appeared in August 1920 with the usual propaganda tidings. Its only points of interest are that it identified the Federation as the "Balkan-Danubian Communist Federation," and that it carried the names of the people who had signed the document. Perhaps these names may serve as a tentative list of the personnel or leaders of the Federation for this period. Signers for the central committee of the Bulgarian Communist Party were Blagoev, Kolarov, Kabakchiev, Dimitrov, T. Lukanov, N. Penev, and T. Kirova; for the Yugoslav party, V. Miloikovich, L. Stefanovich, P. Pavlovich, S. Markovich, and F. Fillovich; and for the central committee of the Greek Socialists, N. Dimitatros. There was no signer for Rumania—further evidence that the Rumanians had little or no part in the Federation at its inception.[78]

Another of the rare early documents of the Balkan Communist Federation is one issued in the summer of 1920 because of the Russo-Polish War. It appealed to the Communist parties of Greece, Bulgaria, and Yugoslavia to take common action against the counterrevolution in the Balkans, and especially against those who might give support to the Poles in their fight against the Russians. There was a special appeal to transportation workers to prevent the shipment of munitions to the Poles.[79] Once again, Rumania is not mentioned.

Norway

The reports of affiliation from the countries of southern Europe—Italy, Switzerland, Bulgaria, Yugoslavia, and Greece—were supplemented by similar reports from the small countries of northern Europe. In the Netherlands, Sweden, and Norway, parties or factions contributed to the bandwagon impression of Communist success. The Netherlands, which presents special problems, will receive separate treatment later, but the Scandinavian parties may be studied as a unit. The Comintern made sporadic efforts to encourage the same kind of geographical federation in Scandinavia as that which the Communist parties in the Balkans wanted to form.

In Scandinavia, the first important victory for the Comintern came in Norway. The Norwegian Labor Party, like the Italian Socialists and the Bulgarian Tesniaks, went into the Comintern *en bloc* in the spring of 1919, and like the Italians, it began to have troubles with the Comintern once it obtained detailed information about what Moscow expected. The Norwegian labor movement was historically oriented toward pacifism, anarchism, and syndicalism rather than toward Marxism; it did not share the Marxian-Bolshevik theories about the need for the exclusive leadership of the proletariat.[80]

In 1918, the Left wing of the party, led by the Bergen housepainter Martin Tranmael and the trade union organizer Kyrre Grepp, won control of the party. It adopted a resolution inviting all working people to unite behind the Labor Party and the trade union organization for the forthcoming election, so that the party could seize power by legal means. Meanwhile, the party reserved the right to take "revolutionary mass action in the fight for economic freedom."[81] In other words, even the party's Left wing was not completely opposed to winning power by legal means and not dedicated to the Soviet system. The Norwegian Laborites provide a typical example of a party attracted by the socialistic revolution in Russia, but not willing to take direct guidance from Moscow.

The news of the First Congress of the Comintern stimulated considerable interest within the party, which culminated in a congress held at Christiania on June 7–10. The congress voted overwhelmingly in favor of joining the Third International, but this action reflected an emotional, rather than a doctrinal, preference. The Norwegian Labor Party gave a partial endorsement to the Soviet system, but ruled that the country's farmers and fishermen must have equal rights with the industrial workers, who were relatively few in number.[82] A reservation of this kind, based on Norway's ocean-oriented, non-industrial economy, was unlikely to cause trouble with the Comintern; but the party also made the more dangerous statement that it intended to retain a large measure of freedom over internal policy. It expressed hesitation about the need for arming the workers for violent conflict, as the Comintern wanted to do.[83] The party's pacifist preferences went much further than the so-called pacifism of the Bolsheviks; the Norwegian Laborites preferred to deal peacefully even with their class enemies, if circumstances would permit. They also saw no need to purge the party of its moderate elements.

If the Comintern office in Petrograd learned of these reservations, it did not give them any attention in the *Communist International*. It seemed satisfied that an affiliation had been achieved.[84] Apparently the Bolsheviks were not so concerned about the reformist elements in the Norwegian party as they had been about those in the Italian movement. Indeed, Norway was seldom mentioned in Comintern literature at all. Early in 1920, Zinoviev expressed gratitude to the Norwegian party and working class for their demonstration of solidarity with Soviet Russia;[85] and there was an occasional mention of a "bureau" in the Norwegian capital, a reference to the fact that Christiania Socialists sometimes served the International by relaying messages to Western Europe when other forms of communication were slow.[86]

In April, the Right wing of the party made an effort to withdraw the organization from the Comintern, but it was thoroughly defeated.[87] The Norwegians sent one of the largest delegations from outside Russia to the Second Congress in July. All the superficial signs suggested a high degree of understanding with the Bolsheviks.

Sweden and Scandinavian Communist Cooperation

In Sweden, the Comintern did not win the nominal endorsement of the whole Socialist movement as in Norway; but it encountered a situation more to its liking in one respect. The break between the Left and Right Socialists had already occurred during the war; about a fifth of the Socialists, under the leadership of Mayor Zeth Hoeglund of Stockholm, had broken away from the Social Democratic Party and formed the Left Social Democratic Party, partly because the main wing of the party had adopted a somewhat partisan attitude toward the Allies during the war. Most of those who had composed the anarcho-syndicalist factions within the old party joined the new party.

Before 1919, the Swedish Left Social Democrats were hardly "leftist" at all by Bolshevik standards. Only their name and their opposition to the main branch of the Socialist movement gave them a semi-revolutionary appearance. In an election program ratified in February 1919, the Left Socialists called for a series of suffrage reforms, fiscal and economic changes, and social adjustments, all of which implied a gradual, peaceful revolution rather than violence.[88] By June, largely owing to Bolshevik propaganda, the party had shifted its position substantially toward that advocated by the Comintern. The party was relatively well-informed about the Comintern and its program; the communications blackout that troubled the Petrograd headquarters seems to have been less severe between Russia and Stockholm than elsewhere.

At a national congress in Stockholm on June 12–17, 1919, party delegates engaged in a long debate, and finally adopted a program that came very close to Bolshevik standards. The party's statement called for world revolution, for the dictatorship of the proletariat, for both direct and parliamentary action against the bourgeois system, and for revolutionary propaganda.[89] The party voted to affiliate with the Third International and rejected a resolution imposing conditions on the affiliation.[90] A party referendum later ratified this decision. The Swedish Left Social Democratic Party thus came nearer to meeting the Comintern's standards of purity than did the Norwegian party. It was, on the other hand, much smaller; the Norwegian party claimed about a hundred thousand members late in 1919, whereas the Swedish group had only about seventeen thousand.[91]

The Swedish Left Socialists took the initiative in creating contacts among the various Scandinavian groups that sympathized with the Third International. Their earliest work of this kind appears to have been done among youth organizations in Sweden, Norway, and Denmark. One of the early organizers was Otto Grimlund, the Swedish Left Socialist who had attended the First Congress in Moscow and had returned to Sweden to help convert his party to the Comintern. A few weeks after the June congress in Stockholm, he and a score of other Leftists from Norway, Denmark, and Sweden met in Denmark and constituted themselves the First Congress of Young Scandinavian Socialists. They claimed to speak in the name of 50,000 young Socialists in these countries.

In Denmark, there was no substantial support for the Third International, and the Comintern had no organization there until near the end of 1919. At a summer congress, the Danish Socialist Party voted to remain within the Second International, and only a small group on the extreme Left objected to this stand. It was this group that Grimlund and his associates apparently hoped to stimulate by assembling in Denmark. However, the Danish government expelled Grimlund from the country a few days after the conference opened.[92] In spite of the presence and influence of the Norwegians and Swedes who had come for the meetings, a small group of Danes still resisted the Third International. The vote to affiliate carried by sixty-eight to five.[93]

In December, a general conference of Left Socialists and syndicalists in Scandinavia was called in Stockholm, again on the initiative of the Swedish supporters of the Comintern. This congress attracted 269 delegates, according to an official Comintern account, and it included delegates who claimed to represent Finland, although none of them had come direct from that country to the Congress. This meeting recognized exiles, just as the First Congress of the Comintern had done.[94] The delegates established an inter-Scandinavian committee to coordinate activities in the various countries and to give aid to the Soviet regime. Some Swedish reformists attended, but their views had little chance of approval in such a leftist assembly. The Congress issued the usual declarations on behalf of Russia and the proletarian revolution, and against capitalism and the Second International.[95]

Comintern sympathizers controlled the meeting, but no direct representative of the Petrograd headquarters could attend. Zinoviev sent a message expressing regret at being unable to send a delegate.[96] The Comintern's affairs had to be entrusted to persons not under the immediate supervision of the Russian leaders. No important deviations from the Moscow-Petrograd line occurred in this case, as they did later when another federation experiment was tried in Amsterdam.

Conclusion

The Bolsheviks did not control any of the European revolutionary parties that associated themselves with the Third International during 1919 and early 1920. They served as an inspiration and a model, but they lacked the necessary contacts for instructing or dominating their European supporters until the summer of 1920 or—in some cases—later. The organizational successes of the Comintern in capturing the allegiance of Socialist movements in Italy, Switzerland, the Balkans, and Scandinavia compensated in part for the defeat in Hungary, and allowed the Bolsheviks to continue to say—and probably to believe—that their cause was flourishing. As for other defeats that the Communist movement suffered from time to time, these were explained away as being temporary.

The fact that by the end of 1919 the Bolsheviks were winning the civil war and defeating the intervention also gave cause for optimism. And when, early in 1920, they were able to establish more or less regular communications with affiliated parties in Europe, their confidence increased still further. Victories in these matters seemed to be preliminaries to the victory over capitalism.

Not all countries, of course, were equally responsive to Communism. The Comintern made no real progress in Belgium in 1919, despite the sufferings caused by the war, and despite the degree of industrialization there. By all current Bolshevik standards, Belgium should have had a vigorous revolutionary movement. When, in 1920, a Belgian Communist group finally did get started, it assumed a position that Petrograd considered incorrect. In Czechoslovakia, another country in which, theoretically, Communism should have been popular, nationalism and a fear of Hungarian Bolshevism stunted the movement. No important pro-Communist group emerged until 1920.* Similarly, in Spain and Poland, although the Comintern was heartened by the development of small groups, there was no marked shift toward Communism either within an existing Socialist party or within the labor movement.

The Comintern's main interest, though, was in none of the countries covered in this chapter. It lay, rather, in Germany, France, and Great Britain, and it was in these countries that the Third International learned many of the lessons which shaped its programs in 1920 and beyond.

* A Slovak Soviet Republic was organized on June 16, 1919, at Prešov, but it was a creation of the Hungarian Soviet regime, and its leaders fled when the Hungarian Red Army retreated from Slovakia in July. See Toma, pp. 203–15. Zinoviev sent greetings via Budapest to the short-lived republic on June 27, but otherwise the Comintern headquarters seems to have had no role in its affairs. *Kommunisticheskii Internatsional*, No. 3 (July 1919), col. 374.

Chapter five   Germany

Whereas the experience with Hungary taught the International that it should avoid dealings with the Social Democrats, the situation in Germany taught the opposite lesson. There, as in Hungary, a Communist party existed at the beginning of 1919, the Spartakusbund having officially become the German Communist Party (KPD) on December 30. In the next eighteen months, the Comintern leaders learned that much could be gained from working with certain Social Democratic groups in order to raid their memberships and disrupt their programs. Their sabotage was aimed in particular at the Independent Social Democrats (USPD), and they eventually devoted more energy to courting the USPD than to developing and improving a purely Bolshevik KPD.[1]

The Misfortunes of the KPD

This change of approach may be partly explained by the difficulties of the KPD, and by the failure of the German workers to produce the anticipated immediate revolution. Initially, the Comintern leaders placed great hopes on Germany and her new Communist Party. There were many signs that the events of the Russian Revolution were being re-enacted in the homeland of Karl Marx. The destruction of the imperial order, the widespread hunger and war exhaustion, the creation of soldiers' and workers' councils, the strikes among laborers and military personnel, and the effort at government by a moderate Socialist regime all had a familiar ring to the Bolsheviks. Propaganda directed to the German troops in Eastern Europe in 1918 had been obviously effective in many instances.

If, however, the stage was set for a Communist revolution, the actors themselves were not ready. At the beginning of 1919, most Germans were putting their hopes on the Paris Peace Conference rather than on any solution Moscow could offer. The armistice document included a clause promising to send food supplies to Germany, and although the Allies were slow in fulfilling this promise, the anticipation of relief from the West was an inducement to peace rather than violence. No such deterrents to revolution had existed in the Russia of 1917. In addition, the German Communists failed to gain control of any substantial number of workers' or soldiers' councils, as the Bolsheviks had done in November 1917. This failure was particularly serious in view of the fact that the coalition government under Friedrich Ebert had extensive support from these councils, far more than the Russian Provisional Government had possessed. Finally, the German Communists lacked the advantages of the anti-war agitation that had been so helpful to the Bolsheviks in their final preparations for seizing power.

Soon after the end of hostilities, the Russians had dispatched a special agent to Germany, as they had done to Hungary; but their organizer in Germany, Karl Radek, had much less success than Kun did initially. Radek, a former member of the Left Socialist movements in Poland and Germany who had worked closely with Lenin in the Zimmerwald movement, had served the Bolshevik cause in Sweden before the October Revolution, and in Russia after that time. He entered Germany illegally in December 1918. Undoubtedly, one phase of his mission was to encourage the German revolutionary Socialists to support the idea of a Third International, just as Tomann was to do in Austria and Kun in Hungary. Thus in a speech that he made in Moscow shortly before his departure for Germany, he hailed the approach of a new day, "the day of the Third International."[2]

Radek was more consistent and more intelligent than Kun, but he was also faced with a more difficult situation. The German Left Socialists were not warm in their welcome. Luxemburg was still alive, her prestige was high, and she had firm convictions about the need to postpone the creation of an International. To make matters worse, she nursed an old animosity toward Radek, and for some time after his arrival she refused to see him. Her coolness toward him, coupled with her attitude about a Third International, probably discouraged him from giving much time to promoting the idea. Also, he may not have known that a new sense of urgency was developing in Moscow about the creation of the institution.

At the end of December 1918, when the Spartakusbund and other small revolutionary Socialist groups gathered in Berlin to create the KPD, Radek spoke briefly of an International in which Germans would cooperate as members of a great league of the working class, but he made no effort to win support specifically for Lenin's proposed International.[3] The program of the Spartakists, drafted at this congress, called simply for "the immediate establishment of relations with fraternal parties in other countries in order to put the socialist revolution on an international basis, and to plan and assure peace by means of the international fraternization and revolutionary uprising of the world proletariat."[4]

Not only did the Berlin Congress of December 30–January 1 produce a vague attitude toward the contemplated International, but it failed to achieve the degree of duty within the revolutionary Left that the Comintern later regarded as essential. The new KPD absorbed a Bremen pro-Bolshevik group as well as the Spartakusbund. Another revolutionary faction, the shop stewards, remained outside the new party and retained its affiliation with the USPD even though it was far more radical than most members of that party. Luxemburg did not want the shop stewards within the KPD because she was afraid the militants among them would try to seize power before the proletariat was ready. Liebknecht, on the other hand, negotiated privately with Richard Müller, the leader of the shop stewards, in an effort to achieve unity. His efforts failed, but Luxemburg's precautions did not prevent the troubles she anticipated. On January 6, the shop stewards and other extremist elements within the USPD started demonstrations in Berlin that threw Germany into chaos for ten days. In spite of its efforts to avoid connections with this movement, the KPD became identified with the uprising. When the government crushed the demonstrations, Luxemburg and Liebknecht were arrested, and their captors put them to death on the night of January 15–16.[5]

The murder of Luxemburg and Liebknecht may have served the

Bolsheviks' cause temporarily by removing an obstacle to the creation
of the Third International, but in the final analysis it hurt the revolutionary movement in Germany. They were the most respected leaders
of the KPD. Radek had no chance to fill the vacuum because he had
been forced to go into hiding during the uprising, and he was discovered, arrested, and placed in solitary confinement.[6] The government
declared the KPD illegal, and for a year its operations were severely
handicapped. Unlike the pro-Bolshevik parties of other major European countries at the time, the KPD was forced to work underground
for several months. This seriously retarded its propaganda program
and paralyzed intra-party communications; consequently, the Comintern's cause floundered.

The KPD in Berlin had inherited a newspaper, *Die Rote Fahne,*
from the Spartakusbund, but this had to cease legal publication on
January 16. The paper reappeared on February 3 illegally, but its operation was erratic for the remainder of the year because of government pressure. At one time it apparently suspended publication for
several months.[7] Other editions appeared elsewhere in Germany during the year, notably in Munich and Mannheim; the Munich edition
apparently suspended operation on May 1, and the Mannheim one
appeared fairly regularly throughout 1919.

In other cities, branches of the party published other periodicals.
In Frankfurt, for example, the KPD unit issued the *Spartakus,* which
managed to offer its readers a report on the Moscow Congress on
March 18, less than two weeks after the conference had ended. Few
newspapers in Central or Western Europe produced a news report on
the Congress earlier than this. It obtained its information from a copy
of *Pravda* that contained a statement by Lenin on the founding of the
Third International.[8] The Munich *Rote Fahne* carried a brief account
of the Moscow Congress on March 21, and during the short period of
its existence, the journal published quite a large number of documents
from the Russian and Hungarian branches of the Comintern.[9] The
Leipzig *Rote Fahne,* however, did not print an account of the First
Congress until the end of April, more than a month after the Frankfurt branch and the leading Socialist newspapers of France and Italy.
The Leipzig branch of the KPD had had access to the Manifesto of

the Congress on April 20, but the editors of the journal lacked details of the Congress,[10] and only on April 27 did they finally produce a good account of the proceedings.[11] The information was even slower in reaching Mannheim. There, the *Rote Fahne* did not publish a report on the Congress until May 6, and even then the account was brief. In three subsequent issues, the paper published parts of the Manifesto, offering it to the readers piecemeal.[12] This great variation in the publishing of basic Communist news and documents shows how little coordination there was among the various branches of the party and between the KPD and Moscow-Petrograd.

With Luxemburg gone from the scene, the various branches of the KPD were quite willing to accept the idea of a Russian-led International. Radek cannot be given credit for this change of attitude, since he had little contact with any section of the party during the early months of his confinement, when the change was taking place. Perhaps the Comintern's efforts to create a martyrology helped to bring about acceptance for the International. The Leipzig *Rote Fahne* received messages of regret from Moscow-Petrograd over the deaths of Luxemburg and Liebknecht even before it had obtained an account of the Moscow Congress.* Zinoviev's first success in the German Communist press was to transform the KPD's martyrs into Comintern heroes.[13]

The man who emerged as the new leader of the KPD, Paul Levi, was an admirer and pupil of Luxemburg. He, too, was firmly convinced that rash revolutionary developments should be avoided while the proletariat was still unready to act. For Levi, the grim lesson of the January riots was that the KPD must move slowly toward any future revolutionary action. He even felt that the Communists' separation from the USPD and the creation of a separate party had come too early.[14] He devoted much energy during the next year and a half to re-establishing organizational contact with the Left wing of the USPD, and his goal was achieved near the end of 1920. One of the many ironies of the early history of the Comintern is that at the very time when the hopes of a German revolution were highest in Moscow

---

* The later murder of Leo Jogiches, another KPD leader, was also worked into the martyrology.

and Petrograd, leadership of the German Communists had passed to a man who wanted to prevent an early revolt. The Comintern could exercise no real control over the situation until the summer of 1920.

Discouraged and fragmented, the KPD limped through the spring and summer of 1919 without making any important contribution to the Communist International or gaining any real help from it. The only exception in this period of lethargy came in Bavaria, where the brief revolution and the short-lived Soviet republics served to reinforce Levi in his cautious approach, and also to confirm briefly the predictions and hopes of the Comintern headquarters.

The Bavarian Soviet Republics

Events in Munich in the late fall of 1918 had followed the same general pattern as those in Berlin.[15] The Social Democrats had proclaimed a Bavarian republic, and Kurt Eisner, an Independent Socialist, became the first premier. There was a strong body of opinion in favor of establishing a separate Bavarian state, since the Prussian-led unification of Germany in 1871 had always been unpopular with Germans in the south. Both monarchists and Left revolutionaries in Bavaria had reasons for wanting to see this moderate Socialist regime fail, and on February 21, 1919, a royalist sympathizer assassinated Eisner on a Munich street. This provoked a riot in the local parliament (Landtag), and the ensuing chaos reduced the chances for a stable republican regime.

During the next few days, local units of the SPD, the USPD, the KPD, and anarchist groups formed themselves into the Workers' and Soldiers' Soviet, and this body decided almost immediately to proclaim a socialist republic to replace the Landtag. The KPD representatives, expressing their fears about overhasty action, voted against the proposal. The motion carried 234 to 70.[16] In the meantime, a section of the SPD led by Johannes Hoffmann tried to save the Eisner Republic, and for more than a month an interregnum existed in which Hoffmann held office precariously. Finally, the proclamation of the Hungarian Soviet Republic on March 21 gave the Bavarian radicals the necessary push;[17] on April 7, they seized power in Munich and proclaimed the first of the two Bavarian Soviet republics.

A motley group of politicians came to power in that first April *coup,* and Communist commentators have taken pains to disassociate their party from it.[18] The regime, under the leadership of Gustav Landauer, identified itself as the Zentralrat, and the Communists quickly dubbed it the "Scheinräterepublik," or "sham Soviet republic." Its leaders included a number of intellectuals and anarchists who had no idea of how to organize a revolution and little understanding of the problems of the proletariat. The KPD conducted a campaign against the Zentralrat during the whole week of its existence from April 7 to April 13. On the day the regime was proclaimed, the Munich *Rote Fahne* appealed to the workers not to follow the "sham" Soviet government but to remain faithful to the instructions of the KPD; and it tried to brand the new government as a bourgeois trick.[19] In these circumstances, it is understandable that Communist commentators should have done their best to discredit the Zentralrat. But what they fail to mention is that, in contrast with the KPD, the Comintern and the Moscow Bolsheviks endorsed the regime.

Moscow-Petrograd and Budapest quickly accepted the Zentralrat as a legitimate part of the Comintern.[20] As early as April 9, *Pravda* acclaimed the *coup* as a victory for the International.[21] On about April 12, the Zentralrat Foreign Minister, Dr. Franz Lipp, received a dispatch from Chicherin that contained an endorsement from both the Russian government and the International. It asked for as full a report on conditions as radio communication would permit (radio communiqués being audited by the "whole world"). It also asked about the relationship of the Munich Communists to the USPD and the SPD. Information would be relayed through Budapest, Chicherin said, and he promised that further material from the Comintern Congress would be transmitted. The message confessed almost complete lack of information about the situation in Bavaria.[22] The Bolshevik leaders obviously did not know that the KPD was opposing the regime, and it did not occur to them that non-Bolshevik groups might have adopted the Soviet form. Moscow and the Comintern headquarters were not fussy in their choice of allies during this period of rampant idealism. Once again, as in the earliest phase of the Hungarian Soviet regime, officials of the Moscow government had apparently bypassed Zinoviev and the machinery of the Comintern in Petrograd in order to encourage the revolution beyond Russia's borders.

The KPD, too, was in an embarrassing position. It knew that the Hungarian Communists were pleased about the establishment of a Soviet regime in Bavaria, and there was little it could say except that the Hungarians would be even more pleased if a true Communist regime were established.[23]

This situation, however, did not last long. On April 13, the Zentralrat, barely a week old, collapsed in the face of public disorder and the revolt of a local military garrison. After several hours of confusion, the KPD took over the government of Munich. Ruth Fischer has written of this transition: "It has often been asked in Communist literature why the party let itself be forced into a policy that from the onset it judged disastrous. Very simply, the Communists could not resist the drive of the Munich workers, who, irritated after the garrison coup, wanted to defend Munich."[24] It is impossible to prove or disprove that the Communists were forced to take power because of the irresistible demands of the proletariat. One must be suspicious of a conclusion that fits Marxian doctrine so closely and has so little supporting evidence; it is possible that the workers would have been satisfied with a moderate Socialist regime or even with the restoration of the Wittelsbach dynasty, if there had been leaders disposed to guide them in either of these directions. In the absence of definitive evidence, it is reasonable to suggest that the KPD put aside its reticence about the premature assumption of power because of the frustrations it had suffered under the Zentralrat. The KPD leaders undoubtedly worried about the fact that Moscow and Budapest were endorsing a "sham" Soviet regime; perhaps a desire to prove they were truer revolutionaries, combined with an urge to share the glory that Moscow and Budapest were directing toward the Zentralrat, prompted them to take power at this time. If so, then the Third International was at least indirectly responsible for the KPD's action. Direct responsibility cannot be assigned with any certainty, since it is not clear whether the headquarters in Moscow, or Zinoviev's staff, had anything to do with the favorable messages issued on the Zentralrat.

When the Communist Soviet government came into existence in

Bavaria, the leadership of the Munich KPD included two men of Russian origin who became the most prominent members of the regime. Eugen Leviné, the son of a wealthy merchant, had spent his youth in Petrograd (then St. Petersburg), where he attended German schools, and he had become acquainted with Russian revolutionary groups in his early years. He participated in the 1905 revolution in St. Petersburg, and spent several years in Siberia as a result. He had escaped to Germany, where he associated with the USPD and eventually the KPD. He arrived in Munich in March 1919. Unlike Kun and Radek, he was not a disciple of Lenin, but as a Russian and a Communist, he was attractive to the revolutionary elements in Bavaria.

Leviné's associate was Max Levien, a native of Moscow who had also gained his revolutionary training in Russia in 1905. He had been arrested for his activities and eventually emigrated. He came into contact with Lenin in Switzerland before the war, served in the German infantry during the war, and at the end of hostilities took his revolutionary ideas to Munich. He identified himself with the Spartacist movement there, and with the Soldiers' Soviet that was formed in February.[25]

Neither of these men, nor any of the other leaders of the Bavarian Communist movement, had been in contact with Lenin during the years when the idea of the Third International was taking shape. The mystique of the Communist International, which meant so much to Kun and Radek and Fernand Loriot (the Frenchman whose extensive services to the Comintern will be examined later), did not affect them. In their writings and proclamations they mentioned the organization favorably, of course, but there was an absence of the intense romanticism that existed in Moscow, Petrograd, and Budapest. To the Bavarian Communists, it seems, the Comintern was not a super-government or a spiritual union of the workers; it was merely an organization.

Moscow was unable to keep abreast of the chaotic developments in Munich by relaying messages through Budapest. Judging from *Pravda*'s accounts of events in Bavaria, the Bolsheviks had only scanty reports on developments there during the seventeen days of the second, or Communist, Soviet republic. Apparently, Moscow did not hear about the transfer of power of April 13 until two or three days after the event, and even then its data seem to have been fragmentary. On April 17, for example, *Pravda* reported the "restoration" of Soviet power in Munich, not knowing perhaps that the new Soviet regime was a repudiation of the old one.[26] More precise information was available on the following day—five days after the Communist *coup* in Bavaria.[27] This information was obtained from a monitoring of the German radio station at Nauen, rather than from Budapest or Munich. Thus the Comintern became aware only slowly that its spokesmen in southern Germany had not been in control all along, and that the original Soviet experiment there did not meet their standards.

The Leviné government broadcasted a message to Russia and Hungary on April 15, describing itself as the true Soviet regime.[28] There is no evidence of a dispatch from Lenin or other high-ranking Bolsheviks to the Munich Communists until April 27. On that date, Lenin composed a message to the Bavarians, but it is questionable whether he was replying to the document of April 15. He asked for information on domestic matters, primarily relating to preparations for a civil war.[29] At approximately the same time as Lenin's message was composed, the Communist government of Leviné was replaced by a more nationalistic regime headed by Ernst Toller, which survived for only three days. Lenin's message arrived in Munich on April 29, but by that time, troops of the Freikorps,* together with Social Democratic volunteers, had been assembled from other parts of Germany and were ready to recapture the city from the Communists. They entered Munich on May 1, and after fierce fighting put an end to the Third International's outpost in Bavaria.[30] Apparently there was no chance to answer Lenin's inquiry, which was the only significant dispatch to be exchanged by the two revolutionary governments between April 13 and May 1.

Zinoviev's headquarters, it seems, did not have an opportunity to play any part in organizing, guiding, or even communicating with the Bavarian Soviet republics. Those messages that reached Munich from Russia originated in Moscow, not Petrograd. The only message from Zinoviev was a brief greeting telling the Bavarian revolutionaries that

---

* Semi-official, volunteer military units led by former officers of the Imperial Army.

they held a crucial position in the struggle for Germany and Europe.[31] The first number of the *Communist International,* in which the new Bavarian and Hungarian Soviet regimes were acclaimed, was published on the day the Communists were being overwhelmed on the streets of Munich.[32] The news of the collapse filtered through the communications system to Moscow only three or four days later.[33]

The failure of the Soviets in Bavaria did not have nearly the impact in Russia that the collapse of the Hungarian regime was to have a few months later. At this early stage, the reversal of Communist fortunes seemed only temporary, since the Bolsheviks were convinced the revolutionary movement was growing in Germany. The Russian leaders, partly owing to ineffective contacts, never became personally involved in the Bavarian situation as they were to be in the Hungarian. The defeat furnished Comintern propagandists with new material for use against the Allies and the Social Democrats, and after the execution of Leviné and other leaders of the uprising, it gave them another contingent of martyrs for exploitation.[34] But the long-range effect of the Bavarian episode on the Comintern's operations was negligible.

A New Program: Levi vs. Radek

For the KPD outside Bavaria, the failure of the Munich Soviets was taken as additional proof that much more popular support would be needed before the Communists could assume power. Borkenau has accurately described the fall of the Munich Soviets as the end of one phase of the German Communist experiment.[35] After this experience, Levi endeavored to find new strength for his party by shifting it toward the Right, and by proclaiming an "anti-Putsch" policy that he hoped would prevent further useless uprisings. His specific objective was to attract membership away from the USPD, and he sought to adjust the KPD program accordingly. At the party's founding congress in Berlin at the beginning of 1919, the KPD had voted 62 to 23 against participation in elections for the constituent assembly that was to create a new republic. Luxemburg and several other leaders had preferred to participate in the elections, but the majority decided to put exclusive faith in a new system of Soviet-type organizations that were also being started in Germany at this time.[36]

A congress of Workers' and Soldiers' Soviets had convened in Berlin in December 1918, but supporters of the USPD and the SPD had controlled the meetings, and the Spartacist element—then still within the USPD—had little voice. When a second congress of the Soviets met in April 1919, only a single Spartacist-Communist participated.[37] The Soviets did not meet again in a congress after this, so the Communists had no opportunity to use them to develop a power center against the government.

At the founding congress of the KPD, the party had also denounced the existing trade unions, claiming that they were led by reactionaries and class traitors. In the confusing months that followed, however, they did nothing to remove party members from the unions or to create rival factions. Levi decided that withdrawal from the trade unions would only increase the party's isolation and reduce its effectiveness. Many trade union members belonged also to the USPD, and since Levi sought more rather than less contact with that faction, he felt Communist participation in the unions was desirable.[38]

Levi's shift toward the Right aroused considerable suspicion within some units of the party, and it also seems to have worried Radek in his prison cell.[39] Only a month after his arrest and confinement, the Executive Committee of the Comintern appointed Radek as its secretary, but this had no immediate effect in Germany because his contact with the KPD was negligible for several weeks. In August, however, his solitary confinement ended, and although he remained in jail a while longer, he was allowed to have visitors and exchange messages. From this time until his departure from Germany early in 1920, he maintained a continuous if imperfect communication with the KPD leaders. Radek's status as secretary of the International, though, did not impress Levi enough to assure complete agreement on tactical and theoretical matters; their differences on the question of party alliances and parliamentary activity are a case in point.

A few weeks after his release from solitary confinement, Radek became worried that the KPD would make an unrevolutionary compromise with the Left wing of the USPD. In September, he wrote a long article, part of which warned the KPD against the wrong kind of understanding with the Left Independents. Such Left USPD leaders as

Ernst Däumig and Richard Müller, he said, had revealed a Utopian tendency after the revolutionary failures of January and March; after this they had moved into a "Putschist-Blanquist" phase, and finally into a "Proudhonist" one.[40] Although he did not direct his remarks specifically to Levi, he obviously had the KPD's new efforts at reconciliation and its "anti-Putsch" doctrine in mind. He insisted that the USPD Left must give more evidence of revolutionary intentions and renounce its present rightist leadership. He attributed the failures of the Soviet regimes in Bavaria and Hungary to collaboration with the "Independents." Although he probably did not know that Moscow-Petrograd was adopting a similar line with regard to the Hungarian Communist defeat, he employed the standard Comintern arguments with only minor variations. Kunfi and his associates were "Independents," according to Radek's interpretation.[41]

Another of Radek's warnings was that "the only parties eligible for membership in the Communist International are those that refuse every compromise with the bourgeoisie and its Social Democratic lackeys." By the same token, the means of struggle that a party selected determined its eligibility to participate in the Comintern, and this brought up the question of parliamentary activity. Whether or not the KPD adopted parliamentary means must be made secondary to the need to broaden and deepen the revolution and to increase the social crisis of capitalism. He then added that one of the main aims of the party must be to advance the Comintern as an International Federative Soviet Socialist Republic.[42] In other words, he regarded the parliamentary question in itself as of secondary importance, but if it led to improper collaboration with the USPD, this would be a matter of primary concern to the Comintern. It is interesting that Lenin, only about two weeks earlier, had taken an almost identical position concerning a British dispute over parliamentary activity.[43] Early in 1920, the Comintern shifted its attitude substantially on this issue.

Levi pursued his program without any notable concession to Radek's point of view. Most KPD leaders did not visit Radek in jail because of the danger of compromising themselves, but couriers passed messages back and forth. A measure of Levi's disregard for Radek's warning is evident in his handling of the second party conference in

Heidelberg on October 20–24. Levi had decided to present a program endorsing parliamentary action and urging Communist participation in the existing trade unions. He intended to expel from the party all who opposed this principle, notably the syndicalist and "Putschist" elements, whose efforts to capture the potentially revolutionary factions within the USPD were handicapping the Communist cause. The program that he presented at the beginning of the Heidelberg Congress—and it was finally adopted by the majority—sounded in places like a polemical answer to Radek's warnings. It said the question of participation in elections was subordinate to the need to intensify the revolutionary struggle, and it endorsed the idea that parliamentary action could be used as a revolutionary means. But it also made clear that cooperation with non-Communist groups could in some instances advance the cause of revolution.[44]

Radek learned of Levi's intention to expel automatically any members who voted against the program, and he sought to avoid the rupture. He admitted that he had no objection to KPD participation in parliamentary elections, in the legislative chambers, and in the trade unions.[45] But he begged Levi to avoid creating a schism in the party. Levi nevertheless proceeded according to his original plan. Near the end of the conference, a series of votes brought about the endorsement of his platform and the exclusion of the minority.[46] Thus Radek's influence had failed to avert a further numerical diminution of the party.

The expelled members did not consider themselves out of the party immediately after Heidelberg; for a time they represented themselves as a "Left Opposition" within the KPD, and their leaders flirted with an odd movement known as "national Bolshevism." Eventually, after a long period of bickering (which will be examined shortly), the "Left Opposition" or "Putschist" elements of the KPD announced their own split and formed the Kommunistische Arbeiter-Partei Deutschlands (KAPD). This development, which came in April 1920, complicated the efforts of the Comintern leaders to unify the revolutionary elements. The KAPD linked itself with other parties of similar persuasion in the so-called West European Bureau of the Comintern and thus became one unit of a group that threatened to change the direction Moscow-Petrograd had given to the International.[47] National Bolshevism was a movement that contemplated the union of German military and nationalistic zealots with the Bolsheviks in order to upset the Versailles Treaty and to drive the Allied powers from Europe. Two of its leaders were Hamburg Communists—Heinrich Laufenberg and Fritz Wolffheim—whom Levi had ejected from the KPD in October. They annoyed the Comintern and incurred the criticism of Lenin in 1920.[48]

Another intriguing fact about the Heidelberg Congress is that an unnamed representative of the Third International, possibly from Russia, participated. He made one brief comment on the structure of the Communist party in Russia, and another in support of Levi's proposal to engage in parliamentary activity. He said withdrawal from parliament by party members at some future date could serve as a revolutionary act, and he remarked that a "true Communist does not need to be afraid of a compromise in parliament."[49]

This person cannot have been a very dynamic spokesman for the Comintern cause, because the conference did not issue any of the typical expressions of enthusiasm for the world revolutionary movement. The documents from the Heidelberg meetings lack the kind of dramatic pronouncements for the International and for Bolshevism that appeared earlier among the Hungarian Communists and during the same period at the meetings of the British and French supporters of the Comintern. Perhaps the underground status of the party and the desire to avoid untimely revolts influenced the decision not to propagandize for the world revolution; perhaps Levi and his supporters were so preoccupied with internal problems that no attention could be given to such external matters. Perhaps, too, Levi, as a disciple of Luxemburg, was less than enthusiastic about a Russian-led organization.

As Levi succeeded in shifting his party toward the Right—toward the USPD—Radek seems to have gained renewed interest in attracting the USPD toward the Left. In November, writing under a pseudonym, he considered the possibility that at least part of the USPD could become revolutionary enough to merit membership in the Third International. His remarks were still uncomplimentary, but his hopes for a reconciliation of the two parties on Communist terms had improved since the summer.[50] Thus in November, both Levi and Radek saw that the future of the revolutionary movement could depend on developments within the party. The KPD had suffered from the Heidelberg schism to the extent that it soon lost nearly half of its membership, which had been estimated at about 107,000 before the division. The heaviest membership losses were in Berlin and other parts of north Germany.[51] The only way to compensate for this loss, Radek and Levi both decided, was to raid the ranks of the USPD.

The Transition of the USPD

Initially, the spokesmen for the Comintern had an intense distrust of the USPD and made no distinction between its revolutionary elements and those of its leaders who, like Kautsky, were close to the position of the SPD in their political views. Lenin, in his article on the Berne Congress, was nearly as harsh in his treatment of Ernst Däumig as he was in dealing with other "Philistines," although Däumig had attempted to ally himself with the Bolsheviks.[52] The Comintern headquarters usually identified the whole party with Kautsky, whom Lenin had scorned late in 1918 as a "renegade" within the labor movement. Zinoviev, in one of his early articles for the *Communist International,* said that whereas the USPD appeared to be adopting a more radical position, its leaders could not be trusted and the German Communists were wise to stand apart from the party.[53] Radek's early warnings to the KPD to avoid careless agreements with the USPD mirrored the attitude of the Comintern during the early summer of 1919. At this point, the Bolsheviks apparently ignored the revolutionary potential of the party.

The Bolsheviks' distrust of the USPD leadership was not based merely on the party's failure to support a revolution in Germany during the war, or on the fact that the party had participated for a few weeks in the provisional government after the November *coup* in 1918. The Bolsheviks hated the USPD because of its connection with the Berne Congress; some of the party's leaders had gone to Berne and, along with the representatives of the SPD, had voted for the Branting resolution that criticized the dictatorial methods of Bolshe-

vism. Kautsky had spoken for the resolution, and had specifically
charged the Bolsheviks with creating "a new militarism."[54] He explained and defended this position at a party congress on March 2–6,
1919, and he met opposition from Klara Zetkin, the aged revolutionary who shortly afterward shifted to the Communists. Däumig, like
Zetkin, approved the Communist position on the dictatorship of the
proletariat, although, in the tradition of Luxemburg, he disliked the
"Putschist" policy that the Communists sometimes developed as a
result.[55] Däumig, Richard Müller, Kurt Geyer, and Walter Stöcker
gradually emerged as spokesmen for the Left wing within the party,
and sought to discredit the liberal, gradualist policies of leaders like
Kautsky, Hugo Haase, and Rudolf Hilferding. At this congress the
USPD endorsed the Soviet system of government, but many party
leaders defended the parliamentary system, and no significant change
of day-to-day policy resulted.[56] Such indecisive conduct annoyed the
Bolsheviks and caused them to believe that the USPD leaders were
only mouthing slogans in order to deceive the workers.

Kautsky had been appointed to the permanent commission that was
created at Berne to follow the Versailles Conference, and he participated in the efforts to rebuild the Second International. Since the moderate Socialists at Berne had expressed high hopes for a just peace at
Versailles, their position was damaged when the Versailles Treaty
handled Germany harshly. In addition, the USPD, which had opposed
Germany's war efforts during the later part of the conflict, tended to
support the Allies' thesis that Germany was the most guilty of the
powers that had engaged in the war. This view was less attractive to
many members of the USPD than the KPD view that the bourgeoisie
and imperialists of all countries shared the war guilt, and that the proletariat of all lands were uniformly innocent. Finally, Kautsky's cause
languished within the USPD because the moderate, democratic International that he advocated had not yet been established.

Kautsky was one of the leaders of an effort to revive the Second
International at a conference in Lucerne during the first nine days of
August 1919. Five USPD spokesmen participated; they formed one
of the largest single delegations at the meetings. Once again, as at
Berne, the conference delegates quarreled over whether dictatorial, un-

democratic methods could be tolerated by the restored International. The majority resolution that resulted from the meetings showed that most of the delegates still insisted on democratic institutions and liberties, while only a minority was willing to consider dictatorial methods of revolution as a concession to Bolshevism.[57] The USPD delegates again supported the majority, even though their March platform had given qualified endorsement to the Soviet system of government; they did not regard the Soviet system as necessarily dictatorial.

More important than anything the Lucerne conference did, however, were the things it failed to do. It made no substantial progress toward re-establishing the Second International. It did draft a provisional constitution for the future organization, and it confirmed plans for a constituent congress to be held in Geneva in February 1920, but many participants were disappointed by the absence of more specific progress and by the continuing sharp disagreements. Some expressions of discontent reached the German Socialist press,[58] and these must have contributed to the sense of frustration of the USPD members who wanted international affiliations. The humiliation of Versailles, the acceptance of the theory that Germany bore much of the war guilt, and the failure to reconstruct the old International all served to erode the influence of the Kautsky-Hilferding school in the party. Kautsky admitted shortly after Lucerne that the idea of the Third International was gaining ground. He tried to convince his fellow party members that the Bolsheviks hated the USPD so much that any thoughts about dealings with Moscow should be abandoned, but he recognized the danger of the Bolshevik appeal under the circumstances.[59]

After August, the Left wing intensified its agitation for support of the Soviet system and crystallized its position on the issue of the Third International. Geyer made the question a central consideration at the party conference in September.[60] This trend in the Left wing coincided with Radek's increased activity from his prison cell, and he may have influenced the members of the USPD who went to visit him.

In the meantime, the party membership grew—from about 300,000 in March to about 750,000 by the end of 1919.[61] Since the KPD was illegal, most of those who were radical but not inclined or able to go underground in their politics went to the USPD; the party also attracted a number of Left-wing pacifists and assorted Socialists who objected to the majority Socialists for various reasons. The ambiguity on the question of parliamentary or Soviet government allowed for some of this increase in size.

The drift to the Left that Kautsky sensed in August and Geyer tried to accelerate in September received new impetus on October 8, when an assassin fatally wounded Hugo Haase, the influential moderate leader of the party. No one of his stature remained within the Center of the party, and his death early in November deprived the projected Second International of one of its most effective advocates.

The internal dilemma of the USPD and its members' increasing interest in the Comintern were funneled into a party congress that convened in Leipzig early in December. This conference was more important to the evolution of the Third International than any other European gathering between the First and Second Congresses of the Comintern. It resulted in a decision to repudiate the Second International and to seek the establishment of a new International that would include the Comintern and other revolutionary groups in Europe. Consistent with its tradition of equivocal language, however, the USPD wrote its statements on the Third International in terms that raised questions about whether it would actually endorse the Moscow-Petrograd program. Despite this lack of precision, the example of Leipzig counted heavily in a congress held by the French Socialist Party in February, and in an Easter conference held by the British Independent Labour Party. After Leipzig, the Comintern headquarters had to alter its dogmatic attitude about Social Democrats; exceptions could be made to the lesson of Hungary, once it appeared that a numerically strong party was considering affiliation.

The Leipzig Congress was a turning point in the acceptance of the Comintern by a considerable part of European Socialism, and it deserves more consideration than it has generally been given by Comintern historians. It lasted from November 30 until December 6—a relatively long period for a European Socialist congress. The length of the session and the fact that the supporters of the Third International had a more vigorous policy than their opponents helped the cause of Moscow. The cause was also helped by the fact that virtually all hope and support for the Second International had vanished within the party. Finally, the pro-Bolshevik wing used to good advantage a device that they and their colleagues were to employ again later: they managed to present at an early session of the Congress a respected pro-Communist speaker from abroad. Otto Grimlund, the leader of Left Socialism in Sweden who had attended the Moscow Congress, urged the party to affiliate with the Comintern.[62]

On December 4 and 5, during the main portion of the debate on the Internationals, three resolutions were offered for consideration.[63] The first, sponsored by Hilferding, represented approximately the position of such men as Kautsky and the deceased Haase. Hilferding argued that although the Second International no longer offered a basis for international cooperation, the Third International could not be regarded as acceptable either. He cited its modest beginnings and the fact that it sought to exclude much of the Socialist movement, and he stressed the extent to which it had rejected the USPD. He said the party would have to change its entire orientation to come to terms with the Third International. He proposed the creation of an organization with a liberal Western philosophy, some kind of body that would not represent a complete break with the traditions of the Second International but would be a more radical version of it.

Stöcker, as spokesman for the party's Left wing, offered a resolution involving unqualified affiliation with the Comintern. He granted that the Third International had been established somewhat prematurely, but he contended that it was motivated by the correct principles. Reformist Socialists would have to be excluded to protect the movement from the misfortunes of the past. He believed that by affiliating with the Comintern, the German Socialists could become the leaders and shapers of post-war Socialism.[64]

The third proposal, offered under the name of Ledebour, reflected disenchantment with the Second International and distaste for the Third. The faction that supported this resolution favored the dictatorship of the proletariat and the Soviet system, but it had been offended by the Bolshevik propaganda; Ledebour deplored the insults the Comintern had thrown at the USPD and criticized some of its leaders. He recommended that the German Independents seek a conference of all Socialists who demonstrated revolutionary preferences.

None of the three resolutions had enough support to be adopted without a compromise or coalition. Although Hilferding and Ledebour blocs shared a distaste for the conduct of the Comintern, this did not provide a basis for a coalition. Instead, a compromise was worked out on the basis of a common desire—expressed by all three groups—for some kind of international conference that would bring together the Bolsheviks and other party representatives in the West who had repudiated reform Socialism. The compromise resolution instructed the party's central committee to begin immediate negotiations with all revolutionary parties for the establishment, "in conjunction with the Third International, of a united proletarian International, capable of action."[65] The resolution was deliberately vague, except that it definitely withdrew the USPD from the Second International and announced a boycott of the proposed Geneva conference. It anticipated the creation of a new and larger International that would absorb the Comintern as well as some of the Western parties Moscow had consistently berated. At this point, it appeared that Stöcker's faction had made little headway in winning unqualified endorsement for the Russian-inspired Comintern.

Late in the debate, however, the Left wing managed to add an amendment that changed, or at least clouded, the original meaning of the compromise resolution. It said that "If the parties of other countries should not be willing to enter into the Third International with us, the union of the German Independent Social Democrats must be undertaken alone."[66] This paragraph was appended on a vote by show of hands. Its language implied the possibility of simple, total acceptance of the Comintern, and thus it conflicted with the tone of the original compromise resolution. The dichotomy that resulted in the final statement was to create confusion among the German Socialists and to work to the benefit of the pro-Bolshevik wing in the French Socialist Party two months later. The Left wing of the USPD had handled its case so deftly that even though it failed in its main objective, it won an important victory. It obtained an obscure endorsement for the Comintern despite the fact that a majority of the delegates—those who initially supported Hilferding and Ledebour—had opposed endorsement.

The West European Secretariat

At about the same time as the USPD was changing its orientation, an effort was being made to establish a branch office of the Comintern in Germany, known as the West European Secretariat.* Radek may have had a hand in guiding the early organization, but the main responsibility rested with a Bavarian Communist who identified himself as J. Thomas, and with M. J. Bronsky, a Polish associate of Radek. Little has been discovered about the origin of this office; it is even questionable whether Moscow or Petrograd was consulted about its establishment.[67] However, since Radek was secretary of the Comintern, it may not have been thought necessary to obtain specific permission from Russia.

The first official act of the Secretariat seems to have been the issuing of a manifesto, dated October 1919, observing the second anniversary of the Bolshevik Revolution. It was primarily an appeal to the workers of Europe to resist the continuing interference by the West in the Russian civil war.[68] Publication of messages of this kind became one of the main functions of the Secretariat. Late in 1919, the Berlin branch of the KPD began to issue a newspaper called *Spartakus* which carried a number of the messages and articles that Radek had written, under a pseudonym, for the Secretariat.[69] It also reproduced some of the documents of the Petrograd headquarters.

In December, an effort was made to broaden and strengthen the Secretariat. Delegates from several European countries gathered secretly, presumably in Berlin or Hamburg, and exchanged reports. Sylvia Pankhurst, the English propagandist, attended, and wrote a guarded account of the proceedings a month later. She said a decision had been made to "appoint a Secretariat for Western Europe." It appears that the persons attending the conference were given the impression that they were creating the Secretariat on behalf of the Com-

---

* This should be distinguished from the West European Bureau established later in Amsterdam. The Bureau and its relationship to the Secretariat are discussed in Chapter 8.

intern.[70] The scope of the Secretariat's activities increased after this clandestine meeting.

The action of the USPD at Leipzig gave the Secretariat its first responsibility on a matter of membership. All three factions at Leipzig had proposed some kind of a conference with the Socialist and Labor parties of other countries in order to establish a new International. About a week after the Leipzig Congress ended (i.e., mid-December), Artur Crispien, a co-chairman of the party, began to investigate the prospects for such a conference, and one of his messages to foreign party leaders suggested negotiations involving all Socialist groups and the Comintern. In this, although speaking for the entire USPD, Crispien reflected the "reconstructionist" attitude of the Center faction only, thereby annoying the Left in his own party and the Comintern in Moscow.

The Secretariat responded to Crispien's proposal on January 15 in terms less than cordial. By this time, Radek had left Germany and was en route to Russia; it is questionable whether he could have had much part in shaping the Secretariat's response to the USPD proposal. The substance of the response, however, had much in common with the views he had expressed about the USPD earlier.[71] Since the USPD had been hesitant to join the Third International, even though it repudiated the Second, the party had put itself in a foolish position, the Secretariat felt; it had not removed doubts about whether it was truly revolutionary. If the USPD proposed negotiations between the Comintern and parties that still contained "social patriots," the Secretariat refused to have anything to do with such proceedings. The statement specifically characterized negotiations with the Dutch, Swedish, and Austrian Social Democrats as "impossible," and it made similar comments about the French Socialists and British Independents under their existing leaderships and policies. It even expressed reticence about negotiations with the USPD. In any case, it said, negotiations should be carried on in public and not in secret conferences.

The Petrograd headquarters responded more slowly than the Berlin Secretariat, and Zinoviev probably did not know of the German reply when he prepared a statement of his own.[72] His answer was dated February 5, and in general his position was the same as that of the

Secretariat.[73] He gave much more attention to the theoretical problems than the Secretariat had done, and chastised the USPD in detail for past conduct. He also advocated open negotiations rather than closed-door conferences, but he took a different approach on the possibility of negotiation. In fact, he invited leaders of the USPD to travel to Russia for consultations:

The Executive Committee of the Communist International considers it highly desirable to engage in negotiations with the parties who declare themselves ready for a final break with the Second International. With this in view, the Executive Committee summons the representatives of these parties to come to Russia, where the Executive organ of the Communist International has its seat. . . .

The Executive Committee is aware that because of the complexities and specific peculiarities of the development of the revolution, complete account must be taken of these peculiarities. We are perfectly prepared to extend the Third International, to take into consideration the experience of the proletarian movement in all countries, to amend and extend the program of the Third International on the basis of Marxist theory and the experience of the revolutionary struggle throughout the world.[74]

Zinoviev tried to give the appearance of tolerance even while he rejected the idea of cooperation with the Right wing of the party. His willingness to negotiate, and his suggestion that the ECCI might yield on some points, showed a relaxation of the line the Bolsheviks had taken immediately after the fall of the Hungarian Soviet regime. In a sense, the Berlin Secretariat still applied the lesson of Hungary at this time, whereas Zinoviev, for tactical reasons, temporarily disregarded it. Both his earlier comments and his later conduct prove that he had no real intention of negotiating on the terms the USPD suggested. During 1919, German Social Democrats of all types had been special targets of the Comintern's wrath.[75] As will be seen later, Zinoviev's purpose in inviting delegates to Moscow was not to negotiate with them, but to convert and overwhelm them.

The Comintern's preoccupation with the affairs of the USPD worked to the disadvantage of the KPD. Zinoviev's answer to the USPD did say that the Independents should have expressed a willingness to amalgamate with the KPD, but this was rather scant attention to the party that Moscow-Petrograd regarded as the most nearly correct in Germany.[76] In fact, the *Communist International* contained very little news or comment on the KPD throughout 1919. This relative silence was the result of the party's lethargy, its illegal status, and the absence of contacts. Lenin, like Radek, had been disturbed by the news of the Heidelberg schism, and had declared the unity of the German Communists to be "essential."[77] This pronouncement, however, had no effect in Germany. Levi firmly believed that the welfare of the party demanded the expulsion of the anti-parliamentarians, and he held to this attitude right through the Second Congress of the Comintern, at which he quarreled with Lenin on the issue.

The Communists whom Levi had expelled at Heidelberg had been troublesome before the schism, and they became even more difficult after it. One important unit of the Left Opposition existed at Hamburg, under the influence of Laufenberg and Wolffheim,[78] and another was based in Berlin. This latter controlled a newspaper plant, which issued an edition of *Die Rote Fahne*.[79] During the summer of 1919, when Levi had been trying to guide the party back into parliamentary and trade union activity, the Berlin organization had offered strong journalistic opposition.[80] When the expulsion occurred, the evicted anti-parliamentarians had accused Levi of imposing a "dictatorship of the leader" instead of a class dictatorship, and *Die Rote Fahne* mentioned that the opposition had considered the possibility of creating a new party.[81]

As we have seen, a separate party, the KAPD, was not actually formed until April 1920. In the meantime, the Berlin organization continued to identify itself as part of the KPD and as the legitimate representative of the Comintern. The main KPD organization also occasionally spoke on behalf of the Comintern, as in October, when it issued a message to the workers of Europe asking them to strike on November 7 in commemoration of the Bolshevik Revolution.[82] Occasionally, too, because of its close relationship with the West European Secretariat, the party had its views expressed through that agency. In February, for instance, the Secretariat issued a statement of tactics that was virtually an expression of the main themes of Levi and the KPD. It cautioned against overhasty class action, and criticized anarchism and syndicalism; this remark was obviously directed against the Left Opposition.[83]

These tangled affairs of the German Socialists and Communists made the position of the Comintern very unclear during the first two months of 1920. The large USPD—formerly chastised as "social patriots"—seemed almost willing to join the Third International under certain conditions. The KPD and the West European Secretariat, which to a large extent were interlocking, regarded this prospect with suspicion and preferred to refuse all negotiations. At the same time, the Left Opposition of the KPD insisted that the majority had become too opportunistic, and the executive of the party was using the West European Secretariat as a weapon in this internal struggle. Obviously, the Comintern had to seek some kind of reconciliation and order in the chaos, but before it could do so, new complications were added. These were caused by the Kapp Putsch.

The Kapp Putsch and Its Effects

The circumstances surrounding the Kapp Putsch gave the German Communists one of their moments of choice, and their decisions gave the Comintern theorists enough new material for analysis and criticism for many months. On March 13, 1920, German generals leading the Reichswehr invaded Berlin and proclaimed a government. The existing republican regime, including the Social Democrats, fled. The figurehead leader of the new government was Dr. Wolfgang Kapp, a reactionary Prussian official. An effective counterattack came not from the Socialist or Communist organizations, but from the trade unions, led by Karl Legien. He called a general strike of the workers, and four days later the Kapp regime fell.

At the time Legien called the strike, Levi was absent from the KPD headquarters, and his subordinates issued a leaflet opposing the strike. Those responsible for the decision considered it wrong to aid the existing regime, even if it were under attack from extreme reactionaries. On the second day of the strike, when it appeared to be successful, the KPD reversed its stand, largely because its members were observing the walkout. The Left wing of the Independents, meanwhile, supported the strike and even encouraged street fighting against the Reichswehr.[84] This slow conduct by the KPD brought it much humiliation later, and even Levi upbraided those who had been responsible.[85] After the strikers had destroyed the Kapp regime and it became necessary to form a new government, Legien asked the USPD leaders whether they would cooperate. Before giving an answer, the USPD consulted the KPD to find out how the Communists would react to such an arrangement. The Communists had long regarded Legien as a class traitor, and since the majority Social Democrats would also participate in the contemplated government, the KPD could hardly endorse it. But in view of the threat from the reactionary elements that the Kapp Putsch had demonstrated, the KPD spokesmen—Jakob Walcher and Wilhelm Pieck—agreed on March 18 that the Communists would not try to overthrow such a government if the USPD remained faithful to its program. The KPD would become a "loyal opposition," Walcher said.

Again the KPD central committee procrastinated. It could not decide whether to endorse the promise made by Walcher and Pieck, and in the meantime the Left wing of the USPD stepped into the picture and demanded that their leaders renounce the proposed agreement with Legien. Rather than split the party, the USPD leaders yielded, and the issue facing the KPD became academic. This rapid sequence of events made the Left wing of the USPD appear more radical than the KPD, and once again there was plenty of material for the journalistic mills of the Communists.

One of the first direct results of the Kapp Putsch was the creation of the KAPD. For the Left Opposition group ejected at Heidelberg, the KPD's delays over the general strike and the Walcher-Pieck agreement were inexcusable. These events had proved, they said, that the KPD was both unrevolutionary and "opportunist." They denounced its *Führerpolitik,* which allegedly worked against the spontaneous revolutionary impulse of the masses, and announced that they would follow a course of direct action based upon the will of the masses.[86]

On April 4 and 5, 1920, the Left Opposition held a conference in Berlin at which it formally proclaimed the foundation of the KAPD.[87] The founders pretended to have the approval of Comintern spokesmen for their venture, since they were anxious to establish themselves as the legitimate representatives of the Third International in Germany, at the expense of the KPD.[88] The KAPD claimed it did not need to seek admission to the Comintern in view of its record and its revolutionary attitude; it had only to proclaim membership in order to establish it. One of the missions of the KAPD, the conference declared, was to fight against the KPD as an enemy and betrayer of the revolutionary movement. The KAPD thus solidified and gave voice to that wing of the German Communist movement that believed in the imminence of the revolution and the immediate need for violent action.

The Comintern offices in both Petrograd and Berlin responded negatively to the new party's claims. The West European Secretariat issued a disparaging statement within a month after the KAPD conference. It accused the party of having undesirable connections with "national Bolshevism" and with the perpetrators of the Kapp Putsch, because at one point Laufenberg and Wolffheim had tried to ally the Left Opposition with nationalist military groups. It disapproved of the party's terrorist theories and its endorsement of individual acts of sabotage, an attitude that might harm the revolutionary movement as a whole. Finally, it criticized the KAPD for having attacked the KPD while the latter was affiliated with the Comintern.[89] The tie between the KPD and the Secretariat was apparent in this document.

The Comintern headquarters in Russia naturally responded more slowly, and its answer revealed the larger context in which it operated. The ECCI issued its comments on June 2, having learned of the new party only after "some weeks."[90] It tried to deal gently with the KAPD and to encourage a reconciliation with the KPD, but it also spoke with a commanding, paternal voice about the errors of the extreme Left. It denied that Comintern representatives had contributed to the founding of the KAPD. Then, apologizing in advance for having to cause pain to the "honest revolutionary workers" in the party, the ECCI proceeded to catalog their errors. They had been wrong, the Committee said, in opposing the KPD, an action that constituted an "open deviation from Communism." They had been wrong in resisting participation in existing trade unions. And they had been wrong in permitting the "national Bolsheviks" Laufenberg and Wolffheim to play a role in party affairs, since these two men had flirted with reactionary militarists and nationalists. The ECCI ordered the KAPD to expel the two Hamburg members.

To soften its criticism, the ECCI allowed that some of the KAPD's objections to KPD policy had been valid. It was true that Levi's party had failed to "assume a firm position," and it was true that the creation of a "cult of the leader" was no business for Communists. However, although revolt against party leadership was in some cases essential, the revolt of the KAPD did not fall under this category, the ECCI contended. It found the party guilty of "vacillation in the direction of petty-bourgeois anarchist policy," and it suggested that an agreement be reached with the KPD before the Second Congress of the Comintern, which was scheduled for mid-July.[91]

Meanwhile, the Comintern headquarters continued its efforts to capture USPD membership by ridiculing the party's leaders and identifying their success in the Kapp affair with the Comintern's cause whenever possible. The response to Crispien's proposal had been rather meager. The French Socialist Party and the British Independent Labour Party approved the plan for a broad conference, and a few relatively minor parties from other countries had given their endorsement; but the attitude of the Comintern killed the idea. The USPD leaders, under the Leipzig mandate, had tried to negotiate with Moscow, but Moscow insisted that USPD representatives come to Russia for negotiation. Also, Comintern publications during the spring of 1920 implied that the Leipzig Congress had intended cordial negotiations with the Comintern but that the USPD leadership was sabotaging this objective; obviously this was a distortion of both the intent of the Congress and the conduct of the USPD executives. On two occasions, Zinoviev and Radek used the pages of the *Communist International* to accuse the party's leaders in this manner and to insist that the USPD send delegates to Russia for consultation. On one occasion, the ECCI appealed over the heads of the leaders to the local party groups.[92] These tactics had the desired effects. At a June conference, the USPD decided to send a delegation to Russia to attend the Second Congress of the Comintern, even though this had not been intended or foreseen at the time of the Leipzig Congress.[93]

The Comintern's letters to the KAPD during the same period had less productive results. The leaders of that small party were not obliged by party policy to seek reconciliation, as the USPD leaders were; in fact, their whole program was against conciliatory action. The KAPD answered the Comintern's criticism by saying that it would not make peace with the KPD; it declined to expel the members to whom the ECCI objected; and it refused to commit itself in advance to endorsement of the work of the Second Congress, as the Comintern had requested.[94] It did agree, however, to send a delegate to Moscow in the hope that he could be heard and that he would win support for his ideas.

The Kapp Putsch served to point up a number of facts. In fifteen months of dealing with the German parties, the Comintern had found itself gradually forced into a position of defending a party—the KPD —that was tactically clumsy and overcautious in a revolutionary situation. It had had to seek the favor of two rival parties—the KAPD and the USPD—that had shown themselves eager for action and in some respects more attuned to the revolutionary spirit of the Comintern than the KPD. Yet each of the two more aggressive parties was resisting the Comintern's domination. By the middle of 1920, the ECCI was rapidly abandoning the view that the KPD was the correct revolutionary party in Germany; its attitude was becoming more like that of a father who wants to impose a compromise among three quarreling children.

Ideologically, the British parties of the Left were divided in much the same way the German parties had been at the beginning of 1919. The large Labour Party, corresponding to the SPD, had shared the government's war efforts and was committed to parliamentary institutions and to peaceful revolution. The Independent Labour Party (ILP), led by Ramsay MacDonald, resembled the German USPD in that it had repudiated the main Labour Party's war efforts and held a more sympathetic attitude to Bolshevism. Further Left, the British Socialist Party (BSP) had much in common with the Spartakusbund-KPD, notably its small size and its extremist Marxian orientation. And to the far Left were three other small groups that shared some of the ideas of the German extremists who eventually created the KAPD; but by virtue of the energy of the personalities involved, this sector of the British revolutionary movement had much more impact on Comintern affairs than the KAPD did.

Historians have generally concluded that Bolshevism never gained wide support in Great Britain because the political climate and traditions there were more hostile to revolutionary ideology than in some of the Continental countries.[1] Loyalty to the Crown and parliament undoubtedly did figure in the refusal of the British working class to adopt revolutionary methods. But there is evidence, too, that the British Communist Party, by the very circumstances of its creation, engaged in activities that dissipated whatever opportunity existed for winning any sizable segment of the proletariat to the Comintern. The examination of these activities will occupy the first part of this chapter. The second part will deal with the question of why the

Comintern, in its appeal to the ILP, had less success than it did with the USPD in Germany, aside from the political traditions.

The Dilemma of the BSP

The Manifesto of the First Congress had called upon the revolutionaries of each country to form a united Communist Party if one did not already exist. There was no such party in Great Britain. The Bolsheviks had made it unmistakably clear, both in the Comintern pronouncements and earlier, that they wanted no dealings with the leaders of the main wing of the Labour Party, but this party could not be rejected *en bloc* because of its peculiar nature. It was a loosely organized federation ranging from the moderate Right to the far Left. In fact, both the ILP and the BSP were part of the Labour Party, although they rejected many of the views of the majority. They participated in Labour Party conferences and affairs, and acted, in the British tradition, as a "loyal opposition" rather than as independent entities. They maintained, however, complete freedom of action.

On one occasion during the war, Lenin had identified parts of the ILP and BSP as representing the "Third, or real Internationalist, trend" in Great Britain.[2] The ILP, though, did not respond to Moscow's overtures. MacDonald, who commanded considerable respect in the party, wanted more time to watch the experiments with the Soviet system. Moreover, he had been an active participant in the Berne Congress, and he questioned the need to abandon the Second International. In spite of the frequent attacks on him by the Bolsheviks and their allies, no substantial group in the ILP rejected his leadership to participate in the formation of the British Communist Party.

It remained for the small BSP, on the extreme Left wing of the Labour Party, to try to form an organization that would meet the wishes of the Third International. Chicherin's message of January 24 announcing the First Congress had mentioned the BSP as one of the eligible groups, and it also invited the participation of the Socialist Labour Party (SLP), a tiny group engaged in pro-revolutionary action on the Clydeside. This was one of the organizations to the Left of the BSP that declined to affiliate with the Labour Party. Two other groups that reacted favorably to Chicherin's invitation and to the reports of the First Congress were the Workers' Socialist Federation (WSF) of London and the South Wales Socialist Society (SWSS). None of these groups, however, knew of the invitation or the Congress until about two weeks after the sessions had closed.[3]

The Labour Party had the direct support or affiliation of millions of persons. The ILP had about 60,000 members and contained a large proportion of the leaders of the labor movement.[4] The BSP claimed a membership of about 10,000, but recent scholarship has estimated its active membership at only 2,500.[5] The SLP, the WSF, and the SWSS had no more than a few hundred members each; the responsibility of organizing a Communist Party thus fell to numerically insignificant bodies whose only hope was to win over support from the ILP or the main wing of the Labour Party. Although the Bolsheviks could help to inspire this effort, they were not yet in a position to guide or control it; they needed efficient British agents.

In theory, the BSP had more in common with the Bolsheviks than any other British party.[6] In 1914 and 1915, the party's leader, Henry Hyndman, supported the British war effort, but in 1916 a split occurred within the organization over this issue. At the Easter Congress of that year, the pacifist wing won, and Hyndman's group left the party;[7] this division explains why Lenin endorsed only part of the BSP and not the whole organization during the war. Also in 1916, the party established a newspaper, *The Call,* as its propaganda organ. The paper consistently opposed the war effort, publicized Socialist theory, and expressed an internationalist point of view. Both the party and the newspaper endorsed the Zimmerwald movement.

Like Lenin, the BSP had assumed an increasingly unfavorable attitude toward the Second International, with which it had been affiliated through the Labour Party. Like the Bolsheviks, the BSP regarded the leaders of the old International as class traitors, and felt that such elements should be removed. The party did not, however, take up the crusade for a third International to any significant extent during the war. In July 1918, *The Call* printed a series of articles on the subject of a new International, and some of these anticipated accurately the theories of the future Third International.[8] Lenin and the Bolsheviks probably had no more than an indirect influence on this transition. The BSP was a Communist Party *avant la lettre*. It advocated the cause of the Soviets and especially of the Bolsheviks during the period of the Provisional Government, and it gave complete endorsement to the October Revolution. It objected vigorously to the British Intervention in Russia in 1918 and 1919. In all important points, it was a logical candidate for the International Lenin had conceived.

One feature of the BSP, however, caused confusion and difficulty as the party sought to offer itself as the nucleus of a Communist Party; that was its connection with the Labour Party. In 1920, the Comintern was to specify that it wanted its member parties to affiliate with the larger, non-Communist groups in order to attract the membership of those groups; but in 1919, the value of such affiliation was not generally recognized. As a result, the BSP eventually sacrificed its connection with the Labour Party in order to organize the new party.

Because the BSP initially remained within the revisionist, gradualist Labour Party but identified itself as a party of revolution, its position was somewhat vague. Until the end of 1919, it had not clearly defined the relationship between the revolutionary objectives it proclaimed and such traditional institutions as parliament. E. P. Fairchild, the party's chairman during 1918 and part of 1919, led a faction that assumed the revolution could be achieved by winning control of parliament and using it to build the new proletarian order. In a manifesto issued during the election campaign of 1918, the BSP appealed to the workers to vote for Socialist and Labour candidates to hasten the end of capitalism, and the party's propaganda claimed that the Soviet system of government was "infinitely more democratic than the parliamentary system." However, there was no specific recommendation for the abolition of parliament or for violent revolution.[9] It is understandable that the BSP did not make unfriendly references to parliament while attempting to elect members to it, but this attitude extended beyond the election period, partly owing to Fairchild's leadership and his belief that parliament could aid Socialism.

Another group, led by J. F. Hodgson and John Bryan, opposed the Fairchild faction and suggested abolishing parliament as a governmental institution. The issue arose at the annual party congress at Sheffield on April 20, 1919, and the Hodgson-Bryan contingent won the day, although their position did not become final policy until later. The debate continued throughout the spring and summer,[10] and then in the autumn the quarrel subsided. The arguments in favor of parliament ceased to receive attention in *The Call*. However, the party leaders still did not announce a policy, although most of them agreed that parliament should eventually be replaced. They argued that it was necessary to use the legislatures and the electoral process as a forum for revolutionary propaganda until the revolution had replaced these institutions. Thus, by autumn 1919, the BSP was approaching the position that the Russian Communists were advocating, although its members knew little or nothing about the Bolshevik attitude on this point then. The party held a referendum in the fall that confirmed its affiliation with the Comintern.

The BSP did not reach this position entirely on its own initiative. The shift to the Left on the question of parliamentary action was partly the result of pressures from the SLP, the WSF, and the SWSS. The BSP, as the unifying agent for the Comintern in Britain, felt it necessary to respond to some of the demands of these groups, and this helped crystallize its own policy toward parliament.

The Anti-Parliamentary Left

The three small parties of the extreme Left exerted an influence altogether out of proportion to their size and popular support. The SWSS had only a few hundred active members and apparently no regular journal. There is little documentary material on this organization, and its spokesmen did not have an important part in the debates over unification, although the party was recognized as a negotiating unit by the other pro-Bolshevik parties. It held an anti-parliamentarian viewpoint and it objected to the Labour Party, and in some of the negotiations, as will be seen later, its voice counted nearly as heavily as that of the BSP.

The SLP was the second largest of the four parties that took up the

Third International's suggestion for unity and affiliation. It probably had about a thousand members.[11] It deliberately remained small and exclusive by permitting membership only to those who belonged to no other political organization.[12] As early as 1904, it had applied for admission to the Second International but had refused to affiliate with the Labour Party in order to attain membership. Its leaders were involved in the Clydeside shop stewards' movement that gained prominence by industrial agitation during the war. Thus it was a regional group with strong trade union ties, and its attitude toward parliamentary conduct was more clearly defined than that of the BSP. Three SLP candidates stood for parliament in the election of December 1918, admittedly using the campaign and seeking election only as a means of agitation. The party consistently refused contact with the reformists.

Like the other small parties of the extreme Left, the SLP endorsed and adopted many of the ideas of the Bolsheviks when they seized power in Russia. In the 1918 election, the party issued a fourteen-point statement that was clearly influenced by Moscow. Among the proposals was one for a federation of Socialist states.[13] The organization had a monthly newspaper, *The Socialist,* which claimed about 8,000 subscribers. It occasionally criticized the BSP for its association with the Labour Party. The SLP's criticism, however, had much less effect than that of the fourth small party of the Left, the WSF, led by Sylvia Pankhurst.

Pankhurst approached Communism indirectly. She had originally worked for the women's suffrage movement in England and did not adopt Bolshevism until after the October Revolution. The suffragists had more nearly resembled the British utopian socialists of the nineteenth century than the Marxian Socialists. Besides seeking voting rights for women, they engaged in various pacifist programs and undertook such social relief measures as distributing eggs and milk to needy mothers and babies.[14] Pankhurst edited a weekly newspaper, *The Woman's Dreadnought,* which, like *The Call,* had international interests.* Initially, the internationalism of the *Dreadnought* was incidental to the agitation for the franchise, as opposed to the interna-

---

* Later, when the emphasis shifted, Miss Pankhurst changed the name to *The Workers' Dreadnought.*

tionalism of the BSP, which was an integral part of the party's Socialist dogma. The *Dreadnought* had a Leftist point of view during the early years of the war. It advocated more benefits and rights for the working class, but it was not originally revolutionary. In 1915 and 1916, the WSF concentrated on winning seats in parliament with a view to getting social reforms made. Pankhurst seems to have regarded women's suffrage as a panacea for the social evils of her day, until 1917 or early 1918 when the Bolshevik revolution caught her imagination.

In the late summer of 1917 she still agitated for broader suffrage,[15] but by January 1918 she was changing her position. When the Bolsheviks dismissed the Constituent Assembly in Petrograd on January 18, 1918, without allowing it to do the work for which it had been elected, she endorsed their action, even though it violated the suffrage principles she had previously advocated. Persons of leisure and wealth have an undesirable advantage over the poorer classes in bourgeois election systems, she argued, and the Soviet system "is more closely in touch with and more closely represents its constituents than the Constituent Assembly or any existing Parliament."[16] In other words, Miss Pankhurst and her party had completely reversed their position on parliamentary activity, and they carried their new conviction with the fervor of converts into the Communist unity discussions of 1919.

Bids for Comintern Approval

Like most other left-wing groups in Western Europe, the British proto-Communists learned of the First Congress only after considerable delay. *The Workers' Dreadnought* (as it was now called) had its first report of the Congress more than three weeks after it had closed, gathering most of its information from French newspapers.[17] *The Call* could offer detailed information only on April 17,[18] and many documents of the Congress did not become available until several months later. The early information to the four small parties made it clear that the Comintern wanted a single unified Communist Party to assume Britain's seat on the Executive Committee. In April, an exploratory meeting of representatives of the four groups produced no results, and there seem to have been no further important meetings until June, when a Unity Committee from the four parties assembled. At that time, all spokesmen held to the previous policies of their organizations. The BSP favored both parliamentary action and affiliation with the Labour Party; the SLP recommended parliamentary activity outside the Labour Party; and the WSF and SWSS opposed both parliamentary politics and affiliation. None of the groups yielded on any point at this session.

In August, during a second meeting, the BSP representatives agreed that the decision on whether to affiliate with the Labour Party and to participate in parliamentary action could be postponed until three months after unification had been achieved.[19] This was an important concession for the future of the Communist Party; it meant that the BSP—which was fairly large by comparison with the other groups—was willing to surrender its status within the Labour Party in order to win the confidence and support of the smaller parties. The SLP delegates, who had been "afraid of being absorbed in the opportunism of the Labour Party, and dubious about the British Socialist Party, which had a record of social reformism and opportunism," accepted the BSP's offer to postpone the decision until after unification, and asked the SLP executive committee to approve the unification. But the committee rejected their suggestion, and this destroyed the possibility of unity for several months.[20]

Pankhurst's organization acted even more dramatically than the SLP in rejecting the BSP's proposals. Without pursuing the efforts at compromise, the WSF withdrew from the negotiations in June and constituted itself as the official Communist Party. It issued a manifesto to all Communists, posing as the legitimate representative of the Third International: "The Communist Party, refusing to take part in Parliamentary and Local Government elections, knowing the futility of Parliamentary action, and the confused and artificial character of the Labour Party, instructs such Branches as may be affiliated to the Labour Party, immediately to withdraw, and to agree to support and encourage the formation of Workers' Committees and Soviets."[21]

This attack on the principles of the BSP set the pattern for the future conduct of Pankhurst's Communist Party. She herself became secretary of the new party, the position she had held in the WSF. Although the membership remained small, Pankhurst's journalistic activity was a potent force within the extreme Left. It was her literary skill that helped to prod the BSP toward the Left. As the only intellectual to participate in the founding of the Communist Party in Britain,[22] she wrote articles in her tiny newspaper that aroused reactions in the more important publication of the ILP in Glasgow,[23] and won recognition even in Petrograd and Moscow.

Pankhurst was the first of the British Leftist leaders to make an effective contact with the leaders of the Third International. Her articles and opinions attracted attention before those of any of her colleagues or rivals. This fact accounts, at least in part, for the influence she and her party subsequently had in the unity efforts of the leftist fragmentary groups. During the first five months of the Comintern's existence, her interpretations of the British situation were accepted as authoritative by the ECCI and by Lenin. Her articles appeared in four of the first five numbers of the *Communist International* in its various language editions. She referred in her early articles to the betrayal of the working class by parliament, and referred in general terms to the correctness of the "industrialists" (i.e., industrial workers) who opposed parliaments.[24] In a letter that reached Russia in August and appeared in the September issue of the *Communist International,* she became more specific on this point—an action that later had serious consequences on British efforts to achieve unity.

The September issue of the *Communist International* published a letter dated July 16, the writer of which was not identified by name. Pankhurst was revealed to be the author only several months later. The letter was directed to Lenin, and it purported to explain the reasons for the delay in forming a unified party in England. A large group of "revolutionary industrial workers" existed in Britain, the letter asserted, and these workers were ready to join a Communist Party; but the BSP and SLP, which were more interested in winning seats and taking part in politics than in forming a true Communist Party, insisted upon parliamentary action: "The BSP and the SLP still cling to the idea of running parliamentary candidates and this is repugnant to the revolutionary industrial workers, the WSF, and the SWSS." According to the letter, the WSF was the party closest in spirit to the mass of the workers, and the question of parliamentary action was "keeping everything back." The letter appealed to Lenin to resolve the issue.[25]

Lenin took the letter at its face value, relying on it heavily for his appraisal of the British situation. In his reply, he agreed that the party should adopt an anti-parliamentary position if this were necessary for the unification of the revolutionary elements; the WSF later used this statement to support its opposition to parliamentarianism. He said the question of parliamentary activity was secondary. The party's chief aim should be to form a "revolutionary vanguard" that could control the Leftists in parliament and "make real revolutionary propagandists of them." Then, after wishing for the creation of a single party either for or against parliamentary action, he suggested an interesting alternative. If no union could be achieved because of this controversy,

then I should consider it a good step forward to complete unity if *two* Communist parties were formed immediately, that is to say, two parties which stand for the transition from bourgeois parliamentarianism to Soviet power. Let one of these parties recognize participation in the bourgeois parliament, and the other renounce it; this disagreement is now so immaterial that it would be most reasonable of all not to split over it. But even the mutual existence of two such parties would be an immense progress in comparison with the present position, would most likely be a transition to complete unity and the quick victory of Communism.[26]

In this instance, Lenin adopted a stand that conflicted basically with the one he was to assume a few months later in the case of Germany. It will be remembered that when elements of the KPD broke away to form the KAPD because of a disagreement on this same issue, Lenin deplored the existence of two parties. Of course, in the case of the KPD, the creation of two parties constituted a step toward disunity, whereas in England the creation of two Communist parties would be a move toward unity. In England, for practical reasons, Lenin was temporarily willing to tolerate an exception to the Comintern's demand for a single Communist party; in Germany he was not. His pragmatic approach superseded the provision in the Manifesto of the First Congress that specified the creation of a unified party.

Lenin's letter indicated that he did not receive the Pankhurst document of July 16 until August 27, and the text of his reply did not become generally known in England until nearly five months later. The

English-language edition of the *Communist International* for September did not reach the editors of *The Call* until March or April 1920. Members of the BSP did not know of the reports Pankhurst had been making about them in Moscow, and when they did obtain the information, they reacted vigorously to prove that the BSP was a truly revolutionary organization and not merely a party of parliamentary opportunists. This had a substantial effect on the unification efforts.

The BSP had renewed efforts to achieve unity early in 1920, and then it began to get wind of the remarks in official Communist journals. Another unity meeting had been held in January, with representatives of the BSP, the WSF, and the SWSS participating. The SLP, which was engaged in an internal debate over whether to accept the BSP's offer to delay a decision on parliamentary activity, sent no delegates. The other three parties considered a proposal from the BSP for creating a Joint Standing Committee to handle the details of amalgamation. Completely avoiding the question of parliamentary action, the BSP proposed to allow the Committee to give preliminary attention to finances, publication, and organization to prepare for a national Communist congress at Easter. It would be empowered to issue documents and manifestoes for all three parties, and to act as British secretariat of the Third International. The WSF and SWSS, however, hesitated on the grounds that they did not want to act without the SLP, and the conference ended without result.[27] Pankhurst's group and the Welsh organization were obviously trying to avoid absorption into a party that might later become parliamentary.

At about this time, BSP leaders began to get hints that a "leading English Communist" had written unfavorable remarks about them in a letter to Lenin. The first indication came from the *Newcastle Daily Journal,* which had taken its information from the Swedish pro-Bolshevik journal, the *Folkets Dagblad Politiken.* In this roundabout manner, the BSP leaders learned what was being said of them: that they were "too much occupied with electoral successes, and after the election their representatives, elected by the workmen, usually forget the workmen and their interests." Thomas Quelch, a leading BSP spokesman, responded to this charge by saying that the BSP had not had any representatives in parliament since it split with the "social patriots" during the war. He pointed out, correctly, that the "leading English Communist" had given Lenin a false idea of the attitude of the working class in Britain, and he repeated the arguments that British Communists must participate in the parliamentary elections as a means of rousing the masses and creating conditions for assuming power.[28]

This was a prelude to new trouble in February, when a French edition of the *Communist International* for September 1919 was partially translated for the use of the BSP; once again the party leadership became aroused and annoyed.[29] A complete text of the Pankhurst and Lenin letters did not become available in England until April, seven months after they appeared in Moscow. On April 22, *The Call* published the letters in full for the first time, and it also identified Pankhurst as the "leading English Communist." It accused her of misleading Lenin and of describing the British situation falsely, and it observed that *The Workers' Dreadnought* had never mentioned Lenin's answer.[30]

Although the BSP eventually won the skirmish and redeemed itself before Lenin and the International, Pankhurst's cause actually prevailed, since she put the BSP on the defensive and required it to prove that it was revolutionary rather than "parliamentary" or "revisionist" in character. Moreover, in addition to the unfavorable reports she sent to Moscow, she repeatedly criticized the Socialists in her own newspaper. Judged from the frequency with which other British Leftists answered the *Dreadnought,* Pankhurst's attacks had considerable effect. The spokesmen for the anti-parliamentary wing of the SLP also angered the BSP leaders at times, but their statements generally had less impact than hers. Pankhurst's diatribes helped the BSP to resolve its internal debate on whether parliament could ever serve the workers' cause, and later, after the victory of the anti-parliamentarians, probably contributed to the gradual repudiation of the Fairchild faction.

It took a long time for the BSP to renounce the institution of parliament as a matter of party policy. In February, Quelch had written that parliament must remain a vehicle for revolutionary propaganda until after the revolution.[31] This implied a repudiation of the institution; a year earlier such a stand would not have gone unchallenged within the party. After the annual party conference in April 1920, *The Call* observed that certain "static" elements that had been in the party in 1919 were fortunately gone during the current year; this was an obvious reference to the reformists and supporters of parliament.[32]

The BSP and the WSF continued their argument without interruption until the end of April, when another unity conference was assembled.[33] At this meeting, under the leadership of Pankhurst, the representatives of the SLP, the WSF, and the SWSS adopted a motion to the effect that the new Communist Party would not be affiliated with the Labour Party. The BSP representatives opposed this proposal again, but the structure of the meeting allowed the three small parties to win. The BSP, the SLP, and the WSF each had three representatives present and the SWSS had two, so the BSP was outvoted eight to three.[34] Although the BSP leaders regarded this as a serious error, they were so eager for unity after more than a year of delay that they agreed to plan a national unification convention on this basis for the four parties. After some argument, the meeting was finally set for July 31 in London.

Meanwhile, Lenin had interceded in the British dispute, just as he had tried to do in the German controversy in the spring of 1920. He wrote a number of statements that favored the BSP position, the most notable being *"Left-Wing" Communism: An Infantile Disorder.*[35] Pankhurst ceased to be a regular contributor to the *Communist International,* and the new commentators on the British scene were Quelch, Alfred Inkpin, and William MacLaine, who presented the BSP point of view. Pankhurst and William Gallacher, a contributor to the *Dreadnought,* were identified by Lenin as examples of the "left-wing communists" who held incorrect views on parliament.[36]

When this change became known in England, it strengthened the position of the BSP. During the preparations for the July 31 Unity Conference, there were indications that the committee in charge of planning might permit the questions of parliamentary action and Labour Party affiliation to be raised, in spite of the previous decision to unite without affiliation. As this possibility developed in the weeks before July 31, Pankhurst once again acted unilaterally. For the second time in thirteen months, her WSF announced that it was constituting itself as a "Communist Party." The *Dreadnought* reported the event: "We Revolutionary Communist delegates and individuals pledge ourselves to the Third International, the Dictatorship of the Proletariat, the Soviet system, non-affiliation to the Labour Party, and to abstention from Parliamentary action; and decide not to take part in the August 1st Unity Conference, or the unity negotiations concerned with it."[37]

This action irritated the BSP leaders and those members of the SLP who sought a compromise merger, and it also brought another statement from Lenin. On July 8, he wrote that Pankhurst and her party were wrong in refusing to join in the unity program.[38] Communications between Russia and the West had improved markedly by mid-1920, and Lenin's reaction was soon known in London. Pankhurst remained unmoved, however; Lenin had stated that he would defend this point at the forthcoming Congress of the International in Moscow, and she answered him in an open letter that was frankly sarcastic: "My reply to you is that I also would desire to defend my tactics in the Moscow Congress, but I have been refused a visa by two intervening countries. If you, through the influence of the Labour Party or your Parliamentary friends, can obtain for me a passport, I shall gladly meet you in debate."[39]

Pankhurst's battle with the BSP and Lenin reached a climax at the Moscow Congress after all; she managed to travel to Russia illegally in time for the last few meetings in August. She had her debate with Lenin, became temporarily reconciled to his position, and for a short time acted as a Communist on his terms.[40] Meanwhile, the Unity Conference that she had so strenuously opposed accomplished its work on July 31 and August 1 while she was on her way to Russia. The new party called itself the "Communist Party of Great Britain" (CPGB) to distinguish it from Pankhurst's "Communist Party (British Section of the Third International)." By a vote of one hundred to eighty-five, the Conference voted to affiliate the Communist Party with the Labour Party. It also formally repudiated the "reformist" view of parliamentary action, and it criticized the "disruptive action" of the WSF.[41]

Although the BSP had won its point about parliament and the Labour Party, it had taken such a long time to do so that the Communist movement got off to a critically slow start in England. Also, when the CPGB sought to affiliate with the Labour Party, its petition was decisively and repeatedly denied. For many years, the CPGB tried to regain the status within the Labour Party that the BSP had sacrificed in order to placate the groups on the extreme Left.[42]

The British Leftists had the difficult task of establishing a Communist movement without the help of the kind of Bolshevik-trained leaders who were available to the Hungarians and the Germans. No Kun or Radek was on hand to act with authority from Russia. The fact that Pankhurst established the earliest effective contact with the Comintern gave her brief authority, but her influence worked against party unity, rather than for it. The Communist-oriented factions in Britain had as much difficulty achieving a common program and organization as their counterparts did in Germany, and when the British Communist Party was finally organized, it had little success in preying on the membership of the ILP because it had set its initial course away from the traditions of that party. In addition, the internal affairs of the ILP worked against the Comintern program.

The ILP's Opposition to Bolshevism

The ILP was not a Marxian party. Although it approved and praised the Russian revolutions of 1917, it did not feel any need to imitate the Bolsheviks. Ramsay MacDonald was the most prominent figure in the party, and, like Kautsky in Germany, he had considerable influence both within his own party and in the European labor movement. He participated in the Berne Congress, and he supported the Branting resolution with its language against the dictatorship of a single class. His opinions appeared regularly in *Forward,* a Glasgow newspaper, and he used this medium to oppose the concept of a Third International as soon as he learned of the Moscow Congress. Philip Snowden, another prominent member of the ILP and the editor of the Manchester *Labour Leader,* shared with MacDonald a preference for restoring the Second International, and consequently Moscow's cause received little favorable consideration in the party's two leading organs.

MacDonald's opposition to the Third International quickly extended beyond Britain. Early in April 1919, he wrote a letter to *L'Humanité* criticizing the founders of the Comintern for trying to split the Socialist movement and for trying to impose a uniform procedure on all countries.[43] Shortly afterward, he told his own readers that "two Internationals will be the worst thing that could happen to the revolutions now going on and to the general Socialist movement."[44] He felt strongly about the need for Socialist unity, and he wanted the Bolsheviks included in the all-encompassing, rebuilt International that he contemplated.

At the ILP conference at Huddersfield in April, no real interest in the Third International was shown; most of those present apparently endorsed MacDonald's hope for an early revival of the Second.[45] Despite the lack of interest in the Comintern at home, MacDonald worried about the reports from abroad. He was disturbed by the news that the executive committee of the Italian Socialist Party had voted to join the Comintern, and by reports that the Swiss Socialists were enchanted by Moscow's overtures. He felt that his efforts to rebuild the old International were being threatened, and late in May he traveled to those two countries to see what he could do. He was accompanied on the trip by his colleague Roden Buxton and the French Socialist leader Jean Longuet. The three men visited Rome, Milan, and Berne during the first few days of June.[46] They were warmly received, but could not convert the party leaders whom they contacted. When MacDonald returned to Britain, he wrote that he had found much popular resentment against leaders who were believed to have betrayed the working class, and he had also discovered a loss of faith in parliamentary democracy in Italy.[47] In Switzerland, the executive officers had pointedly refused his proposal, and had issued a statement against the supporters of bourgeois democracy and in favor of the Bolshevik concept of violent revolution.[48]

MacDonald thus emerged as one of the two or three outspoken Socialist opponents of the Third International during the first weeks of its formal existence. In the eyes of the founders of the Comintern, he was one of the most hateful of the class traitors, as obnoxious as Kautsky or Longuet. When the Comintern headquarters heard about MacDonald's article in *L'Humanité*, they regarded it as of sufficient importance to merit Lenin's attention. Lenin composed an answer on July 14 that followed the general pattern of his earlier attacks on Kautsky. He accused MacDonald of a spectrum of sins and errors. This answer became a major propaganda piece for the Comintern.[49]

MacDonald continued his efforts to build a Social Democratic International despite the attitude of Moscow. At the Berne Congress, an executive committee had been appointed to arrange future meetings of the Second International, and MacDonald was one of its most active members. But when the moderate Socialists presented the proposals of Berne to the Versailles Peace Conference only to have them disregarded in the final draft treaty, and when the Allied governments refused to permit a Socialist delegation to travel to Russia, as the Berne Congress intended, MacDonald realized that his cause had been damaged. The Allies' conduct lent credence to the Bolshevik charge that nothing could be expected from bourgeois governments.[50]

MacDonald also participated in the Lucerne conference, and shared the disappointment of Kautsky and others who hoped to revive the Second International there. Nevertheless, he continued to hope for a moderate International, and retained the allegiance of most of his party in spite of these failures. The ILP, however, was not completely behind MacDonald on this question; the British Independents, like the USPD, began to be dissatisfied about the delays. And MacDonald, like Kautsky, was regarded as a "Rightist" within his own party, even by those who supported him on most issues. One segment of the party shared his distrust of the Third International but had no desire to revive the Second; this group increased in size after the failures at Berne and Lucerne. At regional conferences of the ILP late in 1919 and early in 1920, the growing disenchantment with the old International became evident.

In addition, there was a small group of ILP members who wanted to join the Third International, but had no efficient propaganda outlet. Although they had considerable strength in South Wales, Lancashire, the Tyneside industrial region, and Scotland,[51] they were not powerful enough on their own to change the anti-Comintern policies of MacDonald and Snowden, and they usually ignored the overtures of the BSP and WSF. Among the most active members of this Independent Left were Shapurji Saklatvala, an emotional young Indian orator; Ellen Wilkinson, another youthful agitator; and Walton Newbold, a one-time Quaker who had been won over to Bolshevism.[52]

In the final weeks of 1919 and during the first quarter of 1920, MacDonald and Snowden appeared to be losing to these pro-Communists within the ILP, just as the moderates were losing to the Left wing in the USPD at this time. During the first week of January, a Scottish Congress of ILP members voted overwhelmingly for affiliation with the Comintern.[53] The action of the USPD at Leipzig against the Second International, and that party's approach to the Third, helped to justify such action. Most of those members of the ILP who wanted to affiliate with the Third were relatively young;[54] here, as in many of the Continental Socialist parties, the image of a new labor-dictated civilization in Russia had tapped the idealism of the young. The belief that the Soviet system was the final answer to the world's social problems was cultivated by the small pro-Communist newspapers on the far Left, and in the spring of 1920 a much more important newspaper adopted this line.

George Lansbury, the influential Labourite and pacifist who edited the *Daily Herald,* made an illegal trip to Russia. He stayed there for nine weeks in early 1920, met with Lenin and other top Bolsheviks, and even addressed the Moscow Soviet. He was the first of several important Western labor spokesmen to be temporarily converted to Bolshevism and the Third International. He returned to London in March and immediately advocated affiliation with the Comintern.[55] The left-wing members of the ILP took note of this new support for their cause, and in April, at the party's annual Easter congress, they made their bid. They had not only the arguments of Leipzig and Lansbury, but also the example of the French Socialist Party. In February, the French Socialists had met in Strasbourg and, following the lead of the German Independents, had left the Second International.

At the ILP's Easter conference at Glasgow on April 4–6, many youthful speakers pleaded Moscow's case. Only MacDonald and Mrs. Snowden, the wife of the party chairman, argued for the possibility of reviving the Second International; most delegates wanted a new experiment along the lines proposed by the USPD. The conference voted 529 to 144 to leave the old International. In a second vote, delegates were allowed to choose between a proposal for consultation with the Third International and a motion for immediate affiliation. The former option won by a vote of 472 to 206.[56] Many of those who supported the Third International apparently felt that the original Bolshevik orientation might not be permanent, and that it could be rendered more liberal and democratic.

Like the USPD in Germany and (as will be seen in the next chapter) like the Socialist Party of France, the ILP decided to send a delegation to Moscow for talks. R. C. Wallhead, one of the party's most active propagandists, who had replaced Snowden as chairman after the Easter conference, was made responsible for the consultation. Together with Clifford Allen, the party's treasurer, he traveled to Russia and presented a series of questions to the ECCI. Up to here, from the Comintern's point of view, the ILP had behaved in much the same way as the Socialist parties of Germany, France, and Italy, all of which were sending missions to Moscow in 1920. The ILP delegates, however, reached Russia with an unusual handicap: the Labour Party had decided to send a contingent to Russia for a visit, and Wallhead and Allen traveled with them. The main Labour Party had no interest in negotiating with the Third International as a possible affiliate, since the party was satisfied to work for a restoration of the Second. The fact that the two groups made the voyage together prejudiced the Bolsheviks against the Independents from the start.

Despite the action of the ILP in voting to abandon the Second International, it remained in a sense within that organization owing to its continuing affiliation with the main Labour Party. MacDonald retained his position in the leadership of the commission that sought to restore the old International, and he did not slacken his efforts because of the new stand his party had taken. At a time when the ILP was showing increased interest in the Comintern, MacDonald wrote one of the most perceptive comments of the period on the attractions of the organization:

The Third International is the product of two things—Russian conditions . . . and a dogmatic logic which spins policy from fancied necessity. The grand *coup d'état* in Russia and its successful defiance of the whole of armed and financial Europe have properly roused the enthusiasm of democrats all over the world and have particularly affected the minds of those who have entered the Socialist movements since 1914. They find it impossible to pay tribute to the courage and strength of will of the Russian leaders and to demand that European reaction and spitefulness shall let them alone, without also supporting the Moscow International. I do the first two, but decline to do the third.

He objected to the Comintern's "domineering methods which ally it with theological fanaticism," and added: "It is metaphysical in its spirit and not scientific. It is to impose upon the National Parties a philosophy, a method, a shibboleth and a purge."[57]

MacDonald's ability to separate the issue of the International from that of the intervention and the internal programs of the Bolshevik government was typical of the attitude of most British Labour leaders. His own party eventually rejected the Third International because a majority of its members disliked the Comintern's philosophy and methods. While the British Labourites were making this distinction, the French Socialists were failing to do so.

Chapter seven France

France was an enigma from the Bolshevik point of view. It was at once the home of the modern revolutionary tradition and the source of the most energetic demands for the destruction of Bolshevism. The revolutionary propaganda of the Reds in the civil war had stimulated more mutiny among the French than among any other interventionist troops, but France remained, as Zinoviev wrote in spring 1919, the seat of the most reactionary of Europe's bourgeoisie.[1] No single Socialist or Communist movement outside Russia received more attention from the Comintern propagandists during 1919 than the French one.

As of March 1919, there was much in the French situation to encourage the Bolsheviks, and favorable news continued to come from France for the next two years, reaching a climax with the reports from the Congress of Tours in December 1920. With the split that occurred in the French Socialist Party at that congress, when most of the delegates endorsed the Third International, the Bolsheviks won an important organizational victory; for in the events preceding Tours, the Comintern's agents had played a crucial role.

French Socialism had begun to drift toward the Left during the war. When war broke out in August 1914, every Socialist deputy had voted for war credits, and most party members obviously supported their leaders. As the war continued, however, a growing minority group within the party objected to the government's announced war aims and to prolonging the fighting. Some French Socialists came to regard this controversy within the party as a break in Socialist unity, and they believed that the Tours Congress only confirmed a situation that had

existed much earlier.[2] As early as December 1914, a small faction opposed the party's new nationalistic, pro-war policy; this same group
later became the first advocate of the Third International. It remained
too small to have any important influence during the war.

By spring 1915, a large minority of Socialists was asserting that the
party had become aggressively committed to war and inattentive to
the possibilities of achieving peace. By the end of 1915, two major factions had defined their positions and their membership within French
Socialism: the Majoritaires sought to achieve peace by means of a complete military victory, and the Minoritaires wanted a negotiated peace
at an early date. Translated into Bolshevik terms, the Majoritaires
were "social chauvinists" and the Minoritaires were "social patriots,"
both of whom were "social traitors" because they were not willing to
take up arms against the bourgeoisie of their own country in a class
war. In April 1916, at a national congress, the Majoritaires won 1,996
delegate votes for their program against 960 for the Minoritaires, but
the latter gradually gained strength until they had managed to obtain
a majority in the national congress held on July 29–30, 1918. Their
policy of negotiated peace had gained popularity as the costs and bur-
dens of the war increased.

In February 1919, a majority of the Socialist delegates in a national
convention voted to return to the pre-war Socialist position on war
credits: namely, complete opposition to such appropriations. As the
balance thus shifted to the Left, the breach between those who retained
the war-oriented position of August 1914 and those who were returning to the traditional pacifist position became constantly wider.[3]
Among the Minoritaires—or, as they now came to be called, the ex-
Minoritaires—were such prominent Socialists as Jean Longuet, Paul
Faure, Paul Louis, and Raoul Verfeuil; the ex-Majoritaires were led
by Albert Thomas, Ernest Poisson, and Paul Renaudel.

At the Berne Congress in February, the ex-Majoritaires had supported the Branting resolution with its sharp language against the
Bolsheviks' principles, while the ex-Minoritaires preferred the more
conciliatory Adler-Longuet motion. In addition to these two main
groups, a so-called "Center" faction had emerged under the leadership
of Léon Blum, who tried to hold the two diverging blocs together.

There was also the extreme Left, now led by Fernand Loriot, which had registered the first objections to the war program in 1914, and which sought party endorsement for the Zimmerwald Left during the war. This group was to be the main beneficiary of the tension that existed in French Socialism early in 1919.[4]

The divisions within the French Socialist Party provided only one of the advantages that Bolshevism had in France at this time. The widespread appeal of the Bolshevik Revolution among the French people and the common desire for peace, which the Bolshevik propaganda had exploited, attracted most Socialists. The French revolutionary tradition worked to the advantage of the authors of the new revolution in some instances, and the syndicalist tradition of the French labor movement seemed especially compatible with the doctrine of the dictatorship of the proletariat. Also, all segments of the party's leadership eagerly wanted a renewal of international Socialist cooperation in a formal organization. As early as 1917, at a party congress in Bordeaux, delegates had been unanimously in favor of rejoining the International after the war,[5] and this sentiment persisted in all ranks of the party despite disagreements on other issues. The difficulties encountered during and after the war in reviving the Second International suggested that the old organization was hopelessly dead, an idea that the Bolsheviks were, of course, eager to foster.

The new International that Lenin's disciples offered in place of the old one nullified some of the advantages Bolshevism found in France in 1919. By ruling out the leaders of the Right and Center Socialists in advance, the Bolsheviks diminished their chances to attract the followers of these men. Virtually all the important Socialist spokesmen in France fell into these two categories. The Chicherin invitation of January 24 and the statements of the First Congress refused the possibility of membership to such persons as Thomas, Renaudel, Longuet, Marcel Cachin, and René Compère-Morel, all of whom held responsible positions in the party and influenced the policies of the party's main newspapers. Although the exact conditions for affiliation with the Third International were not known immediately, the general attitude of the organization became known rather quickly. The January 24 announcement had become available in mid-March, and it specifically provided that only the left-wing elements (Loriot's group) would qualify to represent France in founding the Comintern.[6]

Lenin and Zinoviev had picked Loriot as their agent in France on the basis of extensive contacts with him in Switzerland during the war. Loriot, a thin, bearded Norman, had worked zealously in the Zimmerwald Left, and had endorsed the plan for a Third International as early as May 1917 in a journal he published. He was not a major figure in the Socialist Party at this time, but he had gained some attention as the leader of a group called "The Committee for the Resumption of International Relations," which was composed of Socialists of the extreme Left. It operated mainly in Paris, but Lenin had been in touch with it from Switzerland during the first phase of the war, and had endeavored to guide it.[7] Thus, Loriot, like the Hungarian Communist leaders, had had the benefit of Lenin's revolutionary advice.

At the time of the First Congress, the Bolsheviks had new cause to regard Loriot as their best ally in France. He had gone to the Berne Congress in February, and had delivered a letter condemning the Socialists who had endorsed or tolerated the war. His message echoed the basic Bolshevik pronouncements, and although it made no impact in Berne, it won enthusiastic approval in Moscow while the First Congress was in session.[8] The state of communications between France and Russia did not permit any direct contact between Loriot and the Comintern for many weeks, but he undoubtedly knew that he had been designated as the French leader, and he conducted himself accordingly. He and his committee at once set about winning working-class support for the new organization. The immediate reaction of the Right and Center leaders had been cool, and this gave Loriot special problems. Le Populaire, the party newspaper under the political direction of Longuet, and L'Humanité, under the supervision of Cachin, were skeptical about the Moscow proceedings. The writer Amédée Dunois, commenting on the Berne Congress, summarized the view of Le Populaire: "I do not believe, for the moment, in the chances of or the necessity for a Third International. The Second is enough for me."[9] Longuet and his followers insisted that the Second International could be revitalized, and that the Bolsheviks could find a place within it; *Le Populaire* therefore paid relatively little attention to reports of the First Congress.

Although *L'Humanité* expressed more interest, its tone was no more sympathetic. When the Italian Socialist Party announced its withdrawal from the Second International and affiliation with Moscow late in March, the newspaper deplored the act and expressed the hope that the decision could be revoked.[10] It also gave prominent attention to the article by MacDonald, as previously discussed.[11] The editors of *L'Humanité* were not convinced that either the Soviet form or Bolshevik action in general should be made the exclusive standard for international Socialist cooperation.

In these unfavorable circumstances, Loriot began his program. In his central organizing group were Pierre Monatte, Alfred Rosmer, Boris Souvarine, and Louise Saumoneau, all of whom had connections with journalism and organizational work, although not all were Socialist Party members. Most of them had been members of the Committee for the Resumption of International Relations. Their first efforts on behalf of the Comintern were made at a meeting of the Confederation of the Seine* held in Paris on April 13, and at a national Socialist congress a week later. At the Seine meeting, Loriot's faction mustered a substantial minority. Three motions were presented at this time, and the response to them indicated considerable support for the Comintern. Verfeuil, on behalf of the ex-Minoritaires, offered a proposal suggesting continued affiliation with the Second International on a probationary basis, until the future course of that organization could be determined; this motion won 3,999 votes. Loriot offered a proposal for immediate affiliation with the Third International; this won 2,214 votes. And a third motion, calling simply for continued affiliation with the Second, had only 1,305 supporters.[12] This shows the extent to which there was discontent with the old International, as well as an uncritical willingness to endorse Moscow, in the traditionally revolutionary Paris region. At this conference, Loriot broached the subject of revolutionary aims and procedures. He found

---

* This body, a regional unit of the French Socialist Party, usually met a few days before a national party congress to discuss issues that were coming up before the national congress.

his main opponent to be Barthélemy Mayeras, a Socialist deputy of the Right.

The dialogue between Loriot and Mayeras at the Seine meeting was continued at the national congress of April 20–22. Loriot provoked the debate by arguing that the party should not adopt its future program on the basis of vote-seeking in parliamentary elections, but should instead lead the masses to revolution. He read parts of the Manifesto of the First Congress and made his usual criticisms of the Second International. Mayeras responded by attacking the legitimacy of the Moscow Congress. He objected to the claim that French Socialism had been represented by Guilbeaux, whom he regarded as an anarchist. The Moscow Congress, Mayeras said, had been staged simply because Lenin found it in the interests of his own party to do so, and although he expressed admiration for Lenin's cleverness, he argued that French Socialism need not follow the Russians' lead on this point. He asked why the French Socialists should go to Moscow if the Bolsheviks declined to go to Berne, and he chided the Bolsheviks for a willingness to negotiate with the French foreign minister, Stéphen Pichon, at Prinkipo, but not with fellow Socialists in Switzerland.[13] The Socialists of the Right and Center overwhelmingly defeated Loriot. There were 894 votes for temporary adhesion to the Second International, 757 votes for a right-wing motion that would have given strong endorsement to the Second International, and only 270 votes for Loriot's motion in favor of immediate affiliation with the Comintern.[14]

Only a week after this defeat, Loriot and his committee adopted another approach. They began to issue a newspaper, *La Vie Ouvrière,* representing it as a revival of a pre-war periodical. Monatte, who had directed the earlier periodical, became editor. The next step came on May 8, when the Committee for the Resumption of International Relations reconstituted itself as the "Committee for Adhesion to the Third International." Encouraged by large labor demonstrations in Paris and other cities on May 1, the Committee felt the outbreak of violent class war was near.

The newspaper, which appeared weekly, sought to identify various expressions of post-war unrest with the Third International, and it made a special bid for syndicalist support. It represented itself as the organ of the Confédération Général du Travail (CGT), but it rejected the leadership of the CGT's general secretary, Léon Jouhaux, who had supported the war effort. A line written for the first number by Tom Mann, an English Socialist, may be regarded as summarizing the attitude of *La Vie Ouvrière*: "Bolshevism, Spartakism, syndicalism —all signify the same thing under different names."[15] The paper emphasized its loyalty to the Zimmerwald Left idea, and frequently asserted that it represented the purest tradition of French socialism and syndicalism. On July 9, it claimed a subscription list of 1,100.

The Committee organized branches in local sections of the Socialist Party and the CGT throughout France; by the summer it had reported the creation of subcommittees in most of the major cities. In June, a Regional Union of the Southeast was formed, with headquarters in Lyon. It is impossible to determine, from the brief reports in *La Vie Ouvrière,* the size and effectiveness of these groups, but evidently some of the work bore fruit among the syndicalists. At the Lyon Congress of the CGT in September 1919, Loriot and his supporters won the votes of about 30 per cent of the delegates in a contest with Jouhaux over the future program of the CGT.[16] Like similar groups in other countries, the French Committee published a variety of pamphlets written both by its own members and by such persons as Trotsky, Arthur Ransome, and Jacques Sadoul. According to the Committee's own account, its operations were severely restricted by the Clemenceau government. In early autumn, the Regional Union of the Southeast reported that it had been restrained from holding mass meetings, and that speech limitations had been imposed. The Paris headquarters reported that its plenary meetings had been prohibited, and that it was considering going underground.[17]

All during this organizational phase, the Committee's isolation from Moscow was nearly complete; at the end of July, *La Vie Ouvrière* complained of a "total absence of communication" with Russia.[18] This was not technically correct, since there had been indirect messages from Zinoviev, Sadoul, and Trotsky, but the statement was substantially true. The Committee had only a general knowledge of the work and aims of the First Congress, and consequently there was a good

bit of controversy about what Moscow and Petrograd intended. The
Committee knew, for example, that the Comintern stressed the ideological differences between the "pure" revolutionaries and the Socialists of the Center and Right; this principle had been learned from the
Bolsheviks during the war. But the Committee was not sure whether
the International wanted a complete organizational break to be made.

In fact, both the letter and the spirit of the documents of the First
Congress made it quite clear that the Bolsheviks wanted either the
expulsion of the Center and Right from existing parties or the creation
of new parties. However, Loriot and the majority of his committee,
with no documents to refer to, received a different impression from
preliminary reports, and defended their position strongly. Loriot, arguing against those who would have created separate "Communist-
Socialist parties" on the authority of Comintern advice, claimed that
"the Russians are too well acquainted with the Socialist and labor
movements in France and elsewhere to recommend uniform methods
of action everywhere. They know that no argument can prevail against
reality, and that the great majority of the French Communist-Social-
ists, nearly all other groups in the party, and the CGT are opposed to
a split." He argued that the movement on behalf of the Bolshevik
Revolution and the Third International would suffer seriously from a
division with the main body of the syndicalist and Socialist movements.[19] He repeated his arguments on later occasions, and once he
even defended the Center Socialists, L. O. Frossard and Jean Longuet,
when one of the extreme leftists described them as "assassins." In this
way, he managed to stay within the main Socialist movement without
being identified with its policies, and his program of organization and
propaganda prospered.

Loriot managed to maintain a position somewhat to the Right of
the course that the "lesson" of Hungary would have indicated and
somewhat to the Left of "opportunistic" cooperation. In a sense, it was
an ideal position from the Bolsheviks' point of view. He made an error
in assuming that the Bolsheviks did not want "uniform methods of
action" everywhere, but perhaps if communications had been better,
Zinoviev would have been able to modify Loriot's position. The French
Comintern leader had enough respect within the Socialist Party to be

named one of the directors of *L'Humanité* on July 20. He was not able to exercise any great influence on the paper's policy, however, since spokesmen for the Center and Right had most of the directorships, and it is questionable whether Zinoviev would have condoned such an affiliation at a time when his hatred for moderate Socialists had been intensified by the Hungarian experience. Positions of this kind within the Socialist Party gave Loriot's group possibilities that the Socialist Party of Great Britain had been forced to sacrifice because of factional disagreements with other pro-Bolshevik groups.

Loriot was a man of considerable intellect, well able to spread the doctrine of Bolshevism without help from Moscow. His writings demonstrate a consistent political theory, one that was more coherent and intelligent than Kun's. In his writings for the Comintern and *La Vie Ouvrière,* he occasionally dealt with doctrinal and philosophical questions, leaving the more emotional issues to other members of the Committee. He composed theoretical arguments against the Center in France and against Friedrich Adler, trying to prove by reference to Marxian doctrine that there could be no reconciliation between the Second and Third Internationals.[20] His general approach was similar to Lenin's, which is probably a reflection of their association in Switzerland rather than of any immediate guidance received from Russia in 1919. In an article entitled "Revolution and Evolution," in which he argued that the proletariat could never achieve its ends by gradual steps, he justified violence, and made references to the history of Socialism in an intellectual, non-emotional manner not common among the revolutionary journalists who were associated with the International.[21] In later years, Loriot's carefully thought out beliefs caused him to break with the International during the "Bolshevization" of the Western parties. Nearly a decade after he had helped to build the Comintern, he wrote an essay demonstrating that it had been diverted from its course, that the dictatorship of the proletariat did not exist in Russia, and that Lenin's name was being applied to non-Leninist concepts.[22]

Although Loriot's pragmatism and theoretical position permitted him to work within the Socialist Party and the CGT, he did not manage to persuade all his pro-Bolshevik colleagues to do so, too. Some splintering occurred among the Third International's supporters in France, just as it had in Great Britain and Germany. Owing to the refusal of Loriot and most of his supporters to leave the existing Socialist and syndicalist groups, a separate organization was formed under the leadership of Raymond Péricat, secretary of a construction syndicate and a former associate of Loriot. The party called itself the French Communist Party, and expressed itself through a newspaper known as *L'Internationale*. This paper had appeared for the first time on February 15, 1919, with Péricat as editor, and in the first number he had criticized the Second International and advocated the organization of a true International.[23] Although initially affiliated with the Committee for Adhesion to the Third International, Péricat's party began to accuse the Committee of unrevolutionary conduct with the decision not to leave the Socialist Party; there were even charges that Loriot's group had adopted a parliamentary approach toward revolution. Loriot energetically denied the accusation, stating that he would refuse to vote for or endorse any parliamentary ticket, and renouncing any electoral ambitions for himself.[24] The Committee had managed to avoid "left-wing infantilism" in the matter of affiliating with other parties, but in France, as in England, the extreme Left had forced the Third International temporarily into an anti-parliamentarian position.

Several other groups and journals shared the extreme Left with Péricat's party and Loriot's Committee, and they expressed varying degrees of support for the Third International. Souvarine established the *Bulletin Communiste,* which backed the Committee on most issues. Another publication, *L'Avenir International,* shared its headquarters for a time with the Loriot Committee, although one of its most frequent contributors, Emile Chauvelon, disapproved of the Committee's affiliations with the Socialists and belonged to Péricat's party. There seems to have been a high level of cooperation among these extreme Left groups, in spite of their disagreements.[25] One anarchist newspaper, *Le Libertaire,* worked closely with *L'Internationale,* although there was considerable controversy in its columns about whether anarchists should identify themselves with the Third International.[26] These small journals, and several more of the same type, competed for the allegiance of the Left with such large periodicals as *L'Humanité, Le Populaire, Le Journal du Peuple,* and *La Vague.*[27]

Loriot's policy proved more effective than Péricat's partly because all the leading French Socialists wanted to avoid a split. There was at this time a strong desire to save the Socialist unity achieved by Jean Jaurès in 1905. Marcel Cachin, a leader of the Center, was one of the most ardent advocates of unity in 1919. As editor of *L'Humanité* and an important figure in international Socialism, he tried to find a common ground for the Right Socialists and the pro-Bolshevik Left. At this point, he believed it was possible to be a revolutionary Socialist without abandoning the Second International and without giving allegiance to the Third.* He participated in the Lucerne Congress, at which moderate Socialists made another effort to revitalize the Second, for, along with the delegates there, he believed that if the old International were given a revolutionary spirit, it could still win support both from Moscow-Petrograd and from the Bolsheviks' allies in the West.[28]

The pleas for unity, of which Cachin was the most frequent author in 1919, increased in number as national elections approached in the fall of that year. Many distinguished Socialists published appeals for intra-party cooperation. At an extraordinary party congress held in Paris in September, members apparently feared that an open break would develop. The division did not come partly because the revolutionary wing—including Loriot—did not press its demands for direct action or its arguments against parliamentarianism. Loriot chided the Socialists for their moderate approach, but he did not provoke a repetition of previous quarrels. Leaders of both the Right and the Center expressed their pleasure after the congress that a dangerous threat to unity had been avoided.[29] Once again, Loriot's conduct did not strictly agree with Comintern principles; his moderation for the sake of unity would probably have earned Zinoviev's disapproval had communications been better.

Loriot's group did not, however, carry its restraint over into the CGT congress at Lyon in which it participated in the same month. Unity was not a delicate matter in this instance, so the Committee did

---

* He changed his mind later, as the result of a visit to Russia in 1920, and he was one of two men who helped accomplish the split at Tours in December of that year. After the Russian trip, he became a zealous convert to the Third International and took over from Loriot the role of the Comintern's chief agent in France. See below, pp. 181–85, 207–10.

not hesitate to pursue its disruptive tactics there. It sought a repudiation of Jouhaux and of the patriotic policies of the CGT. Although it did not actively seek endorsement of the Third International at this time, it advocated Bolshevik standards for judging the events of the recent past. Monmousseau, Loriot, Monatte, and others made speeches impugning the revolutionary integrity of the incumbent leadership, and provoked a bitter debate.[30] The revolutionary wing finally proposed a resolution asserting that "the CGT, by its various activities on the side of the government, has practiced a policy of abdication and compromise with the bourgeois leaders." The statement called for greater use of the general strike and for direct action.[31] The majority group behind Jouhaux had 1,393 votes against 588 for the radical minority in the final test, but Loriot had made substantial headway. Here, as in the Socialist Party, he and his allies were to advance by a process of gradual attrition until they had reached a point at which a break was profitable.

The Sadoul Incident

An ironic chapter in the efforts of the Third International to enlist supporters in France involved Captain Jacques Sadoul, who had been a consultive delegate to the First Congress. Late in October 1919, while he was in exile in Russia, a controversy developed around his name in France. He became a hero for the Center Socialists, and an object of hatred for the conservatives and nationalists, who identified him as being both a traitor to France and an adherent of the Comintern. The Center Socialists had no desire to associate Sadoul with the Communist International at this time, nor did they have any intention of endorsing the organization; but their defense of him moved them closer to the revolutionary movement, and encouraged the idea that revolutionary action necessarily implied affiliation with the Third International.

Sadoul had gone to Russia as a military attaché to the diplomatic mission in 1917, arriving in Petrograd shortly before the October Revolution. After the Bolsheviks came to power, he immediately made contact with Lenin and other Bolshevik leaders, and dealt with them as the legitimate government. His correspondence to France in the ensuing weeks showed an early sympathy for the Bolsheviks; he quickly appealed to his government to endorse the new regime. When the official French position hardened against the Bolsheviks, Sadoul denounced his government and joined the revolution. He continued, nevertheless, to act on behalf of his countrymen, interceding with the Bolsheviks whenever Frenchmen encountered difficulties, and he even managed to obtain the release of a few French prisoners from Bolshevik jails.[32] His renunciation of the French government, however, made him a traitor in France, especially after mid-1918, when he began to play an important part in the Bolsheviks' propaganda activity against the intervention. He prepared pamphlets for distribution among French troops in Odessa, calling on them to revolt against their officers, and his efforts undoubtedly contributed to the mutinies there late in 1918 and in 1919. In addition, he collaborated in the publication of the French-language newspaper *La IIIme Internationale* during this time.[33]

Early in 1919, the French government announced its intention to prosecute Sadoul as a military traitor, and the Socialists came to his defense. The case received little attention until his name became an issue in the fall election campaign. In October, several Socialist groups in Paris proposed him as a candidate for the Chamber of Deputies, even though there appeared to be no prospect of his returning from Russia just yet. The Center Socialists supported him immediately, saying a vote for Sadoul would help the Russian Revolution and oppose capitalism.[34] He was entered on the election lists for the third *arrondissement* of Paris because the Socialists felt his reputation as a revolutionary would strengthen the ticket in that area. They were particularly anxious to get popular names, since a new law provided that seats would be apportioned to the parties according to the *scrutin de liste* system, which made it necessary for a party to obtain a high average vote-total for its entire ticket before it could win any significant number of seats in a department. The Socialists had eliminated from their ticket those party members who had voted for armament credits in 1919 after the party had decided, at a February conference, to return to the pre-war, anti-armament position. The whole ticket was weighted to the Left, and it was important to gain enough votes on the Left to compensate for the losses on the Right.[35] Sadoul's name appeared likely to attract those revolutionary elements who were being urged to stay away from the polls by the anti-parliamentarians, including the supporters of the Third International. *L'Humanité,* in endorsing his candidacy, underplayed his affiliation with the Comintern.

Whereas the Socialists felt Sadoul would help their ticket, the coalition under Georges Clemenceau, the Bloc National, apparently felt he could be made a liability to the Left if his name were associated with treason. Late in October, the government ordered that Sadoul be tried by a court-martial in Paris on November 6, only nine days before the election. He was charged with military disobedience, desertion to the enemy, and intelligence contacts with the enemy. In view of the proximity of the election, there seems to be justification for the Socialists' accusation that politics motivated the timing of the trial. *L'Humanité* began to de-emphasize Sadoul's conduct against the French military effort and to stress his services to Frenchmen in Russia. It attempted to present him as the victim of governmental persecution, and endorsed a demonstration on his behalf on October 25. He was described as a hero by most French Socialist leaders for the purpose of the campaign.[36]

The conservative press, hoping to disgrace Sadoul and the Socialists together, published documents from the government's dossier to prove that he had signed a Bolshevik document as a member of the Bureau of the Third International and as a Commissar of Foreign Affairs for the Ukrainian government.[37] Affiliation with the Third International was treated as a feature of treason.

On November 9, after a three-day hearing, the court-martial convicted Sadoul and sentenced him to death.* He seems to have had only one brief chance to play a role in the political controversy; on November 1, Longuet reported the receipt of a letter from a member of the British House of Commons who claimed to have received a letter from Sadoul. According to this source, Sadoul accepted his candidacy for office and promised to return to France to serve in the Chamber.[38] It is difficult to assess the impact of his candidacy or his

* The death penalty was never executed. Six years later, Sadoul was pardoned, and he subsequently returned to live in France.

trial on the outcome of the election. Election day came only a week after his conviction, and the Socialists fared badly, partly because the *scrutin de liste* system worked against them. The party received a relatively high number of votes by comparison with previous elections, but it lost 35 of its 104 seats because of the revised voting system. Sadoul did not get enough votes to be elected; he ran badly on the Socialist list in his *arrondissement,* several right-wing Socialists gaining more votes than he. His attraction, then, was less general than the party had anticipated, and it was probably strongest among those Socialists who were least inclined to vote.

One aspect of the election was that the ex-Minoritaires suffered most from the defeat. Several of the leaders of this faction, such as Longuet, Mayeras, Frossard, and Faure, lost their seats in the Chamber. Almost all the Socialists who remained in the Chamber were from the Right wing, despite the fact that the party was generally moving toward the Left.[39] This tended to confirm the ideas held by the extreme Left against parliamentary action. It also weakened the group that had regarded itself as the moderating influence.

Sadoul's affiliation with the Third International cannot be regarded as a central issue either in the trial or in the election campaign. But the injection of the controversy of the Internationals into his case and his campaign served the cause of those who wanted to establish the interdependency of the revolutionary movement and the Third International.

Smolny's View of France

The headquarters of the Comintern in Petrograd had a slight advantage over the Committee for Adhesion to the Third International; more information got through from Paris to Petrograd than in the other direction. While only a handful of messages dispatched from Zinoviev's offices in 1919 reached France, there was a constant, if irregular, stream of newspapers and letters getting into Russia from French sympathizers. Admittedly, much of the material must have been erroneous, and Lenin complained several times during the year about the lack of information from abroad. The issues of the *Communist International* give an indication of the amount of information that arrived from France and the type of reports that the Comintern leaders chose to believe, or at least to repeat.

The Comintern's view of France was filtered through four main observers: Sadoul, Guilbeaux, Serge, and Loriot. The first three were exiles from France who were serving the Soviet government or the Comintern, or both, in Russia. They read whatever French newspapers were available and apparently drew most of their information from this source. The articles from Loriot that appeared in the Comintern publication were generally reprints of his French journalistic efforts. Of the sixteen articles and reports on France in the *Communist International* in 1919, about half were attributed to these four men. The picture created by them coincided almost exactly with the Bolshevik preconceptions about Western Europe.

Their most common themes fall into four categories: (1) capitalism is rapidly dying in France; (2) there are clear signs that it will soon be replaced by the dictatorship of the proletariat; (3) a small group of capitalist evil-doers and socialist-syndicalist traitors is trying, sometimes cleverly and sometimes stupidly, to prevent this; and (4) the great embattled benefactors of the world revolution and of the proletariat, whom the French proletariat must help, are the Russian Soviet government and the Third International.

Most of Sadoul's messages contained statements of what the French workers must do and appeals for action;[40] probably he received this assignment since he was best known in France. Guilbeaux was less a spokesman for the proletariat than an analyst. He wrote articles on the treaties of Brest-Litovsk and Versailles, on a French deputy who was believed to have conspired against the Bolsheviks, and on the general situation in France.[41] Serge, as a staff member, did routine reporting on the French situation on the basis of newspapers and letters. Occasionally, letters from France appeared in the *Communist International,* and several Russians contributed articles. Among them were Trotsky, who had had contacts with French leftists in pre-war years but no special connections or information in 1919, and D. Z. Manuilsky, who had traveled in France recently but, according to Serge, did not understand what he observed there.[42] In many cases, the Comintern propagandists allowed faulty information or wishful thinking to distort the facts according to their preconceived ideas.

Two examples may be regarded as typical. One is an article by E. Blonina, the Russian Bolshevik, who discussed the meeting of the Seine Socialists in April. In general, she had sound information about the meeting: she recorded the victory of the ex-Minoritaires that gave provisional endorsement to the Second International. But she erroneously reported not only that the ex-Majoritaires felt helpless and hesitated to present their resolution, but that the ex-Minoritaires had expressed a willingness to expel the extreme Right from the Second International or else to join the Third.[43]

Similarly, an article prepared by Serge on the November election relied upon conflicting and erroneous election returns. He knew that the Socialist Party had suffered losses in the election and that the Right wing of the party had retained a number of seats. He concluded from the results that the bourgeois dictatorship had reached "a rare degree of perfection" and that the Socialist Party had been repudiated because its leaders were not sufficiently revolutionary. Yet the article acclaimed the vote for Sadoul as a demonstration of the revolutionary spirit of the workers, ignoring the fact that he had finished behind several other candidates.[44] Such a conclusion probably resulted from a combination of faulty information and self-delusion.

The lack of clear information caused confusion in Moscow and Petrograd about who would emerge as the leader of the workers' movement in France as the revolution approached. The Comintern leaders had initially chosen Loriot for the job of organizing a Communist Party, but later in the year they seem to have become confused about his position, or perhaps to have developed doubts about his abilities. They continued to regard him as their chief agent in France, but with less confidence. Sadoul may have planted some of the doubt, because in his report to the First Congress he said the French proletariat had no Lenin or Trotsky—no qualified leader—for the impending struggle. He suggested, somewhat equivocally, that such persons as Cachin or even the rightist Renaudel might make revolutionary contributions; he did not consider Loriot as a leader.[45] In October, he repeated his opinion that the "French proletariat lacks leaders" and that the most ardent revolutionaries had fallen into anarcho-syndicalism. According to his interpretation, no revolutionary doctrine existed in France.[46] About two months later, he made a plea for unity among the small groups that were sympathetic to the Third International, but specified neither the leader nor the terms. He stated emphatically that the Right and Center could have no part in the revolutionary action, and he named Longuet and Cachin as men who were dangerous to the movement.[47] This article probably came under the shadow of the Hungarian failure, when the Comintern was most insistent that no cooperation with the moderates was possible.

No further doubts about Loriot were expressed in Comintern writings for some time. Guilbeaux wrote of him in favorable terms. At the Eighth Congress of the Russian Communist Party in March, a letter was issued to French Communists honoring the Paris Commune of 1871, and the addressee was Loriot.[48] On July 31, Zinoviev dispatched a message to the French proletariat on the fifth anniversary of the death of Jaurès, and it went to Loriot as the representative of the working class.[49] About a month later, however, in a circular letter, Zinoviev said that Péricat's group represented the nucleus of the Communist Party in France. He gave lower status to Loriot's faction as an example of a party which, having remained in the Socialist Party, continued to be parliamentary in tone. He hoped that this organization would soon unite with Péricat's group.[50]

When Trotsky wrote a letter to the French Communists on September 1, he addressed it to Monatte, Loriot, Péricat, and Rosmer because of his "bonds of friendship" with all of them. The French revolution would be in strong and honest hands, he said, ignoring Sadoul's doubts and the differences that existed between Péricat and the others.[51] Lenin, in an article written in October, said Paris had two Communist newspapers, Péricat's *L'Internationale* and Georges Anquetil's *Titre Censuré*. He either forgot or was not informed about *La Vie Ouvrière,* which had been discussed in previous issues of the *Communist International*.[52] On October 28, Lenin wrote a letter to "Loriot and all French friends who have joined the Third International," which indicated that he still felt Loriot to be the chief spokesman for the cause.[53]

The whole nature of Comintern-French relations underwent a change during the early weeks of 1920. Just as the Comintern modified its program in Germany as a result of developments at Leipzig, so it changed its attitude toward the French situation after the Socialist Party Congress at Strasbourg on February 25–29. Here, the Bolsheviks not only received the first reward from the efforts of the Loriot group, but saw signs of the impact the Comintern was making on Socialist parties throughout Europe.

The Strasbourg Congress

Loriot and his allies had a much stronger position in February 1920 than they had had ten months before. The Socialist Party had continued to drift toward the Left, at least partly because of Loriot's organizational and agitation work. As before, Loriot first took his proposal for joining the Third to the meetings of the Confederation of the Seine, which were being held a few days before the national congress at Strasbourg. On this occasion, Loriot's faction received 9,930 votes for their motion, as compared with 5,988 for a Center motion and only 616 for the right-wing position.[54] It was a youthful contingent that produced the victory at the Seine conference, unwilling to heed the warnings of the older leaders like Longuet and Renaudel. When these young delegates reached Strasbourg, they encountered the more conservative representatives from the provinces, and they achieved only half of their objective; the party voted to leave the Second International, but it did not endorse the Third. The debate that resulted during the five-day Congress revealed the extent to which the Comintern was gaining as a symbol of the new Socialist order.

The victory at the Seine conference and the progress made at the national congress cannot be attributed entirely to the work of Loriot's Committee. The Centrists had shifted their position in much the same way as the Independents had done in Germany. Whereas in spring 1919 they had hopes of reviving the Second, by the beginning of 1920 they generally agreed that the Second was hopelessly dead and a new International must be constructed. The action of the USPD at Leipzig completed the evidence on which this conviction rested.[55] Actually, the Center Socialists had not made a substantial change in their position, since they still wanted a broad organization containing all branches of the Socialist movement. But the fact that they now renounced the Second as a possible base was a victory for the Comintern, and they even found themselves trying to claim some of the support that had been generated for the idea of a Third International. Longuet, a leading Centrist spokesman, wrote on February 11 that a Third International indeed was needed; he identified this as an International to serve the "third," or post-war, period of the Socialist movement. Such an International did not yet exist, he asserted; it must include all forces working for the liberation of the proletariat.[56] The fact that he adopted the Bolshevik idea of the Third International testifies to the amount of ground the concept had gained.

The chief aim of the Centrists at the Strasbourg Congress was to get the Socialist Party out of the Second without creating a rush to the Bolshevik Third. They therefore tried to prove that Moscow-Petrograd had created conditions that made a true International impossible, and that the French Socialists could adhere to the Third only if different conditions were acknowledged. The supporters of the Comintern responded with an ambiguous sequence of counterarguments. They may have intended to mislead their audience on the aims and principles of the organization, but undoubtedly poor communications from Russia were responsible for some of the inaccuracies that occurred in the debate. The result was a tumultuous session in which much misinformation was bandied about.[57]

Loriot carried the main part of the debate for his group. He sought to dispel doubts about the Soviet system by saying that soviets would not compete with existing Socialist and syndicalist groups, but would supplement them. He said the soviets were not to be the means of seizing power, but would come into full effect only after control had passed to the proletariat. Then they would become an instrument of proletarian power.[58] This was a corruption of the Comintern's insistence that all power should be in the hands of the soviets. After Frossard had reported to the Congress that the USPD was willing to join the Third International under certain conditions, Loriot claimed to have information that the German party had agreed to join without previous conditions, and he recommended that the French Socialists do the same.[59] One condition that he insisted was necessarily imposed by the Comintern was the purging of part of the membership, and it was precisely on this matter that the Center wanted the Comintern to alter its policy.[60] At the same time, however, that Loriot declared a purge to be a necessity in Moscow's eyes, he assured the Congress that the Comintern would allow "as much autonomy as you could want."[61] He apparently did not know, or would not admit, that the Comintern headquarters was becoming less inclined to tolerate national variations in view of the parliamentary question and the Hungarian experience.

Loriot's insistence on a program of purges caused as much controversy as any other single question in the Congress, creating opposition even within his own group. Louise Saumoneau, one of the most active members of his Committee, said that the French party should not be obliged to expel some of its members because of their past conduct; it was present willingness to affiliate with the Comintern that counted.[62] The resolution that the Committee had proposed in favor of affiliation did not require an automatic purge, and she felt that Moscow would not insist on one.

One member of Loriot's faction who rose to prominence at Strasbourg was Raymond Lefebvre, a war veteran and relative newcomer to the party. A former Minoritaire, he had been opposed to Loriot during the war, but gradually became dissatisfied with the moderates and attracted to the peace propaganda of the Third International. In 1919, he had allied himself with Loriot's Committee, and had contributed articles to *La Vie Ouvrière*. His emotional performance at the conference and a controversy over his right to participate enhanced his reputation as a revolutionary. He was later to have a role in the Second Congress of the Comintern.[63]

The Strasbourg Congress took two votes on future international policy. The first dealt with the question of whether to leave the Second International, and in this case the Center and Left voted together. There were 4,330 votes for withdrawal from the old International and only 337 against the motion.[64] The second vote involved the question of whether to reconstruct a new International along lines that would condemn those who had collaborated with the bourgeoisie during the war, or to join the Third International. The Longuet wing proposed the "reconstruction" motion; the Right, led by Blum, offered an alternative "reconstruction" motion deleting the provisions that condemned the collaborators. The "reconstruction" groups had 3,021 votes in the final count, of which 732 were recorded for the Blum amendment. Loriot's motion received 1,621 votes.[65] This represented a substantial improvement in the position of the Loriot faction over the previous year, and the Left greeted the returns with applause.

The victory of the Center and the endorsement of the plan to rebuild an all-inclusive Socialist-Communist International meant that an understanding would have to be reached with the Moscow-Petrograd International. This is what the USPD and ILP also wanted. The summary resolution adopted by the Strasbourg Congress addressed itself to this issue, which became a turning point in the relations between French Socialism and the Comintern. The resolution instructed the central council of the party to contact and negotiate with other groups, including the Third International in Moscow, the Independents in Germany, and the Socialist parties of Italy and Switzerland, about forming a new multinational organization. It gave wholehearted support to the USPD's suggestions on the subject.[66] Accordingly, the party's executive committee dispatched two Centrist representatives, Cachin and Frossard, to Russia for consultations with leaders of the Third International, with results that were to have long-lasting effects.

Chapter eight Left-Wing Communism

By the end of 1919, the original pro-Communist parties in Germany, Great Britain, and France had reached the same point: each had suffered a period of organizational trouble because of the question of parliamentary activity. In Germany, the KPD had initially renounced parliamentarianism as being unrevolutionary, and when it resumed parliamentary activity for tactical reasons in October, it lost about half its membership. The group that remained anti-parliamentary and that later formed the KAPD became a competitor for the support of the revolutionary proletariat. In Britain, the small WSF and SLP opposed parliamentarianism and Labour Party affiliation so effectively that they prevented Communist unity. In France, the Left extremists had been vociferous enough to persuade the Committee for Adhesion to the Third International to repudiate parliamentary elections. Individually, these anti-parliamentary Communist groups were small and ineffectual, but together they constituted a significant part of the early adherents to the Third International.

Bolshevik theory had long contended that democratic parliamentary institutions should be used by revolutionaries to arouse the masses, to attack bourgeois parties and policies, and eventually to destroy these same institutions. The Bolsheviks had entered the pre-Revolutionary Russian Duma to enlarge their scope for agitation, and Lenin's theoretical writings prior to 1919 had advocated such a policy for other revolutionary parties.[1] The Bolsheviks' position on this point, however, was not generally known in Western Europe. Chicherin's invitation to the First Congress, Lenin's theses on bourgeois democracy and proletarian dictatorship, and the Manifesto of the First Congress,

the three best-known expressions of Comintern doctrine in 1919, gave
no indication that the affiliating parties were to participate in the
affairs or campaigns of bourgeois parliaments. Indeed, they devoted
a good deal of space to attacking parliamentary institutions. In the
January invitation, there was a statement not only against parliamentarianism, but also about the need to bring syndicalist elements into
the Communist movement. In the theses, Lenin's main theme was
that parliamentary systems were a means of oppressing the proletariat
and must be replaced by proletarian dictatorships.[2] The Manifesto
made the same point,[3] and none of the three documents suggested
that the Communists could use parliaments temporarily.

Lenin did not clarify the position until July, when in attacking Mac-
Donald, he mentioned in passing that the proletariat should not fail
to make use of parliamentary activity in its class struggle; this statement did not reach the important European countries until several
weeks later.[4] In the September issue of the *Communist International*,
Zinoviev gave the question a thorough examination for the first time.
He insisted that opposition to parliamentary government did not require revolutionaries to abstain from parliamentary elections and debates in the pre-revolutionary period. On the contrary, a revolutionary
strategy required Communists to use parliament as a weapon. On this
occasion, Zinoviev introduced the argument that Lenin was to defend
in detail in *"Left-Wing" Communism: An Infantile Disorder* a few
months later.[5]

Again, Zinoviev's remarks took too long in reaching the West to
have any effect. The KPD split at Heidelberg, Loriot's abstention from
the French elections in November, and the intensification of the anti-
parliamentary campaigns by the extreme Left in Britain all came after
Zinoviev's discussion of the matter. In point of fact, the problem became even more serious, from the Comintern's point of view, in the
early months of 1920 because the left-wing faction won control of the
branch organization that the Comintern was trying to establish in
Amsterdam.

The Creation of the Amsterdam Bureau

In October 1919, in an effort to overcome some of the effects of the
blockade and civil war, the Comintern had sent S. J. Rutgers to the

Netherlands to open the so-called West European Bureau of the Communist International.[6] He arrived in Amsterdam in November with a mandate to establish a propaganda center in the name of the Comintern, to issue a bulletin in three languages, to communicate with various Communist parties in Europe and America, and to organize an international conference as early as possible.[7] He was instructed to call a new Comintern Congress if circumstances permitted.[8]

The internal situation of the Dutch Communist Party complicated Rutgers' assignment. This small organization was an offspring of the Dutch Socialist Party, which had expelled its revolutionary Left wing in 1908. Those who had been dismissed, the "Tribunists" as they came to be called, formed an alliance with anarchist and syndicalist groups before and during the war, and this association colored the new party's thought and action.[9] The leading figures were David Wijnkoop and Willem van Ravesteijn, who held seats in parliament and edited the party's newspaper, the astrophysicist Anton Pannekoek, the poet Hermann Gorter, and the Socialist leader Henriette Roland-Holst. The last three, representing the anarchist-syndicalist view, disliked the fact that Wijnkoop and van Ravesteijn remained in parliament.

The party's internal controversy did not initially trouble the Bolsheviks. At the First Congress, Rutgers told the delegates of the alliance between the ex-Socialists and the anarchist-syndicalists;[10] such an alliance was consistent with the current desire to bring all revolutionary elements into the Comintern, and from the Comintern's point of view, this was one of several desirable features of the Dutch party. The party had assumed the name "Communist" late in 1918, even before the Comintern's promptings began. It had been one of the first parties to hear of, and react favorably to, the Comintern's initial message, partly because of Beatrice Rutgers' trip from Petrograd to Amsterdam late in 1919.[11] The executive committee had reacted immediately to the instructions of the First Congress; on April 10 it announced affiliation with the Comintern and appointed Wijnkoop as delegate to the ECCI.[12] At a congress in Groningen on June 28–29, the party had appealed to the proletariat to affiliate with the Third International.[13] Pannekoek, Gorter, and Roland-Holst had written ideologically acceptable articles, which appeared in the *Communist International*.[14] When the Bolsheviks dispatched Rutgers to Amsterdam, they had no reason to doubt that the Dutch Party would be helpful in creating the Bureau.

Rutgers discovered, however, that the controversy over parliamentary action was serious. He became involved in the dispute, deciding eventually, in common with the anarchists, that van Ravesteijn did not have a proper revolutionary outlook.[15] This argument did not immediately prevent cooperation in assembling a meeting to establish the Bureau, but it took on larger significance when the meeting opened.

The Dutch Communists made contact with American and British Communists, who began to arrive in the middle of January 1920. They also managed later to gather assorted delegates from Belgium and Scandinavia, and a single delegate from the Left Opposition wing of the German Communists. Efforts to communicate with the KPD and the West European Secretariat had been largely unsuccessful, and it was decided to proceed without them. The meetings began on February 3 with an address from Rutgers, and discussions opened on the following day. Among the active participants were Wijnkoop, Roland-Holst, and other Dutch leaders; Pankhurst, Murphy, Fred Willis, and Hodgson of Great Britain (the last two representing the BSP); Louis Fraina of the United States; Michael Borodin of Russia; and delegates without mandates from the Dutch Indies, China, and Hungary.[16] Although only about twenty people participated, in some respects it was a more legitimate international conference than the First Congress in Moscow because of the high proportion of delegates who held bona fide mandates.

The absence of spokesmen for the KPD and the West European Secretariat embarrassed the participants. The situation was rendered "rather delicate" because the Germans had not arrived, but the group eventually decided to form a bureau that would serve and unite the Communist groups in Western Europe and America. It left to the West European Secretariat the handling of relations with parties in Central and Southeast Europe, hoping by this device to avoid conflicts of jurisdiction.[17]

The delegates assembled in secret—or so they thought—because they wanted to avoid the Dutch police; several participants had entered the country illegally. For four days they discussed strike tactics and trade union problems, pondered the propriety of relations with moderate Socialists, and drafted resolutions on these and other matters. Then they suddenly learned that the police had placed a recording device in an adjacent room, and that their work was being monitored. At about the same time, a sympathizer from Switzerland appeared, and reported that several German delegates would cross the border in two or three days to join the conference. Hoping to consult with KPD agents in a new locale, the delegates decided to recess until February 11.

The official conference sessions never resumed.[18] The police arrested several delegates and ordered them to leave the country, and several more fled to avoid capture. By the time the Germans arrived—with Klara Zetkin, an influential member of the KPD, among them—the founders of the West European Bureau had scattered, and their conference was in shambles. On hearing what had happened Zetkin lost her temper, and stated that the preparations for the meeting had been poor and the conduct of the participants foolish.[19] In spite of police probings and interference, she made contact with some of the delegates at Rutgers' home in Amersfoort, about thirty miles from Amsterdam. The Communists who managed to gather there conducted a kind of "rump conference" for a few days, arguing over whether the decisions reached at Amsterdam were valid. Borodin, Rutgers, and Murphy participated in these meetings, and tried to reach an agreement with the Germans on the relationship between the Bureau and the Secretariat.[20]

Zetkin insisted that a conference which was so badly prepared and so thinly attended could not be regarded as a legitimate meeting of the International; the Dutch delegates defended its authenticity and its work.[21] The only understanding the ex-delegates and the Germans reached was a decision to allow both the Bureau and the Secretariat to operate as propaganda organs for three months, and to "try, meanwhile, to avoid mutual conflict." The compromise provided that a new conference would be held at the end of the three months, "which, it is hoped, will possess the necessary authority for a more definite International Bureau."[22]

Despite its premature termination, the Amsterdam conference established an executive unit and produced several resolutions. Wijnkoop became president of the Bureau, and Rutgers and Roland-Holst were appointed as secretaries. One resolution provided for a three-member executive committee, all of whom must live in Holland. This virtually assured control of the Bureau by the Dutch party. The conference also commissioned the Communist Party of America to create a sub-bureau for North and South America, and to summon a conference in the Western Hemisphere. It announced its intention to publish a bulletin in three languages, to arrange international conferences, and to act temporarily as the Comintern's exclusive agency in issuing appeals and proclamations. It also planned to create archives of the revolutionary movement.[23]

All these ambitious plans reveal that the participants saw themselves as leaders of the Comintern movement. They regarded the Amsterdam Bureau as one of the great revolutionary instruments of the future. In spite of the brevity of their conference, they issued a number of statements of policy. There was a typical resolution about Soviet Russia, calling on the Allied powers to make peace with the Bolsheviks and urging a mass strike in the West against the blockade and intervention.[24] Other resolutions differed from the usual messages of the Comintern headquarters; their authors regarded themselves as more than mere agents of the central authority. A resolution on labor unions distinguished between trade and industrial unions: the former were necessarily impotent instruments of capitalism; the latter were potentially weapons of the class struggle, which must be encouraged and converted to revolution. This resolution came close to adopting the line of the West European syndicalists, who renounced political activity in its entirety.[25]

The conference did not comment directly on the question of parliamentary action; both the parliamentarians and the anti-parliamentarians had been well represented, and a compromise resolution postponed a decision on this matter until a future conference. However, the Amsterdam meetings did produce several statements bearing on the problem. One pronouncement summoned the Communist groups within "the old reformist and opportunist parties" to "sever their compromising relations and unite in the Communist Party (or form a Communist Party if necessary)." This motion carried by a vote of thirteen to two, with only one Dutch delegate and the representatives of the BSP opposing it.[26] The message was obviously aimed at such groups as the BSP, the Italian Left Socialists, the French Committee for Adhesion to the Third International, and the Left Opposition within the KPD in Germany, where the KAPD had not yet been formed. This motion was completely consistent with the mood of the Comintern of early 1919 and with the lesson the Comintern had drawn from the Hungarian collapse, but in 1920 it was out of step with the Comintern's increasing desire to make contacts with existing Socialist parties in order to proselytize.

The conference also dealt with the question of whether "workshop committees and other industrial bodies" should be admitted to the Third International even though many of their members were not Communists and might not accept Comintern doctrines. Moscow-Petrograd had held that only dedicated Communists could become members of the Third International; the organization must not allow itself to be diluted by moderate elements that would direct it into the same errors and treasonable acts as the Second International. The Amsterdam conference, fully aware that it was differing from Moscow, voted 10½ to 4½ in favor of admitting such groups. This position did not become a firm policy of the Bureau, however, since the delegates decided to "circularise all the organisations affiliated to the Third International, and also the Moscow Executive, in order that the views of the Third International as a whole might be ascertained on this question before any permanent arrangement should be made."[27]

These plans and resolutions of the Amsterdam conference testify that its delegates conceived of the Comintern in Western political and organizational terms: some decisions of fundamental importance might be made by consultation among the member parties and contrary to the original line of the ECCI. Nothing in the Bolshevik mentality or in the original Russian concept of the Comintern allowed for this kind of deviation. Although theoretically the Comintern headquarters was responsible to the Congresses and ultimately to the party members, it never occurred to the Comintern's founders that the lower echelons might properly alter a policy that the ECCI had established. The first and crucial error of the Amsterdam Bureau was that it did not recognize this fact, and the initiative that it took at the prompting of legitimate delegates led it into trouble with the Russian headquarters.

The Bureau at Work

The responsibility for operating the Bureau fell primarily to Wijnkoop, Rutgers, and Roland-Holst as members of the organization's executive committee; most of the documents issued by the Bureau carried one or all of their names. The Bureau found itself immediately under attack from part of the non-Socialist press, which reported the Amsterdam conference as an extensive and treasonable conspiracy, lavishly financed by Russia. In response, the Bureau published most of the documents of the conference as a means of refuting these exaggerated accounts.[28] After the Kapp Putsch and the general strike in March that temporarily gave the trade unions a strong hand in Germany, it issued a manifesto to the English, French, and Belgian workers exhorting them to be ready to turn against their own governments and leaders in case of intervention by the Allied powers.[29]

The Bureau leaders took pride in the fact that the Amsterdam conference had not confined itself to uttering "empty phrases," but encouraged revolutionary action. They quoted approvingly Loriot's remarks at the Strasbourg Congress about the willingness of the Comintern to permit great liberty of action to individual member parties.[30] This emphasis on action and on relative freedom for component parties prompted the Bureau to take the side of the KAPD when it became involved in the quarrels with the KPD and the West European Secretariat after the Kapp Putsch.[31] After the KAPD had been created and its position denounced by the Secretariat, a group of young Communists in Berlin took up the KAPD's cause. The Bureau, contrary to the division of territory that assigned Germany to the jurisdiction of the Secretariat, entered the controversy and also protested on behalf of the KAPD.[32] The Bureau thus unwittingly put itself in opposition to Moscow as well as to the Secretariat.

Shortly after involving itself in the factional troubles in Germany, the Bureau repeated the performance in Britain. Early in May, it appealed to its "English friends" to resolve their differences on the basis of non-affiliation with the Labour Party.[33] This appeal merely echoed a resolution adopted at the Amsterdam conference, but by reopening the theme in *The Workers' Dreadnought* at a time when the parliamentary and affiliation controversy was most bitter in Britain, the Bureau thoroughly alienated the BSP.[34]

Somewhat earlier, the Bureau had managed to alienate some of the leaders of the French Socialist Party by a slightly different form of intervention. Roland-Holst had attended the Strasbourg Congress as a representative of the Bureau and had addressed the delegates in excellent French. She claimed to have a mandate from both the Bureau and the Secretariat, a questionable assertion in view of the controversy over jurisdiction.[35] She disconcerted her listeners when, in encouraging the French party to join the Comintern, she pressed for the expulsion of its right-wing members.[36] The possibility of a purge shocked the French Socialists, most of whom were still eager to avoid a serious division. When Frossard went to Moscow on behalf of the party later, he expressed strong disapproval of the Bureau's effort to bring about the expulsion of certain members.[37] His attitude probably represented the majority opinion, and his annoyance resulted at least in part from the remarks of Roland-Holst at the Strasbourg meeting. Even Loriot had been rather circumspect about insisting upon expulsions or division up to this time, and, understandably, Roland-Holst's stand incurred resentment.

The Bureau did engage in some activity that was "correct" by Comintern standards. Technically, its position on expulsions in France and elsewhere agreed with Moscow's. Its propaganda on behalf of the Soviet government in Russia had been "correct." It had issued a statement against the efforts of the Longuetists and the ILP to bring about a broad international conference, and this echoed the ECCI line.[38] But its "errors" in Germany and its general left-wing mood more than counterbalanced these merits.

Only about three months after the Bureau had been created, Moscow radio broadcasted the decision to abolish it. The ECCI had unanimously decided that the refusal to employ parliamentary means or to work within existing trade unions showed an insufficient appreciation of the role to be played by Communist parties as agents of the world revolution. The Amsterdam Bureau (the message did not call it the West European Bureau) had taken a view different from that of the ECCI "on all questions," and therefore a decision had been made to annul its mandate. Its functions were handed over to the West European Secretariat.[39]

The ECCI was put in an embarrassing position by being forced to kill one of its own branches. It had to face accusations that the dissolution was the result of financial irregularities, and it issued a second explanation early in June denying any such reason. The Bureau had been suspended simply because it adhered to "sectarian policy" and was "incapable of fulfilling the task given to it." The ECCI again mentioned the Bureau's "errors" in connection with the KAPD, and made it clear that this was the most important single mistake committed.[40] Those who had staffed the Bureau did not challenge the Moscow-Petrograd decision at this point, but they did not abandon their opinions, and the controversy was resumed at the Second Congress.

Lenin on Left-Wing Communism

Just when the West European Bureau was most active, shortly before its suspension, Lenin wrote his famous essay *"Left-Wing" Communism: An Infantile Disorder,* which became the fundamental Bolshevik statement on the question of parliamentarianism and Communist trade union activity. The basic portion of this work was dated April 27, 1920; its ideas undoubtedly guided the ECCI in its decision to dissolve the Bureau, but it did not become generally known in Western Europe until June or later.

Borkenau has called the Comintern's action against the ultra-left movement in Europe "perhaps the most interesting theoretical debate which ever took place inside the Comintern," and he describes the essay on left-wing Communism as "perhaps the most powerful thing Lenin has ever written." Whether or not one shares these judgments, one is forced to recognize that the attitude of Lenin and the Comintern on this point, and their effort to impose their view upon dissenters, was a milestone in the history of the international Communist movement. For the first time on a large scale, the Bolsheviks undertook to impose their ideological and organizational policy on foreign parties in a specific matter. Much of the language and conduct of the Bolsheviks at the First Congress foreshadowed the possibility of Russian control of the world revolutionary movement, but the ECCI action against the "Left wing" and Lenin's essay were the first extensive attempts to use that control. Lenin had told the Hungarian Communist leaders in March 1919 not to make the error of trying to imitate the Russian Soviet regime too closely,[41] and he gave lip service in *"Left-Wing" Communism* to the need for a correct modification of Communist principles according to the peculiar circumstances in each country. He even said in the essay that the "guiding center" of world revolution could, "under no circumstances, be built after a single model, by a mechanical adjustment and equalization of the tactical rules of the struggle."[42] Taken from their context, these statements seem to imply that Lenin was willing to permit rather wide variations in policy among the various Communist parties, and that he saw a sharply limited function for the "guiding center." This was exactly what many proponents of the Third International in Europe—including such persons as Loriot, Roland-Holst, Welti, and Pankhurst—had been saying on behalf of the organization.

The whole theme of *"Left-Wing" Communism,* however, is to the opposite effect. In the first place, Lenin supported the parliamentarians in Germany and Great Britain completely, and made it an obligation of Communists to participate in parliamentary campaigns and activities.[43] In the summer and fall of the previous year, it will be remembered, he had expressed much more latitude on the question of parliamentary activity; he had written to Pankhurst authorizing one parliamentary and one anti-parliamentary party in Britain and he had pleaded with Levi not to make the parliamentary question a matter of absolute discipline in the KPD; now he was much less tolerant on the point. In the second place, Lenin tried to establish the validity of his new position by frequent references to the Russian situation and to the Bolshevik successes. Contrary to his own admonition to Kun in March 1919, he tried in 1920 to apply the Russian example too closely to the Western situation and to make the revolutions uniform. He constructed an argument to the effect that the long experience and unique successes of the Bolsheviks gave them a special position as models and

guides for future revolutions; he implied the universality and infalli-
bility of the Bolshevik example: "the experience of the victorious dictatorship of the proletariat in Russia clearly has shown those who are
not capable of thinking, or who have had no opportunity to reflect on
the question, that absolute centralization and the strictest discipline of
the proletariat are among the principal conditions for the victory over
the bourgeoisie."[44]

New information had convinced Lenin that parliamentary and
trade union action was absolutely necessary, and he used some strong
language against the "left-wing" elements in Germany, Britain, Italy,
and the Netherlands. He ridiculed the German Left Opposition, describing its boycott of trade unions as childish and unreasonable.[45]
(He apparently did not yet know of the creation of the KAPD on
April 4.) The ECCI, a few weeks later, spoke of the party's "errors"
more gently. By refusing to work within parliamentary institutions
at a time when many workers still relied on them, he said, the leftists
ran the risk of becoming "mere babblers."[46]

Lenin was less abusive toward the British left-wing Communists,
possibly because he had given conditional endorsement to their position only about nine months earlier.[47] The fundamental law of revolution, "confirmed by all revolutions and particularly by all three Russian revolutions of the twentieth century," dictated that most of the
thoughtful and politically active workers must see the necessity for a
revolution and be ready to fight for it. However, he went on, as long
as many of them continued to rely on the old parliamentary institutions, as they were doing in Britain, revolutionaries must fight within
those institutions. Communists must help to bring to power such moderate Socialists as Ramsay MacDonald and Arthur Henderson in order
to demonstrate their unworthiness to the uninformed masses; Pankhurst and Gallacher were not serving their movement well when they
failed to recognize this, he implied. Lenin wrote that he had too little
information on the question of affiliation with the Labour Party to
comment at length on it, but he nevertheless contended that it would
be an error to reject the possibility of compromise.[48]

In his reference to the Italian Left Socialists who repudiated parliamentary and trade union activity, Lenin found himself obliged to criti-

cize the only faction of the Italian Socialist Party that was willing to expel the "reformists" on the party's Right wing. He wrote that the Bordiga faction was "unquestionably" wrong in opposing parliamentary action, but the refusal of Serrati to purge the Turati group justified the existence of the anti-parliamentarians "up to a certain point."[49]

Lenin provoked some resentment within the Dutch Communist Party by initially associating the whole party with the anti-parliamentarian attitude that prevailed in the Bureau. Wijnkoop was not an anti-parliamentarian; as previously noted, he served in the Dutch parliament. He did believe that Communist parties should not be affiliated with any non-Communist groups such as the Labour Party, and he felt anti-parliamentary action should be tolerated in those countries in which the responsible Communist parties preferred it. Although this qualification existed in most of the Bureau's statements, and the Bureau never absolutely repudiated parliamentary action, these distinctions were not evident to Lenin as he wrote. He included several references to the "Dutch Tribunists" who had made Leftist errors because they had had the "misfortune" to be born in a country of privileged and stable legality, thus missing the experience of having both legal and illegal activity.[50] Wijnkoop protested that the accusation of "leftism" against him was unfair, and Lenin corrected the text in later editions. He substituted the expression "some members of the Dutch Communist Party" where he had previously said "Dutch Tribunists."[51]

Lenin did not take Loriot and his Committee to task for their anti-parliamentary position. As we have noted, the Committee for Adhesion to the Third International had abstained from the November elections, and had thus bypassed an opportunity to issue revolutionary propaganda in a political campaign. If Lenin had been concerned with principle, he should have mentioned this error as well as those in Germany, Britain, Italy, and the Netherlands because Loriot's reasoning was essentially the same as that of the other left-wing Communists. The French Communist groups apparently escaped criticism because they did not become involved in the international left-wing movement, as the other groups did, and because their action did not create the kind of schism that hurt the Comintern's position. In other words,

Lenin was concerned more with practical effects than with principle.

This was a basic precept of the essay; opportunism was apparent in nearly every paragraph. In effect, Lenin said that the tactical expedient that worked for Bolshevism was the correct one for the circumstance. In a sense, this was a renunciation of the "no compromise" doctrine that prevailed during the First Congress and immediately after the Hungarian collapse, and a return to the kind of argument that Lenin had used to justify the signing of the Brest-Litovsk Treaty in March 1918. In fact, he referred to the Brest-Litovsk decision in the essay to demonstrate that compromise with an enemy could occasionally serve the larger cause. He did not completely abandon the lesson that Hungary had taught about the danger of compromise with the Social Democrats; it, too, was mentioned in *"Left-Wing" Communism*. He kept this lesson as an alternative weapon, to be used when it was expedient to oppose any given compromise or to criticize an unsuccessful alliance. Lenin and the Comintern had thus endorsed two conflicting principles, but in practice they made them complementary.

"Leftism" in Austria

The abolition of the West European Bureau and the distribution of Lenin's essay did not immediately destroy the effects of the "infantile disorder" or eliminate the problem. In the first place, not all who held such opinions were willing to abandon them simply because Lenin said they should; the Comintern had not yet been reduced to the league of puppets it later became, and some people carried their arguments direct to the Kremlin and the Second Congress. In the second place, these "left-wing" opinions existed among groups not connected with the Amsterdam Bureau. One such example was in Austria, where a modified form of anti-parliamentarianism survived, with the support of another semi-official bureau.

The Austrian Communist Party had maintained its opposition to traditional political activity into 1920 after having boycotted the election for members of the constituent assembly in February 1919. Most of the party leaders continued to feel that the existing situation did not call for parliamentary action. In this view the Austrians were supported by the two leading Hungarian theoreticians—Kun and Georg

Lukács—both of whom were in exile in Austria at the time. Early in 1920, the Austrian Communist press began issuing a theoretical journal, *Kommunismus,* which carried a subtitle describing it as the Comintern's journal for the countries of Southeast Europe. The Hungarian exiles contributed much of the editorial matter, and together with the Austrians they constituted a branch operation of the Comintern based in Vienna. The writings of Kun and Lukács were sometimes thinly disguised by the use of initials rather than full names, but there was no real effort to hide Hungarian participation in the venture. The Austrians and Hungarians tried to assume roughly the same kind of regional function that the West European Bureau and the Balkan Federation had planned, but their association was perhaps a little less formal, and it was better prepared for propaganda than the organizations in Amsterdam and Sofia.

Just as the parliamentary controversy was reaching a climax in Germany and Britain in spring 1920, an article on the problem appeared in *Kommunismus* over the initials "G.L." There is little doubt that the writer was Lukács because the intricate logic and abstract arguments were characteristic of his prose. He did not give a final answer on whether parliamentary action should be employed, but his theories invited a different conclusion from the one the Comintern headquarters was then expressing.

A key point both of Lenin's letter to Pankhurst in summer 1919 and of his essay on left-wing Communism had been that parliamentary action was a matter of tactics, not principle. According to Lukács, such a distinction involved faulty reasoning because principle and tactics could not be separated. Lukács was not challenging Lenin—he probably did not know of the letter to Pankhurst, and the essay had not yet been written—but his views did put him in an opposing camp.[52]

Lukács reasoned that since parliament was the instrument of the bourgeoisie, the proletariat should make use of it only when the working class was on the defensive and had to rally more strength. If the working class were on the offensive in the class struggle, if the time had come when the workers were able to create their own instruments —the soviets—then it would be superfluous to engage in parliamentary elections or activities. By resorting to parliamentary means, the proletariat would be admitting that the idea of actual revolution could not yet be entertained.[53] He also felt that improper action by Communists in parliament could lead to "opportunism," either to a situation in which the parliamentary representatives would become less revolutionary than the masses and try to retard the explosion, or to a case in which the Communist deputies would bring their destructive work to fruition within parliament before the masses had been properly prepared.[54]

The article agreed that an election campaign could be a most effective means of educating the masses, and that under proper conditions, parliamentary action could serve the cause of Communism well. The arguments were balanced for and against this tactic. The assumptions that Lukács made, however, were in effect an argument against parliamentarianism. If parliamentary activity was necessary only when the revolutionary elements were on the defensive, then it should not be necessary early in 1920, when the pro-Bolshevik elements throughout Europe still believed that the revolution was near. If parliamentary conduct by the Communists was superfluous as soon as soviets could be formed, then it was superfluous as Lukács wrote, since scores of reports printed by the Communist press told of the growth of the soviet movement.

Kun, also writing from his Austrian exile in early 1920, gave a different twist to the problem. He joined the controversy in the May 8 issue of *Kommunismus* by advocating an "active boycott" of parliamentary affairs, not as a matter of principle but as a matter of tactics.[55] He was thus theoretically in opposition both to Lenin, who had decided that Communists must use parliament as a matter of tactics, and to Lukács, who argued that principles and tactics could not be separated. He said the syndicalists were wrong to oppose parliamentary action on idealistic grounds, but if a party abstained from an election and at the same time engaged in a propaganda campaign against the other parties and the parliamentary system, it could be much more effective than if it offered candidates. To engage in an aggressive propaganda program against elections and democratic institutions at the time of a bourgeois parliamentary election was to engage in an "active boycott," according to Kun.

When Kun wrote this article, he knew of the controversy between the West European Bureau and the Secretariat,[56] and he wanted to state his views. His prestige among revolutionaries in Europe was high, and his arguments were used in England by the anti-parliamentarians to help justify resistance against Lenin and the official Comintern point of view.[57]

The articles of Lukács and Kun were not the only evidence of agreement between the Vienna Communists and the Amsterdam Bureau. In addition, *Kommunismus* reprinted a number of the Bureau's documents.[58] The periodical was not criticized by Lenin in *"Left-Wing" Communism,* presumably because he did not know about it when he wrote the essay. When he did become aware of the periodical and the articles by B.K. and G.L., he criticized them severely, and equated the Vienna tendency with "left-wing" error.[59]

"Leftism" in Belgium

Another segment of the "left-wing" movement existed in Belgium, where a tiny Communist organization was just beginning to take form in the early months of 1920. Belgium was the only highly industrialized, commercially oriented country of Western Europe in which no Socialist party or group rallied to the cause of the Comintern in 1919.

The nucleus of the Belgian Communist faction was a youthful group within the Belgian Labor Party known as the Jeunes Gardes. In the summer of 1919, the Young Guards established their own journal, *Socialisme,* in which they expressed their admiration for the work of the Comintern; they declared they felt an affinity for the Communists in Russia and Hungary, but were hampered by the fact that the bulk of Belgian Socialists remained faithful to the Second International.[60] They did not at this time entertain thoughts of a split.

By November, the Young Guards had shifted toward the Left and had become more outspoken against the majority; they announced that they would not help the Labor Party in the forthcoming parliamentary elections.[61] This provoked a serious controversy with the parent organization. A central fact in the birth of the Communist movement in Belgium was opposition to all parliamentary activity.

In January about sixty Young Guards, under the leadership of W.

Van Overstraeten, met in a conference and decided to create a group called the Independent Brussels Communists. They began publication of a propaganda newspaper, *L'Ouvrier Communiste,* which gave sympathetic attention to syndicalist movements and the IWW (Industrial Workers of the World).[62] They sent a delegate to the Amsterdam conference, and their periodical, along with *De Tribune, Kommunismus,* and *The Workers' Dreadnought,* gave the theories of the West European Bureau considerable publicity. Following the Bureau's lead, *L'Ouvrier Communiste* favored the KAPD over the KPD when the Kapp Putsch provoked a crisis among the German Communists.[63] The Brussels group remained too small and too local in its interests to have much impact on the Socialist movement within Belgium or the Communist movement abroad. For this reason it escaped the attention, or at least the wrath, of the Comintern.

In October 1919, pro-Communist groups in Antwerp, Louvain, and Gent created a small Flemish Communist society, which published a journal called *De Internationale.*[64] This group, also, had no national or international influence. Its efforts to unite with the Brussels faction and other French-speaking Communist units failed during 1920; consequently, no national Communist party existed in Belgium at the time of the Second Congress. The Brussels group resisted unification because it felt the Flemish organization should expel certain members from its ranks.[65]

The Brussels group did, however, take the initiative in bringing the French-speaking Communists together by convening a conference on May 22. At this conference, the Communist Federation of Wallonia was formed, which adopted an official statement repudiating parliamentary activity; propaganda in parliament and in elections could not be effective, the Federation said, and the disadvantages of parliamentary tactics outweighed the advantages.[66] When Van Overstraeten left Belgium to attend the Second Congress of the Comintern, he and his party were completely committed to the "left-wing" position.

This uncompromising anti-parliamentary attitude among many of the Comintern's supporters in Western and Central Europe was one of the two most difficult organizational problems that Moscow-Petrograd faced in 1920. The other involved those Center Socialist parties of Europe that wanted to negotiate with the Comintern. Delegates from these parties were descending on Russia in spring 1920, the very time at which the ideological struggle with the "Left wing" reached its peak. The Left wing wanted to reject all dealings with the Independents of Germany and Britain; the Comintern had denounced this inflexible attitude, but did not want to alienate any revolutionary support from the Left. It now had the delicate problem of wooing and overwhelming those Center Socialists whom it had invited to Russia without alienating the left-wing Communists, who were most eager for an early and violent revolution.

Chapter nine Encounters in Moscow

For the men who regarded themselves as the directors of the world revolution, the European situation still looked promising in spring 1920. The revolution that they hoped would sweep the world in the year of the founding of the Comintern had not come; in fact, even the few bases outside Russia that had been won early in 1919—in Hungary, Bavaria, and Slovakia—had been lost, but this did not shake the faith of the Bolshevik leaders.

The existence of Communist-oriented groups in a dozen European countries seemed to testify to the vitality of the revolutionary movement. The marked improvement in the Bolsheviks' internal situation since the previous summer, and the obvious disintegration of the intervention, gave further cause for optimism. To the Bolsheviks, the Allies' failure to press the intervention more vigorously was due to revolutionary pressure from the masses, rather than to war exhaustion or the scruples of Lloyd George and Wilson.

The improved military situation not only cheered the Bolsheviks; it also enabled them to communicate more readily with their allies and potential allies in the West. Now they could engage, for the first time, in the manipulation that was to become a standard feature of the international Communist movement. The change in the Comintern's personality in 1920 was the result partly of enlarged possibilities and partly of recent experiences.

Spreading the Message: The Second Phase

In what specific ways had the Comintern headquarters changed since it was first established? An important difference was that Radek, having returned from Germany and taken up his duties as secretary, now had an active role in Comintern affairs. According to Guilbeaux, who was one of the leading propagandists for the Comintern at this time, Radek introduced a new degree of corruption into the operation because he felt that there was nothing money could not buy.[1] In view of testimony about the free use of money by Béla Kun in Hungary, it is questionable whether Radek added anything new to Comintern policy in this respect. Perhaps the Comintern's expenditures and briberies abroad increased in 1920 as a result of improved communications rather than because of Radek's influence.

The physical accommodations of the Third International at Smolny had apparently improved considerably since the day when Serge and Mazine faced each other across a bare table and began to plan propaganda. Balabanoff, who attended a meeting there in spring 1920, spoke of Zinoviev's "magnificent" offices,[2] and the American anarchist Emma Goldman, arriving in the same period, was impressed "by the magnitude of it all." Later, she also commented on the "gorgeous quarters" of Radek and Zinoviev.[3] Apparently the Comintern leaders lived elegantly by comparison with the miserable standards of most Russians at the time, and although there was a food shortage, they usually got the best available.[4]

In spite of these material comforts, the Comintern leaders had not streamlined their conduct of affairs since the early days. The two delegates of the British ILP who visited Petrograd in May found it impossible to have satisfactory business dealings with the Executive Committee. R. C. Wallhead told his colleagues at home that "the business methods at the headquarters of the Third International were extremely dilatory. Engagements carried no weight, and time appeared of no account whatever." Wallhead finally had some informal conversations with Radek and a meeting with the ECCI, but Zinoviev did not attend these sessions, and Wallhead did not meet him until the night before he was to leave Russia. Commenting on the Comintern generally, he was apparently impressed by the fact that "it was entirely an *ad hoc* body. It had no formal constitution or rules, and its Executive had not been elected upon any constitutional method by the various Socialist bodies who had given their adherence to the new In-

ternational organization."⁵ Wallhead's traveling companion, Clifford
Allen, shared this impression.⁶

The personnel of the headquarters had changed relatively little. Bukharin, who had been rather closely associated with Comintern activities in the first year, seems to have become even more closely involved
when the representatives of the Socialist parties of the West began to
arrive. Serge remained as a leading translator and journalist. Balabanoff had reappeared on the scene from her unofficial exile in the
Ukraine to find that her secretarial office in Moscow and her title of
Comintern secretary had been given to Ian Antonovich Berzin, an old
Bolshevik whom the ECCI members undoubtedly found less difficult
than Balabanoff.⁷ She nevertheless occasionally attended meetings of
the Executive Committee and participated in its affairs through the
Second Congress.

For all the similarity in organization and personnel, the Comintern
leadership had undergone an important adjustment in emphasis between the First Congress and the spring of 1920. Zinoviev summarized
this change at mid-year in an article entitled "What the Communist
International Has Been and What it Must Become."⁸ His key point
was that previously the Comintern had been merely "an organ of *propaganda and agitation,*" but now it was becoming a "*fighting organization* that will have to give direct guidance to the movement in the
various countries."⁹ He emphasized that the Comintern intended to
take a much more detailed part in organizing and advancing the work
of its member parties. The intention of the Third International to
guide and to influence member parties had been announced in the
official documents of the First Congress, but it had not been possible
to put such control into practice. Not only were communications improving in 1920, but also recent events in Europe—the feuds in Germany and Britain, the "errors" in Hungary, the "secularism" of the
Amsterdam Bureau—had persuaded the Bolsheviks that their own
exclusive experience must be brought to bear on the non-Russian parties to a greater extent. Zinoviev's summary statement was only one
of several that carried this message in the weeks before the Second
Congress.

Closely related to the Bolsheviks' new emphasis on control was their
concern about the interest being expressed by the "Center" or "recon-

struction" Socialists. Even though the Comintern headquarters had urged the German Independents and the French Socialists to send delegations to Russia for consultation, it felt obliged to issue many warnings against allowing the "opportunists" to gain entry to the Third International. In his statement on the fundamental tasks of the Second Congress, Lenin declared that the French Socialists, the ILP, and the USPD had passed resolutions conditionally favoring affiliation with the Third International. He represented them as being "willing to adhere," although their delegates had only been instructed to negotiate. Lenin thus misrepresented, or at least oversimplified, the positions of these parties, and he used their so-called desire for affiliation to stress the need for careful selection of future members of the Comintern.[10]

Zinoviev also took this line in his propaganda writings. His famous statement, written in May, to the effect that "We must lock the door and place a trustworthy guard at the gates of the Communist International" stemmed from the fear that these Center parties were applying for membership because they hoped to undermine the revolutionary quality of the Comintern.[11] Indeed, Lenin and Zinoviev were partly right; the three major Center parties of the West did want to bring about a more tolerant attitude on the part of the Third International, and would have worked toward a more moderate position had they been allowed to join on the terms they wanted. The Comintern leaders, however, saw their interest in a more insidious light, claiming that the Centrists were conspiring to repeat the treasonable acts that the Hungarian Social Democrats had allegedly performed against the Soviet government in Budapest in 1919.[12] The very representatives whom the Bolsheviks had invited from Britain, Germany, and France were received as potential traitors, and they were treated as suppliants seeking admission, although they had been encouraged to come by the Russians themselves.

Another manifestation of the Comintern's shift of emphasis from propaganda to organization was the modified attitude toward the creation of soviets. Early Comintern writings stressed that soviets should be organized as soon as possible. The Manifesto of the First Congress had urged the workers to unite under the banner of the soviets.[13] Lenin's "Theses on Bourgeois Democracy and Proletarian Dictator-

ship" made it one of the main tasks of the Communist parties to organize and control soviets in industry, agriculture, and military units.[14]
The Comintern, of course, did not abandon this position now, but
warned that it was possible to organize soviets prematurely and under
the wrong conditions.

In the spring, Zinoviev wrote an article entitled "When and Under
What Conditions Soviets of Workers' Deputies Should be Formed."[15]
He contended that proper soviets could not be established unless an
acute economic crisis were causing power to slip away from the existing government, unless a strong revolutionary impulse existed among
the workers and soldiers, and unless a serious decision had been made
within the ranks of the Communist Party to begin a systematic
struggle for power. Nothing here is substantially different from Lenin's "Theses" of 1919, except the tacit acknowledgment that in some
countries the revolutionary impulse might not be prevalent and power
might not be slipping away from the bourgeois government. Zinoviev
went on to say that the "social traitors" in Germany who had tried to
create soviets under different conditions and to make them part of a
bourgeois-democratic constitutional system were trying to deceive the
workers. Once again, it had become less important to propagandize
for action than to see that the action occurred under proper guidance.

If this essay by Zinoviev is read along with the article published by
Lukács in *Kommunismus* a few weeks before, it will be seen that a
remarkable similarity of views existed in Petrograd and Vienna on
the question of when soviets should be organized. Lukács had said
that parliamentary action by Communist parties was necessary when
the situation did not permit immediate revolution and when the organization of soviets was not possible.[16] Zinoviev, having decided
that parliamentary action was imperative and that the organization
of soviets could sometimes be legitimately delayed, had implied that
the Comintern was dealing with non-revolutionary situations. Although Lukács's position, to the extent that it invited anti-parliamentarian conclusions, had been denounced in a general way, his assess-
ment was correct. The Comintern was not yet admitting it, but the
revolutionary potential was waning in Europe, and the adjustments
of early 1920 were responses to this fact.

The Comintern was advancing in its organization, but retreating in fervor and conviction for immediate revolution. The shift in emphasis from propaganda to organization, the invitations to the Centrists and the simultaneous concern about the danger they represented, and the willingness to demand parliamentary Communism while retarding the development of soviets abroad were all facets of this complementary offensive and defensive strategy. In July, circumstances gave a slightly different hue to the situation: the Russo-Polish War, which reached a climax in that month, seemed temporarily to revive the hope for immediate victory; and the proximity of the Second Congress stimulated renewed revolutionary zeal. But earlier in the year, when the delegates from abroad began to arrive in large numbers, the Comintern was altering its course, de-emphasizing the appeals for early revolution.

The British Delegations

The first groups to arrive from the West were the British. There were two British contingents, the ILP-Labour Party visitors and two representatives of the BSP. Wallhead and Allen of the ILP left England, together with the main Labour Party group, on April 26 and reached Russia about two weeks later. They spent six weeks in Russia, and although their chief purpose was to obtain information "relative to the constitution and conditions of affiliation to the Third Socialist International," they also traveled with the members of the regular Labour Party delegation, who were paying an unofficial visit to the country.

In Moscow and Petrograd, the Bolsheviks made elaborate preparations for the British representatives. They prepared banquets, parades, theatrical shows, and public demonstrations to impress and please their visitors. The melody "The International" was played for them frequently, and they were offered some of the best quarters and finest food available in Russia. They were also provided guides and interpreters, who served incidentally as informers.[17] The Bolsheviks obviously hoped to win over some of the delegates by special treatment and to single out the unreceptive ones by spying on them.

As we have noted, Wallhead and Allen were unimpressed by the Comintern's way of conducting business. When they finally managed to obtain an audience with the ECCI, Radek and Bukharin were the only persons who discussed anything with them. Balabanoff also attended this session, but did not take part in the discussion. Other members of the ECCI, whom Wallhead could not identify, came mainly from "the small border States"—Latvia, Finland, and Lithuania—and sat silently while the ILP delegates presented their questions.[18]

Wallhead and Allen told the ECCI that they were not seeking admission to the Third International; they wanted only to submit the inquiry the ILP had drafted, to offer and to obtain information, but not to negotiate. If Wallhead and Allen made this point clear to the Bolshevik high command, it was ignored, since both Lenin and Zinoviev later mentioned the ILP as one of the parties that sought admission.[19]

The Comintern officials were slow to respond to the ILP inquiry. They waited three or four weeks after the interview with Wallhead and Allen, and then gave the Britishers an answer only an hour before they left Moscow for their return trip to England. The questions were so simple and the Comintern's eventual answers so similar to earlier statements that no special policy decisions were involved. Perhaps the delay was the result of tactical considerations; the answers were harsh and unsatisfactory from the standpoint of the majority of the ILP, and the Bolsheviks may have wanted to prevent any possibility of a response from the ILP delegates while they remained in Russia.

The Bolsheviks gave all the usual answers. They maligned the Center Socialists, reiterated the old arguments about the dictatorship of the proletariat and the need for revolution, and gave the newly enunciated reasons for parliamentary action. Finally, they noted that only about a fourth of the membership of the ILP was sympathetic to the Comintern, and suggested that this faction should break away from the party and unite with other Communist elements.[20]

As the ILP-Labour delegation was leaving Russia, another contingent was on its way from Great Britain. Quelch and MacLaine of the BSP arrived shortly before the Second Congress and persuaded the Comintern leaders that the British Communist Party—when it could finally be completed—should be affiliated with the Labour Party. In *"Left-Wing" Communism* Lenin had reserved judgment on this point, and he later credited MacLaine and Quelch with removing his doubts.[21] This change of attitude by Lenin and the Comintern created another paradox in early Comintern history; for it came shortly after they had encouraged the Leftists within the ILP to withdraw from their party, or—in effect—to leave the Labour Party. Had the Comintern instructed the BSP and other Leftist parties to join with the Left wing of the ILP inside the Labour Party, instead of ordering the ILP to affiliate with the Communist Party, the long-term objective of the Comintern would have been better served. In fairness, it should be pointed out that the Comintern leaders probably did not know the extent to which the BSP had agreed to accomplish the unification of the new Communist party outside the Labour Party, and no one could have known conclusively that the Labour Party would consistently reject the Communists' applications for affiliation over the next several years. At any rate, the Comintern leaders were so eager to establish their control over the ILP Leftists that they risked the ILP's position within the Labour Party—a position they wanted to maintain—in order to establish that control.

None of the Labour Party or ILP delegates stayed on in Russia for the Second Congress of the Comintern. One member of the ILP, who was not connected with the first delegation, did arrive and attend part of the Congress, but she did not participate actively and was not a part of the official voting group. MacLaine and Quelch remained to serve as spokesmen for the BSP, and they were joined by some of their rivals and colleagues from the other small British parties.

One last observation from a British delegate is warranted before we move on to another group of visitors from the West. Mrs. Snowden, although not specifically assigned to deal with Comintern officials, recorded impressions of them and of the general Bolshevik attitude toward the organization. According to her, Communists in Moscow —whom she did not identify—held out little hope for the Communist International because of its irregular creation, its rigid discipline, and the domineering attitude of the men who operated it.[22] Perhaps she gathered this impression from her talks with Angelica Balabanoff, who accompanied the British visitors during part of their trip and who was becoming disillusioned.[23]

At any rate, the entire leadership of the ILP had gained an unfavorable impression of the Comintern, both for its organization and for its philosophy. They had few illusions about the chance for compromise with the Comintern once they looked with care at the replies to their questions.

The Italian Delegation

The second important group of delegates to arrive were the Italians. In this case the Comintern faced a different problem from that presented by the assorted British groups. Whereas the various pro-Communists in Great Britain were hesistant to unite or cooperate, the Italian Socialist Party had entered the Comintern as a bloc, and its members were reluctant to make the kind of division that Moscow-Petrograd wanted. Among the British, the Comintern wanted to induce unity, and among the Italians, disunity. In each case, the ultimate aim was better control from Comintern headquarters.

The Italians did not travel to Russia primarily for the sake of consultation or information regarding the Comintern. Representatives of the Socialist Party and the Federation of Labor visited Russia to learn what kind of technical aid and supplies they could give to the Soviet government. They brought with them cases of canned food, medicines and soaps, and other supplies as a token of their support for the Bolshevik regime. They received a mass welcome when they arrived in Petrograd. Like the British delegates, they were given preferential treatment and allowed to travel extensively in Russia with special guides and observers.[24]

Serrati, the most prominent figure in the Italian delegation, came armed with the belief that the unity of the Italian Socialist Party was a desirable asset, and that the Bolsheviks' suggestion for a purge of the Right wing should be ignored. On several occasions during his stay, he insisted that the factions within the party were of little importance, and he declined to be identified as the leader of any one them. The Bolsheviks persisted in identifying him with one school of thought, and by gradual degrees they sought to discredit both him and his school.

Soon after the delegation arrived in mid-June, Zinoviev asked that the "most radical" members be sent to him for consultation. Although Serrati recognized this as the first step in dividing the delegation, he was unable to resist the later developments effectively. A short time afterward, most of the delegates left Moscow to travel in southern Russia, but Nicolo Bombacci, vice-president of the party, and Antonio Graziadei, a Socialist professor, decided to stay in the capital for "important work." It later became evident that the Comintern had selected them as its future agents. Bombacci prepared an article for the *Communist International* in which he said the failure of the majority of the Italian Socialists to split with the reformist wing was "paralyzing" the party's activity.[25]

Early in the Italians' visit, Zinoviev suddenly announced the plan to convene the Second Congress in the near future, and he asked Serrati and his colleagues to participate and to vote as representatives of their party. Serrati objected on the grounds that the party had not sent them to Russia to attend an official congress, and no mandates had been provided. Zinoviev overcame this argument while Serrati was traveling in the South; he made contact with the executive of the Italian Socialist Party and obtained credentials for Serrati, Bombacci, and Graziadei to serve as delegates to the Congress.[26]

The Bolsheviks had other maneuvers for putting Serrati on the defensive, but used them only after the Second Congress got under way. One of the main objectives of the Russians was to prove that Serrati did not have the support of the Italian workers, and to undermine his leadership in his own party. Zinoviev invited Bordiga to come to Russia for the Second Congress, even though his anti-parliamentary point of view was in disfavor in Moscow. Lenin had criticized the Italian left-wing Communists along with those in other countries, but had partially excused the Italians on the ground that the party leaders had refused to expel the undesirable parliamentarians on the party's extreme Right.[27] This was to be the cue to another Bolshevik attack on Serrati; he was judged guilty of the radicalism on the Left because he would not expel the moderate elements on the Right.

The Comintern leaders had set the stage well for handling the Italian question in the Second Congress. When the Congress opened on July 19, Serrati became a member of the presidium. He was the best known and most admired of the Italian delegates, and it might have been strange if any other member of the delegation had been honored in this way. The Bolsheviks had so arranged matters that he was in a minority within the delegation that he theoretically led, and they had no cause for concern. His position on the presidium did not give him any advantages; it only made him an easy target for his critics.

The French Centrists

Marcel Cachin and L. O. Frossard, the representatives of the French Socialist Party who traveled to Russia as a result of the Strasbourg Congress, reached Moscow just in time to see one of the large receptions given for the Italian delegation, and they knew that no such welcome had been planned for them.[28] The Italians were treated as members of the true faith, and regarded themselves as such; the two Frenchmen, Frossard tells us, felt like "pilgrims in search of the truth." For this reason they were more vulnerable to Bolshevik prose-lytizing than most other Socialist representatives who visited Russia in 1920. According to Frossard's memoirs, Cachin showed signs of being prepared to accept Bolshevism even before they reached the Russian border,[29] and throughout their visit, he was more receptive to Bolshevik ideas than Frossard.

When they arrived, the two Frenchmen were regarded as "social traitors" because of their status as Centrists and their past affiliations with bourgeois-oriented governments. At about this time, two members of the Committee for Adhesion to the Third International also arrived in Russia, and by receiving these latter visitors with great warmth, the Comintern officials emphasized their distaste for the Centrist position. One of the Committee representatives, Lucien Deslinières, a man of no particular importance in the Committee, won praise on his arrival from the president of the Comintern, who then alluded unfavorably to the present leaders of French Socialism.[30] Whether Zinoviev had met Cachin and Frossard by the time he wrote this article, and whether it referred to them, is uncertain, but they could hardly have missed the point. Deslinières was allowed to participate in some of the sittings of the ECCI early in June, at a time when the leading representatives of French Socialism were being treated as outcasts. Shortly afterward, another member of Loriot's Committee reached Russia and also received special honors. This was Alfred Rosmer, who knew Trotsky and had a reputation as an acceptable revolutionary. He was soon made a member of the ECCI, and he later became a member of the presidium of the Second Congress.[31]

Before Rosmer's arrival, Cachin and Frossard were invited to attend a meeting of the ECCI to explain their mission. On June 19, the two attended a session in Moscow, and delivered statements on the purpose of their visit and the attitude of their party. Lenin, Radek, Zinoviev, Bukharin, Serrati, and several others were there. Cachin's report emphasized the efforts of the French Socialist Party and labor movement to support the Russian Revolution, and he avoided touching on the differences between moderate Socialism and Bolshevism.[32] Frossard handled the more delicate question of the attitude of his party to the International. He contended that the Comintern should adopt a more favorable approach to such parties as the ILP, the USPD, and his own party, since all were revolutionary and in agreement with the general aims of the International. He also objected to the Comintern's demands that certain members and factions be excluded from his party, asserting that the French Socialists would join an international organization only if all their members were accepted. He concluded by asking that representatives of both his party and the German Independents be allowed to participate in the Second Congress with a consultative voice.[33]

After they had delivered their statements, Cachin and Frossard were subjected to questioning and a lecture from Lenin that was intended to expose their reformist errors. He chastised Cachin, as editor of *L'Humanité,* for failing to use the paper properly to prepare for the revolution, and he attacked Frossard's views against expulsions. In passing, he turned to Serrati and criticized him both for allowing "reformist" views in *Avanti!* and for opposing a purge. Lenin dominated the meeting and apparently made the first important steps toward converting Cachin.[34]

The Bolsheviks did not neglect the opportunity to impress and entertain their guests. Zinoviev usually remained in the background on these occasions, probably because he was notoriously haughty and poor at dealing with those he disliked. Cachin and Frossard saw a great deal of Bukharin, and they were also frequently accompanied by René Marchand, a French journalist who had endorsed the Bolshevik cause, and Sadoul, now one of Bolshevism's most trusted spokesmen.[35]

The Bolsheviks quickly saw the possibility of taking Cachin into the fold. Within a few days of his arrival, he was engaged in speaking before the All-Russian Central Committee of Soviets in Moscow.[36] On subsequent occasions, he shared a platform with Graziadei and Bombacci. Since none of these men spoke Russian and their hosts provided the translators, the Bolsheviks ran little risk of spreading undesirable doctrine.

Frossard was not enchanted by the arguments and the oratorical opportunities that Cachin accepted. He remained more interested in the consultations that were the purpose of their mission. The Bolshevik leaders did not reply immediately to his question about whether representatives of the French Socialist Party could attend the Second Congress. The Dutch delegate Wijnkoop, who arrived in Russia after the initial hearing of the ECCI, raised objections to allowing representatives of such parties to participate. A majority of the ECCI, including Rosmer, favored the proposal to allow them to attend on a consultative basis.[37]

Shortly before the Congress opened, Cachin made his decision: the French Socialist Party should join the Third International, and a recommendation to this effect should be made immediately by radio-telegram, rather than by a personal report when he and Frossard returned to Paris.[38] The process by which he reached this decision and the extent to which the timing was suggested by the Comintern leaders cannot be documented, but there is little doubt that his action was encouraged by the Comintern high command. By winning a convert of Cachin's stature on the eve of the Congress, the Bolsheviks gained a propaganda victory that could affect both the French Socialist Party and the delegates from other parties then arriving in Moscow. In fact, the Bolsheviks got the appearance of two converts, because

Frossard followed Cachin's lead, although somewhat reluctantly. Frossard tried to dissuade his colleague from sending the telegram, but without success. He finally yielded and signed the message himself after Cachin threatened to send the telegram over his own signature alone.[39]

The message reached Paris on July 20 and took the French Socialist Party by surprise;[40] as Renaudel wrote a few days later, it forced French Socialism to come to a decision.[41] Loriot and his associates had done much to prepare the way for the triumph of the Third International, but the conversion of Cachin and Frossard was what eventually threw most of the Centrist wing into the Comintern's camp. It remained only for Cachin and Frossard to return to France and to follow their initial proposal with a series of speeches. They reaped the results at the Congress of Tours in December.

Once the two Frenchmen in Moscow had accepted the faith, at least on paper, the Comintern leaders had further work for them. Cachin zealously accepted the role of the repentant sinner, and again he swept Frossard along with him. Shortly before the Second Congress opened, the two signed a statement addressed to the ECCI: "You are right on your part when you reproach us for not having shown the energy and force that were necessary. . . . We ought to have come to your assistance in due time, and we did not have the courage to accomplish this brotherly duty. . . . Briefly, we ought to follow the same path as the one followed by Russia, where the proletarian revolution has triumphed."[42] Besides publicly acknowledging their error, Cachin and Frossard—or at least the former—helped the Comintern managers in their dealings with members of the USPD. They had thus been transformed from suspected traitors into missionaries in slightly more than a month.

Cachin and Frossard did not reap any immediate benefits at the Second Congress; they still received only the status of consultative delegates. Frossard continued to have misgivings, which caused him to boycott part of the Congress. Their main service had been performed, however, from the Comintern's point of view, and their conduct during the Congress was an anticlimax.

The only important members of the Committee for Adhesion to

the Third International who managed to get to Russia for the Congress were Rosmer and Lefebvre. Most of the other leaders of the group—Loriot, Monatte, Verfeuil, and Souvarine—had been arrested by the government in Paris shortly after violent strikes had broken out on May 1.[43] They remained in jail for several weeks and thus became heroes in the eyes of the Second Congress.

The German and American Delegations

The Comintern leaders had their organizational program for the British, Italian, and French delegates well under way by mid-July, but they still had not had the opportunity to deal with the German situation, which remained uppermost in their minds. They were especially eager to interview the USPD representatives, but this group of German delegates did not reach Petrograd until July 19, the day the Congress opened there. When they did arrive, however, they were taken to Moscow, where the ECCI interviewed them and gave them the same kind of inquisitorial reception that Cachin and Frossard had received a month earlier.[44]

When the USPD decided in June to send representatives to the Second Congress, it made a balanced selection. Two members of the four-man delegation, Artur Crispien and Wilhelm Dittmann, represented the attitude of the moderates and reconstructionists, who at the Leipzig Congress had favored a broad, tolerant International including both the Comintern and the Center Socialists, but not the large Socialist parties (like the SPD and the Labour Party). The other two delegates were Stöcker and Däumig, who had supported the Comintern's cause in an outspoken manner before, during, and after Leipzig. The Bolsheviks had plans to exploit this disagreement in the same way they had exploited the conflicts in the Italian delegation. Since the German Independents arrived so much later than the other important European groups, the Comintern's stratagems coincided with the work of the Second Congress, which is the subject of the next chapter. Only the earliest experiences of the delegation will be considered here.

Cachin and Frossard were among the first to contact the USPD representatives. They told the Germans of their decision to encourage the affiliation of the French Socialist Party, adding that they wanted their party to maintain a large measure of autonomy; they implied that the conditions for affiliation then being proposed by the Bolsheviks were not of critical importance.[45] Frossard, at least, seems to have believed this, since he made the same argument when he returned to France.

After this preliminary exposure, the USPD spokesmen had an audience before the ECCI similar to the ones the British Independents and the two Frenchmen had been given earlier. The meeting came in Moscow on July 21; Lenin was not present, and Radek took the lead in the interrogation. The questioning and criticism followed the pattern that the Comintern's earlier messages to the USPD had established.[46] No new understandings were reached; in fact, several angry exchanges occurred between Crispien and Dittmann on the one hand and their hosts on the other.

There was one interesting development, however; a new organizational configuration became evident to all the German delegates involved in this ECCI meeting. Among those who questioned and heckled the moderate Independents were two leaders of the KPD who had arrived earlier and been given roles in the ECCI's work. Paul Levi and Ernst Meyer, who in Germany were spokesmen for only a small party of 50,000, had undergone a transformation when they reached Russia; like Rosmer, they now spoke as the authoritative voice of the working classes in their country. The fact that their party was only about one-twentieth the size of the USPD counted for nothing; in Russia, Levi and Meyer were the correct revolutionaries, and Crispien and Dittmann, who had claimed to be revolutionaries in Germany, were branded as reformists and opportunists.

Indeed, the KPD representatives, as heirs of Luxemburg and Liebknecht and as leaders of the party that remained the Comintern's main hope in Germany, wielded unusual influence not only by comparison with the USPD representatives, but in general. Levi—like his predecessor Eberlein at the First Congress—gave the Bolsheviks cause to worry on several occasions. For example, two representatives of the KAPD appeared in Moscow while the voting rights and formal status of the various parties were being determined. The Russians initially favored giving the KAPD spokesmen places on the ECCI and decisive votes at the Congress, but Levi objected and threatened to leave if this action were taken. The Russians yielded, and the KAPD representatives received only a consultative voice. A few days later, the Russians sought to amend this agreement by giving decisive votes to the KAPD, the IWW representatives, and the British Shop Stewards. Once again Levi objected successfully.[47] The Shop Stewards and IWW later got their decisive votes, but the KAPD did not because of Levi's threat.

Other delegations reaching Russia in June and July presented fewer difficulties than the groups from Great Britain, Italy, France, and Germany, since their organizational problems were as a rule less complex. An exception must be made for the American delegation. Of the several visitors who arrived from the United States in the weeks preceding the Second Congress, the two most important were John Reed and Louis Fraina. These two men were representatives of rival factions in the American Communist movement and, initially, competitors for the endorsement of the Comintern. An assortment of American anarchists, Left Socialists, and other radicals had gathered in Chicago at the end of September 1919, in response to the urgings of the Comintern to form a Communist Party. Bitter disputes marked this early gathering, and instead of a single party, two organizations emerged. The controversies, though based more on personality differences than on substantive disagreements, could not apparently be settled in America. The one group called itself the Communist Labor Party of America and designated Reed as its international representative; the other assumed the name Communist Party of America and elected Fraina as its international secretary.[48]

Reed had two important advantages in bidding for the Comintern's favor: he reached Russia well ahead of Fraina, and he already had a substantial reputation as a friend of the Bolsheviks. As a witness of the October Revolution and author of *Ten Days That Shook the World,* he did not have to prove himself. Fraina, on the other hand, reached Moscow only in June, and then under double suspicion. In the first place, before he left America he had been accused by fellow party members of being a secret agent for the U.S. Department of Justice. After a tense "trial" within the Communist Party organization, he proved to the satisfaction of most of his colleagues that he was innocent of the charge. When he left the United States en route for Russia at the end of 1919, he believed he had cleared himself completely.[49] When he reached Moscow, he found that the same charges were still pending there, and once more he had to prove his loyalty to the revolutionary movement. The Comintern appointed an investigating committee to rule on Fraina's reliability. The committee members were Rosmer, Rudniansky, and Alexander Bilan, who was an associate of Reed and a member of the Communist Labor Party.

In the second place, Fraina's participation in the Amsterdam Congress of February aroused the Comintern's suspicion. Not only had Fraina been associated with the heresies of the West European Bureau, but he had been one of those who had escaped arrest when police dispersed the conference. Coupled with reports about the "trial," this seemed to cast a doubt over Fraina's reliability. The committee studied the records of the trial, interviewed Reed and other Americans in Russia, and finally decided that Fraina was innocent and could be trusted. His acquittal came in time for him to participate in some of the preliminary work for the Second Congress.[50]

Under the influence of the Bolshevik leaders, Reed and Fraina temporarily resolved some of their differences; they and their associates agreed to work together in the Second Congress as a single delegation.[51] While the Congress was under way, news came from the United States that the Communist Labor Party and the Communist Party had merged in the United Communist Party. Although this union was only temporary and failed to end the factional controversies that had injured the Communist movement in America, it allowed the Congress to believe that progress was being made.

The American Communists at this time held some of the "left-wing" attitudes on the parliamentary question and on trade unions. Neither the Communist Party nor the Communist Labor Party disapproved in principle of traditional political activity, as the French syndicalists and British Shop Stewards did, but they nevertheless had adopted resolutions against electoral activity. More important, both parties rejected the idea of trying to capture the American Federation of Labor for revolutionary purposes. The American Communists felt this organization was too reactionary ever to serve a revolutionary cause, and they adopted a policy of "dual unionism," which meant separate unions for the Communists so that they would be neither hindered nor corrupted by association with non-revolutionary groups.[52] This point of view, of course, had been specifically criticized by Lenin in *"Left-Wing" Communism*. He wanted Communists to join those unions that had mass followings in order to attract their memberships away from conservative and reformist leaders. Reed, Fraina, and a handful of other American delegates arrived in Russia with the conviction that it would be an error to have any dealings with the AFL. They preferred the militant, anti-political unionism of the IWW.

None of the other delegations from abroad were as important as those from Britain, France, Italy, Germany, and the United States. The main objective of the Comintern in the middle months of 1920 was to rebuild the potentially revolutionary parties in these countries according to its own model.

The Russo-Polish War

The Comintern's preparations for the Second Congress coincided with the outbreak of the Russo-Polish War. The dispute over the Russian-Polish border had existed since the end of the World War, and negotiations between the Poles and the Soviet government failed to produce an agreement. Tired of fruitless talks and determined to re-establish the borders of their eighteenth-century kingdom, the Poles attacked Russia late in April and marched rapidly to Kiev. In the first week of May, they captured the city. After a series of defeats, the Bolsheviks rallied and launched a counteroffensive, which was advancing rapidly during the first half of July. Lenin began to see the possibility that the revolution could be carried into the center of Europe by the Red Army. Trotsky did not approve of the effort to make Poland Communistic by force of arms, but Lenin's view prevailed.[53] As the foreign delegates arrived in Russia for the Second Congress, the Red Army was advancing toward Warsaw.

The decision to invade Poland itself, rather than merely to repel

Polish forces from Russia and the Ukraine, was based on the assumption that the Polish peasants and proletariat would welcome Communism. The belief that the people of Europe wanted Communism and were ready to take up arms to achieve it had been a basic element in the Bolsheviks' calculations early in 1919 when the Comintern was formed; by late spring 1920 it had been gradually and silently replaced by the knowledge that careful organization over an extended period of time was necessary before Communism could triumph. The decision to march on Warsaw, based on the belief that the Polish lower classes would assist the invasion, was a temporary return to the earlier assumptions. This helped to set the tone of the Second Congress.

A revealing piece of evidence on this change comes from Lenin's "Theses on the Fundamental Tasks of the Second Congress of the Communist International." In the first draft, dated July 4, he had written: "The duty for the moment of the Communist Parties consists not in accelerating the revolution but in continuing to prepare the proletariat."[54] When the "Theses" emerged from the Second Congress a few weeks later, after the decision to invade Poland had been made and success seemed certain, the passage had been altered to read: "The duty for the moment of the Communist Parties consists in accelerating the revolution, without provoking it artificially until sufficent preparation has been made."[55] The victories of the Red Army in Poland during the second half of July encouraged the Bolsheviks to revive their hope of an early revolution. But though they reverted to this hope for the period of the Second Congress, they did not abandon the preparations for improving the organizational structure and central control of the Comintern.

To what extent was the Bolsheviks' faith in Polish popular support justified? A Communist Workers' Party of Poland had come into existence in the middle of December 1918, composed of the former Left wing of the Polish Socialist Party and an organization called Social Democracy of the Kingdoms of Poland and Lithuania.[56] Like so many other parties formed at this time in response to the Russian example, the Polish organization was small and sectarian. In February 1919 it boycotted elections for the constituent assembly and refused to acknowledge the authority of the newly established government.

Since it declined to abide by the regulations of the government, it went underground when it was less than four months old, and its opportunity to propagandize for revolution was sharply restricted.[57] Nevertheless, the Comintern leaders regarded its existence as a proof of revolutionary potential.

The leading spokesman in Russia for the Polish Communist movement was Julian Marchlewski. The Russians had tried to establish him within the Polish Communist Workers' Party at about the same time they dispatched Kun and Szamuely to Hungary, Radek to Germany, and Beatrice Rutgers to the Netherlands. However, Marchlewski had been arrested in Warsaw and was promptly returned to Russia.[58] His contact with the newly formed party was thus remote, but he acted on its behalf and spoke for it at the Second Congress. He encouraged the belief that the workers and peasants of Poland were eager for a Bolshevik-style revolution and would welcome the Red Army. He spoke at the opening session of the Congress, predicting that the revolutionary cause would advance now that the Red Army was moving to the aid of the Polish workers.[59] Immediately after he had made his remarks, the Congress adopted a resolution that was at once an appeal for peace, a proclamation of the Soviet government's peaceful and defensive aims, and a justification of the continued offensive of the Red Army to crush the "clique of capitalist and Junker adventurers" who ruled Poland.[60]

This militant tone persisted throughout the Congress, which lasted until August 7. When the Congress ended, Russian troops were at the outskirts of Warsaw. A short time later the Bolsheviks' hopes were shattered by the Polish victory at the Battle of the Vistula, but the participants of the Second Congress did not foresee such a turn of events. The Communist Workers' Party failed to produce enough strength to help the Red Army, and the Polish workers and peasants proved, even to the Bolsheviks, that they preferred nationalism to Bolshevism.[61]

The episode of the Russo-Polish War may be regarded as one in a long sequence of Bolshevik efforts to give Europe an immediate revolution. The fact that it came at a time when the Comintern was modifying its dream of rapid victory gave the Second Congress a more complex aspect than it might otherwise have had. The appearance of victory throughout the period of the Congress stimulated the revolutionary zeal of the delegates and concealed the fact that the Comintern, in its preoccupation with institutional forms and regulations, was in retreat.

Chapter ten   The Second Congress

Mid-July 1920 seemed an auspicious time for the Bolsheviks. They had managed to assemble an assortment of foreign delegates who wanted to join or to reach an understanding with the Comintern. The Red Army was advancing into Poland, carrying the hope that a connection could be made with the German Communists, who would facilitate the spreading of the Communist revolution into Central Europe. Important military victories had been won against the White Armies, the Allied intervention was obviously collapsing, and the advocates of a revived Second International were once again having trouble preparing for a unification conference.

The Bolsheviks tried to create an atmosphere of celebration for the Congress, and to keep it up for the three weeks that the meetings lasted. The pageantry at times resembled that of a royal or religious festival. Great public demonstrations were held in Petrograd, where the Congress opened and met for one day on July 19, and in Moscow, where it resumed on July 23. Theatrical performances in honor of the Revolution were staged in both cities; grand military displays were held; and the palaces of the deposed Romanovs were redecorated according to the tastes of the revolutionaries. Delegates were encouraged to visit the Moscow theaters, and were occasionally persuaded to engage in athletic contests with Russians. Against this backdrop of festivity, the Bolsheviks tried to sell their program, as well as their more rigid organizational concept of the Comintern, to those delegates who still had reservations.[1]

More than two hundred delegates attended the Congress.[2] They represented about thirty-five countries, and, unlike the participants in the First Congress, a large percentage of them were legitimate spokesmen for existing groups in the various countries. Nineteen of the pseudo-delegates of the 1919 Congress reappeared at the 1920 Congress and generally followed the predetermined Bolshevik line, but they were greatly outnumbered by the legitimate delegates from abroad. Ten of those who appeared for the second time were members of the Russian delegation: namely, Zinoviev, Lenin, Trotsky, Bukharin, Obolensky-Osinsky, and Balabanoff, as well as Gopner and Skrypnik, who spoke for the Ukraine in the First Congress, Klinger, formerly a spokesman for the German colonies in Russia, and Rakovsky, who in 1919 had posed as the delegate for Rumania and Bulgaria.

Rudniansky still spoke and voted for the Hungarian Communists, Milkich for the Yugoslavs, and Guilbeaux and Sadoul for the French Socialists, even though their connections with the Communist movements concerned were nebulous. The Finnish Communist Party, which was largely a Russian product, was represented by Kuusinen, Manner, and I. Rajha, all of whom had attended the First Congress. Pöögelman, an exile from Estonia of little importance, and Steinhardt of Austria also returned for the Second Congress.

According to the official German-language *Protokoll* of the Congress, 167 delegates had voting rights, and 51 others had a deliberative or consultative status.[3] Of those who could cast decisive votes, 65, or about 40 per cent, were representatives of the Russian Communist Party. Thus not only did the Bolsheviks benefit from the fact that the Congress was held in Russia, and that the Executive Committee and the holdover delegates were predominantly Russian, but they had also given themselves an imposing bloc of votes to ensure their overwhelming influence in the Congress. The second strongest contingent from the standpoint of decisive votes was the Norwegian delegation, which commanded ten votes. Germany, England, America, Finland, and Georgia had six votes each, and France five.* The size and voting strength of the delegations was not based on the size or power of the Communist parties in the various countries, nor were the delegates recognized on the basis of legitimate mandates from

---

* The nomenclature "England" and "America" is the Comintern's.

existing parties. Instead, the crucial test in most cases was the willingness of the individual to accept the predetermined Bolshevik policy.
Thus the Italian Socialist Party had only four votes, even though it
was one of the largest parties in the Comintern. Austria, where the
Communist Party was weak and small, had an equal number of votes.
While the authorized delegates of the French Socialist Party were
accorded only consultative status, five other men—two of whom had
no mandates at all from France—voted in the name of the French
proletariat.[4]

There is no need to belabor the point. Even though the Congress
of 1920 had a more cosmopolitan appearance than its predecessor,
over half the participants having come from abroad, the overriding
reality was the same as in the First Congress. The Russians, with by
far the largest delegation and the virtual right of selecting delegates,
had unquestioned control. To be sure, a few delegates like Serrati,
Wijnkoop, Pankhurst, and Reed disagreed with the Bolsheviks on
some issues and gave the Congress its most interesting moments, but
they never had any chance of success.

Communist speakers and writers described the Second Congress
as a world-wide gathering, and some non-Communist writers accepted this claim. In fact, the 1920 Congress was only slightly better
than its predecessor in gathering representatives from outside Europe
or Russia. The six delegates from "America" were all from the United
States; the only representatives from Latin America were three from
Mexico, two of whom had voting privileges. No delegates from Africa
were listed in the *Protokoll*. There were two delegates each from
India and China, but without votes; and for non-Russian Asia and
the East Indies, there were only ten voting delegates. More than 90
per cent of the delegates were Russian or European. Even though
the Congress made the so-called national and colonial question an
important item on its agenda, most of the its attention remained
focused on Europe.

The July 19 session in Petrograd was simply a formality, consisting
mainly of speeches by Zinoviev and Lenin, and formal greetings from
the Congress to the Red Army and the workers of Petrograd. The
only important business was the selection of a presidium for the Con-

gress; it consisted of Lenin, Zinoviev, Rosmer, Serrati, and Levi.[5] The device of opening the Congress in Petrograd amidst public celebration and then moving it to Moscow indicates that the Bolsheviks wanted to make the maximum impression on both the Russian people and the delegates.

Difficulties developed as soon as the Congress resumed in the Kremlin on July 23. The problem of language plagued the entire proceedings. The First Congress had used German as the official language, and this time the presidium decided that German and French should be used. If necessary, however, a delegate was allowed to speak in his own tongue, and his remarks would be translated into German and French. This worked a special handicap on the English-speaking delegates, most of whom could not speak Russian, French, or German, and the problem became particularly acute when the questions of British Communist unity, parliamentary activity, and trade union affairs were being debated. John Reed attempted to make English an official language at the beginning of the Moscow session, but his proposal was overwhelmingly defeated.[6] He renewed his request on several occasions, and his repeated demands annoyed some members of the presidium. Eventually, on August 2 with the Congress nearing its end, Zinoviev announced that English would be substituted for French as an official language. Six or seven new delegates had arrived, he said, who did not understand French, and the subject then under consideration—parliaments and trade unions—required the use of English.[7]

The official explanation of the change may not be the full story. A British participant in the Congress later wrote another version. The English-speaking delegates had to depend on the "good nature of any linguist who, out of sheer sympathy, was prevailed upon to give them a garbled translation of a particular speech." This situation finally provoked all the British and Americans to stay away from the meeting hall for one whole day in protest. Reed then told the presidium that this constituted a "genuine boycott" and won his point. A number of French-speaking delegates had already left the conference, so the use of their language was no longer considered so urgent.[8]

The language problem was not the only source of irritation to become obvious on the first day of meetings in Moscow. When Zinoviev made the opening speech, he touched on the explosive question of parliamentary activity and the relationship between the Communist parties and the trade unionists.[9] He singled out the anti-political French syndicalists, the American IWW, and the British Shop Stewards for criticism, although he regarded them as "friends and brothers."[10] He restated the usual arguments about the need for joining the non-revolutionary labor movements and for participating in legislative elections as a means of generating revolutionary support; he gave in effect a restatement of Lenin's *"Left-Wing" Communism,* with all its provocations for the "left-wing" elements. As J. T. Murphy wrote in his memoirs, "No sooner had he sat down than the battle royal began."[11]

The British Question

It was the British who reacted most vigorously to Zinoviev's opening speech, and since their delegation was made up of outspoken people with varying shades of opinion, it became the center of some of the most heated debates. A survey of its experiences provides a good commentary on the events and atmosphere of the Congress.

Eleven people from Great Britain attended the Congress, although not all were active participants and some arrived late. MacLaine and Quelch of the BSP extended their stay in Russia to attend. Murphy, Jack Tanner, and David Ramsay, all members of the British Shop Stewards' movement, were strongly opposed to any kind of connection with the Labour Party, and they were annoyed by Zinoviev's initial remarks about their group. Another participant was Dick Beech, a British seaman affiliated with the IWW. Pankhurst and Gallacher, strong anti-parliamentarians, arrived late in the Congress, but in time to engage in its final debates. The other three Britishers were Mrs. Marjory Newbold of the National Young Labour League, Helen Crawfurd of the ILP, and John S. Clarke of the Glasgow section of the SLP.[12] The last two did not act as delegates.

For this speech by Zinoviev, the British delegates had obviously obtained the services of a translator, since they touched off the "battle royal" to which Murphy referred. Ramsay rose to say that the Shop

Stewards' movement had been misunderstood, that it was a legitimate Communist movement even if it chose not to participate in parliamentary politics. MacLaine followed immediately and expressed disappointment because Zinoviev's statement had not specifically provided that a party like the BSP could remain within the Labour Party and still be a Communist organization.[13] After a few inconsequential remarks from Angelo Pestaña, a Spanish syndicalist delegate, Tanner took the floor to attack the positions of both MacLaine and Zinoviev. He concluded with a few telling sentences which challenged the whole program that Lenin and Zinoviev had so laboriously prepared in the preceding weeks:

Only when Zinoviev has been in England and other Western European countries and has studied the conditions and the new outlook of the workers and compared them with the conditions in Russia, only then can he pass proper judgement on politics and their relation to the Revolution.

Let me ask the Russian and other comrades if there is nothing more for them to learn from the struggles, movements, and revolution of other countries. Have they come here not to learn but only to teach? We have to make the Revolution in England; our Russian comrades cannot do that. They can help, but we must do the act and we are learning and preparing for that end. . . .

The Third International must be founded upon such a basis that the different parties could find common ground on the most important principles and methods. Everything else must be left to the various parties themselves.[14]

Such a challenge could not go unanswered. The Hungarian Rákosi defended the official Bolshevik position in a rather feeble reply to Tanner. The Hungarian experience, he said, using the Bolsheviks' favorite illustration, had proved that the Russian example must be followed in the matter of tight party discipline and organization.[15] The next speaker was Wijnkoop, who injected into the debate some of the independence of thought and organizational tolerance that had existed in the Amsterdam Bureau. He said MacLaine's position should not be adopted, and he agreed with Tanner that the Comintern should not become too rigid or dogmatic.[16]

The Comintern leaders now had a small but potentially dangerous rebellion on their hands within the first few hours of the first business session of the Congress. Levi of the KPD and Serrati made a few remarks favoring MacLaine's position, and then the Bolsheviks countered with their most formidable weapons: Lenin and Trotsky took the rostrum to respond to the upsurge that had obviously taken the Comintern officers by surprise.

Lenin began by mentioning points on which there was agreement, a frequent practice with him when dealing with rebels.[17] Then he remarked that although he had previously left open the question of Communist affiliation with the British Labour Party, he had decided after talking to MacLaine and others that such affiliation was essential. At this point, however, he was more concerned about the admonitions that the Comintern must not become too dogmatic.

Comrade Tanner now comes and says not to be too dogmatic. This expression is out of place here. Comrade Ramsay says: Let the English Communists decide on this point for themselves. What kind of an International would it be, if a small part comes and says: Some of us are in favor and some of us are against; let us decide the question ourselves. What need would there be then for an International and a Congress and a discussion?[18]

Lenin went on to propose the creation of a special committee to study the problem raised by the English delegates, and to point out to them that "the correct tactic is affiliation with the Labour Party."[19] Even if the majority of the workers opposed this decision, he said, it was better to follow the correct procedure than to retain a larger following by incorrect methods. His remarks left no room for the possibility that the special committee would come to a different decision.

Trotsky's appearance during the debate was primarily to make theoretical comments and corrections on the statements of Pestaña, Levi, and Serrati.[20] He added little to the debate on the British question. Before the debate closed, a German syndicalist and Ramsay made further statements against parliamentary action. It is difficult to reconstruct from the protocols exactly what the temper of the meeting was, but it seems that the presidium had difficulty closing the debate. It finally brought the arguments to an end by the announcement that it would create the special committee suggested by Lenin. The device of shifting the British question from the plenary session to a special unit effectively contained the young rebellion during most of the Congress. Lenin himself became chairman of the committee, and Zinoviev, Bukharin, Levi, Kabakchiev, MacLaine, and Steinhardt all participated, as well as others known to be sympathetic to Lenin's position. The only men initially appointed to the committee who opposed Communist affiliation with the Labour Party were Ramsay and Wijnkoop.[21]

Official records are not very helpful about what happened within the special committee. It appears that Ramsay came around to the Bolsheviks' point of view, probably within the committee meetings; no more official remarks are attributed to him on this question. Tanner's attention seems to have been diverted to the trade union question. Two British delegates who arrived late—Pankhurst and Gallacher—took part in the committee's work, and their opposition to Lenin's viewpoint was not so easily overcome. They eventually carried the controversy back to the plenum of the Congress, but the presidium managed to delay this until the last day, when debate was rigidly limited.

Before the last day's debate, the British delegates created one other scene on the floor of the Congress, again disrupting the careful plans of the Russians. The act of relegating the British question to a special committee had not eliminated the need for a discussion of parliamentarianism in general; the ECCI still wanted to correct the positions of the "left-wing" Germans, Italians, and Dutch. The Bolsheviks obviously intended to make this task more manageable when they sidetracked the problem of the British Communists and affiliation with the Labour Party; they hoped, presumably, that the British delegation would feel obliged to abstain from the general debate on parliamentarianism. This hope was misplaced.

On August 2, the day on which the debate opened and English became an official language, the newly arrived Gallacher accused the leaders of the Third International of becoming "opportunist" and of advocating a policy of "subservience" to democratic methods.[22] Murphy, who believed in parliamentary action but not within the Labour Party, then charged Gallacher and his allies with inconsistency, since they had occasionally solicited the support of Members of Parliament: "Time and again have the members of the industrial movement, in cluding anti-Parliamentarians, waited upon the Labour members and others in the Parliament to secure their services in the making of protests and the raising of agitation within that institution."[23] Murphy's remarks produced an outburst of anger that is only faintly suggested in the official reports of the Congress. There is no indication in the records that Gallacher responded, but John Clarke later described a scene that was understandably omitted from the official account: "Then Gallacher, who apparently didn't travel through the territory of the Vikings for nothing, became a verbal berserker, with the result that pandemonium reigned for a considerable period both in the Congress and in the smoke-room."[24] Murphy later apologized to Gallacher and withdrew his accusation,[25] but the Bolsheviks obviously had been able to do little about resolving the differences within the delegation.

When the special committee on Britain took a vote a few days later, Lenin and his allies won eleven to four. The dissenters were Gallacher, Pankhurst, Wijnkoop, and Rosmer.[26] Rosmer, a late addition to the committee, reflected the attitude of the French Committee for Adhesion to the Third International.

The minority had a brief opportunity to present its case to the full Congress on the final day of business, August 6. Zinoviev announced that there would be time for only two speakers on each side. Pankhurst and Wijnkoop objected to this curtailment of the debate, but Zinoviev prevailed. Pankhurst made the opening remarks, MacLaine answered her, Gallacher followed, and finally Lenin closed the discussion.[27] The decision that the British Communist Party should be affiliated with the Labour Party carried by a vote of forty-eight to twenty-four;[28] this was not an impressive majority for the Russians in view of all the weapons they had used against the British "Left wing."

Although Pankhurst and Gallacher fought to the end, they accepted defeat in the traditional Anglo-Saxon fashion. They agreed to abide by the decision of the majority. Lenin's personal influence had a lot to do with this. Gallacher later testified that he gradually came to see the "weakness" of his position as "the clear, simple arguments and explanations of Lenin impressed themselves on my mind."[29] Lenin won the temporary allegiance of Pankhurst after the Congress by implying that the decision might be revised in the following year.[30] For the left-wing Communists of Britain, then, the trip to Russia had resulted in a commitment to abandon—or at least to suspend—the ideals they had come to advocate. The tactic of allowing a basically free, if abbreviated, debate had enabled the Bolsheviks to claim the support of their former opponents in the British delegation.

The Role of Serrati

The Italian delegation, though it had only four decisive votes, was one of the most active at the Congress, and its problems were considered important by the Bolsheviks. The Comintern leaders wanted to convert the majority of the Italian delegation to their methods and views, as they had done with the British group, but they apparently had little hope of winning Serrati. Therefore they intensified the efforts they had begun in June to discredit him. One of the most revealing subplots of the Second Congress involves the isolation of Serrati from most of his own delegation, and the efforts to disgrace him before the other delegations.

Serrati, Bombacci, and Graziadei held three of the votes accorded to Italy, and the fourth was held by Luigi Polano, a representative of a youth organization. Five non-voting delegates attended, but only one of them—the anti-parliamentarian Bordiga—joined in the debates.[31] Serrati's position on the presidium did not prevent him from taking part in debates, nor did it shield him from criticism. On the contrary, the records show that on several occasions he incurred the anger of delegates by having to limit a debate or to rule on other procedural matters in his capacity as a presiding officer.

The first personal attack on Serrati came during the discussion on the national and colonial question. When this matter came before the Congress at an early session, two statements of theory prevailed, one supported by Lenin and the other by the Indian delegate, M. N. Roy. Both sought to dedicate the Comintern to freeing the colonies and the exploited nations of Asia and Africa—a subject virtually ignored at the First Congress—but there was a difference in emphasis. Lenin's original draft theses provided that in the backward countries the Communists must support "bourgeois-democratic movements" of liberation as a step toward eventual Communist victory and control.[32] Roy, on the other hand, presented a set of theses in which he contended that the liberation movement could not be confined to the "bourgeois-democratic" elements, but should be extended to the many landless peasants who represented a revolutionary potential. Both men believed that the capitalist stage of historical development, as described by Marx, could be bypassed in the colonial areas of the world, but Lenin believed that it could be avoided only if Europe became Communistic first and aided the transition; he did not believe that temporary cooperation with the bourgeoisie precluded the bypassing. Roy, whose attention was mainly on Asia, held the opposite view: Europe could not be made Communistic unless the colonial nations were made revolutionary first, with special emphasis on the peasantry rather than the bourgeoisie. The two theories were debated by a special commission of the Congress, and both were amended and returned to a plenary session.[33] The meetings of the full Congress were rambling, disorganized affairs, with several non-European delegates giving vent to their frustrations. Many of the speeches had little to do with the subject, and Serrati had the unpleasant task of trying to keep the speakers to the point.[34] He thus accumulated some of the resentment that goes to any conscientious officer presiding over a quarrelsome and spirited assembly.

Despite its chaotic nature, this debate was an important one in the history of the Comintern and Communist revolutionary policy. For the first time, the Bolsheviks were trying to formulate a practical program for adapting their brand of Marxism to Asia. Four years earlier, Lenin had identified imperialism as the highest stage of capitalism, and the Bolsheviks had long been attacking the colonialism of the major European powers and the United States. The discussion at the Second Congress gave the Bolsheviks a chance to match their theories with those of native revolutionaries. In the 1920's, the Bolsheviks slowly turned their hopes toward Asia as their prospects for revolution in Europe diminished; the Second Congress produced the earliest manifestation of this transition.

When the theses of Lenin and Roy emerged from the commission, they had been amended to camouflage the differences between them, each now agreeing to support "revolutionary liberation movements";

but Lenin gave the Congress to understand that he still considered "bourgeois-democratic movements" within this category.[35] Several of the non-European speakers raised objections to Lenin's position, as well as to other parts of the theses, and Zinoviev tried to placate them by urging an immediate vote with the understanding that the matter would be considered further by the commission.[36] Serrati, however, was treated less gently when he entered the debate.

Serrati was disturbed by the vagueness of the revised resolution, and also by Lenin's implication that the Communists should support bourgeois-democratic regimes. In his view, the liberation of the subject nations could be achieved only by means of the proletarian revolution and the Soviet system, and compromises with bourgeois-democratic groups should not be allowed.[37] In taking this line, Serrati was completely consistent with the position the Comintern headquarters had taken after the fall of the Hungarian regime on the question of compromises with the Social Democrats. His views agreed, too, with Zinoviev's recent pronouncement that all revolutions could become Socialist or proletarian revolutions.[38] Nothing he said challenged the Comintern's basic assumptions; he objected only to the ambiguity of the amended theses, and the expression of willingness to assist class enemies. His remarks brought immediate reaction from the floor.

Both Wijnkoop and Roy, who had participated in the work in the commission, made angry personal attacks on Serrati, and Zinoviev spoke for the Russian delegation to intensify the assault. He criticized Serrati for not having made his objections to the commission, and accused him of uncomradely attitudes. Zinoviev then briefly answered Serrati's remarks, claiming that 99 per cent of the Italian workers would agree with the Comintern and oppose Serrati.[39] Here was another attempt to prove that a division existed between Serrati and his party. A few minutes later, as if to give credence to Zinoviev's claim, Bombacci disassociated himself from Serrati's position, and Graziadei gave conditional approval to the amended theses.[40] The personal accusations against Serrati continued, notwithstanding his attempts to clarify his position. The Lenin-Roy theses were ratified without any negative votes and only three abstentions, one of which was Serrati's.

Another opportunity for the Bolsheviks to dramatize the alleged exclusiveness of Serrati came during the debate on parliamentarianism. Bordiga became the leading spokesman for the left-wing Communists on this issue, and although the Comintern leaders officially disapproved of his stand, they used it as a weapon against Serrati. They could attribute Bordiga's "error" to Serrati's refusal to expel the reformist Right wing of the Italian Socialist Party, and therefore each speech by Bordiga helped prove Zinoviev's and Lenin's point about the fallacy of maintaining unity within the Italian party.

The question of parliamentarianism was initially discussed in a commission, and on August 2 it went before the full Congress. Bukharin presented the commission's recommendations, and in all major respects they followed the pattern established by Lenin's *"Left-Wing" Communism*. Bordiga then presented a set of theses of his own, reflecting the anti-parliamentarian point of view. In both of these presentations, Serrati fared badly. Bukharin contended that within the Italian Socialist Party—and thus within the Third International in Italy—about 30 per cent of those serving in parliament were "reformists." He also identified Serrati as the leader of a centrist faction within the party.[41] Although the Italian party was described as "one of our best parties," its leading member was especially blamed for the elements within it that the Bolsheviks disliked.

When Serrati again tried to clarify his position and to correct some of the inferences Bukharin had made, he was heckled and contradicted by Bordiga. Once again, before the entire Congress, Serrati had to defend himself from one of his Italian colleagues. Although he was on the same side as the Bolsheviks in this dispute, he had been given the uncomplimentary epithet "centrist" by Bukharin, and Bordiga's tirade also tried to put him into this category.

Serrati obviously felt a great deal of frustration as these maneuvers against him continued. At one point, Zinoviev took him to task for having used the familiar pronoun "thou" in addressing a class enemy.[42] Lenin interrupted and chided him during one of his speeches.[43] Angelica Balabanoff, who served as translator, later wrote: "I had the feeling that I was participating not merely in a political, but in a personal, tragedy involving some of my dearest friends." Among her friends, Serrati was one of the closest, and one who was most discouraged by what he experienced in Moscow.[44]

The Twenty-One Conditions

The Comintern's humiliation of Serrati can best be studied in conjunction with its formulation of conditions for membership. In drafting these conditions, the single most important piece of business of the Second Congress, the Comintern leaders showed special consideration for the French Socialist Cachin at the same time they were sabotaging the prestige of Serrati. The former "class traitor" from France was changing places with the former hero of international Communism from Italy.

At the beginning of the Congress, the ECCI published a list of nineteen conditions to serve as a basis for discussion.* In a sense, they can be regarded as the products of the Comintern's experience during its first fifteen months of operation. They became the basic organizational guide for the Comintern for the remaining twenty-three years of its existence. They may be summarized as follows.

Point 1 demanded that all organs of the Communist press must be edited by reliable Communists, must consistently spread the idea of the dictatorship of the proletariat, and must denounce the bourgeoisie and the reformists. The author of the Conditions, probably Lenin, was undoubtedly hoping to bring both *L'Humanité* and *Avanti!* under Communist party discipline. Point 2 required the removal from party offices of all "reformists and partisans of the Center," including editors, trade union leaders, parliamentarian delegates, or others with responsible positions. Point 3 called for programs of both illegal and legal party work in all countries, and for "illegal apparatus" to advance the revolution.

Points 4 and 5 dealt with the need for systematic propaganda in both the army and the rural districts of each country. It was specified that the Communists must form illegal cells within the armies. With an eye toward Bulgaria, Point 5 said that to refuse to work in the countryside was to desist from revolutionary action. Point 6 repeated the need for denouncing all forms of "social patriotism" and "social pacifism," and for demonstrating to the workers that the League of Nations could never keep the peace. Point 7 expanded this require-

---

* These were later to become the Twenty-One Conditions. The two additional clauses are discussed on pp. 210–11 below.

ment; it demanded a "complete and absolute rupture with reformism and the policy of the centrists" throughout all circles of the Communist movement. The only reformists specifically named in this original draft were the Italians Turati and Modigliani. The Bolsheviks may have refrained from mentioning the French and German centrists at this point because they were hoping to win some of them over to their cause. Later, the names of other centrists were added.

Point 8 required all parties to oppose colonialism and imperialism, particularly as they appeared in the policies of the governments of their own countries. The question of Communist participation in non-Communist trade unions was covered in Point 9: Communist groups must be formed within the old unions to agitate, and to attract the membership of the masses. A related condition followed in Point 10: all Communists were to oppose the so-called "Amsterdam International" of trade unions, and to support the creation of an "international union of Red trade unions." From this suggestion was to come the Red International of Trade Unions, or the Profintern.

Points 11–14 sought to tighten the control of party leaders over all phases of each party's operation. The central committee of each party must review parliamentary representatives and remove unreliable ones; it must also assert complete control over the editorial policies of Communist newspapers. The party must apply the principle of "democratic *centralism*" (emphasis in the original) and it must be ruled by "an iron discipline, almost a military discipline." "Democratic centralism" was Moscow's term for complete control from the top. Point 14 called for periodical purges to keep the party free from "the petty bourgeois elements that inevitably creep into it."

Under Point 15, each party was obliged to give all possible aid to Soviet Republics in their struggle against the counterrevolutionaries. Point 16 specified that the Communist parties must draw up new programs "in the spirit of the decisions of the Communist International," and must submit these programs for ratification to a future Congress or the ECCI. Point 17 dealt with one of the Comintern's most delicate problems: the extent to which member parties would be allowed to direct their own affairs. All resolutions of the Congresses and of the ECCI were declared to be binding for all parties, but the Comintern and the ECCI were obliged to consider the variety of conditions under which the various parties had to operate.

Point 18 required all parties to adopt the name "Communist," and, as if remembering Hungary, it emphasized that this was not merely a formal requirement but a matter of high political importance. Point 19 called upon member parties to summon special congresses immediately to approve the work of the Second Congress.[45]

These conditions appear to have been hastily gathered together; the organization is random, and some of the material repetitive. Apparently Lenin decided shortly before the Congress opened to put all the conditions together in one brief statement. The result was a distillation of all the most important points the Bolsheviks wanted to get approved at the Congress. It is notable that none of the points urged an immediate uprising, or even contemplated one. So far had the Comintern departed from its mission of March 1919 that not one point specifically told the member parties to call the workers to arms. The nineteen conditions were basically a tract on how to organize and whom to denounce.

The Conditions became a subject of controversy among delegates long before they became an official matter of business. They were discussed at length in a special commission early in the Congress. They especially annoyed Frossard, who apparently had been led to believe that his party might be able to affiliate without expelling any of its members, and he became involved in a quarrel with the Bolsheviks over whether Jean Longuet would have to be expelled. The Bolsheviks, who had long regarded Longuet as a traitor, insisted on his expulsion, and as a result Frossard boycotted the Congress. In this move he was temporarily joined by Cachin.

According to Frossard's account of the incident, their absence caused a stir at the Congress, and the Comintern leaders sent messengers inviting them to return. Cachin complied, but Frossard remained adamant, and for a while even declined an interview with Zinoviev. Zinoviev's messengers assured him that an understanding could be reached if he would confer, or would present his position to the Congress. Frossard finally agreed to meet with Comintern leaders, and he found Zinoviev in a conciliatory mood. Zinoviev said he did not actually

want to exclude anyone. He liked Longuet as a man; it was his principles to which the Comintern objected.[46] This did not placate Frossard, and he prepared to return to France immediately. The Comintern leaders apparently did not want him to leave without Cachin,
and they wanted to formalize the Conditions before their departure.
On the evening of July 28, Zinoviev announced that the discussion on
the Conditions would be moved ahead on the agenda in order that a
decision could be made before the French Socialists left.[47]

On the following morning, Zinoviev opened the discussion of the
Conditions with a long speech on the need for better organizational
control of the various Communist parties. Once more he repeated the
old warnings about the dangers of reformism and the familiar criticisms of the Center parties. On this occasion, however, he made some
mildly complimentary remarks about Cachin. There could be no
question of Cachin's personal uprightness, Zinoviev said; he had been
an honest fighter even if he had made some errors in the past.[48] Zinoviev elaborated on some of Cachin's "errors," but treated them gently,
and his testimonial to Cachin's integrity was the most important statement in his remarks on the French party. Cachin had been a target of
Comintern criticism and of Zinoviev's own vitriolic pen during the
previous year; not only his integrity but his revolutionary qualities
had been challenged. His conduct in Russia in the last few weeks had
changed the Bolsheviks' attitude toward him.

Shortly after Zinoviev spoke, Cachin was called to the rostrum, and
he announced he was speaking for himself and Frossard, but not for
the whole French party. He endorsed many of the conditions for affiliation, and promised that both he and Frossard would fight for their
adoption by the French Socialist Party. He avoided the question of
Longuet's expulsion by saying that had Longuet been there, he probably would have shared the views that Cachin and Frossard had
adopted.[49] He tried to identify himself as one of the Comintern's trustworthy agents, presumably to dispel any doubts aroused by Frossard's
boycott.

When the Comintern leaders embraced Cachin, they aroused the
antagonism of some of the Frenchmen who had previously been their
most faithful followers. Lefebvre, representing the Committee for Ad-

hesion to the Third International, expressed doubts about the reliability of the new converts. There was reason to fear, he said, that Cachin and Frossard might not truly act in the interests of the Comintern because of their "long opportunistic past" and their "former habits of thought." He worried lest their endorsement of the Third International should lead to a gradual dilution of the original principles of the organization. He disliked the idea of entrusting the Comintern's cause to men who "during the last six years have compromised the word 'Socialism' and made necessary the proclamation of Communism."[50]

Even Guilbeaux, a holdover from the First Congress and a prominent member of the French Communist contingent in Moscow, was surprised by the Comintern's change of heart. He saw the new developments as proof that a Right wing was developing within the Third International. He reminded the delegates that the First Congress had identified the centrism of such men as Frossard and Cachin as one of the greatest threats to the revolutionary movement. He observed that the French Socialists, whom the Comintern now seemed to be accommodating, had been guilty of some of the "meanest treacheries" during the war, while the Right wing of the Italian Socialist Party, which the Comintern's leaders now wanted to exclude, had conducted itself in a proper manner during the same period. He elaborated on the contradiction by noting that the lesson of Hungary proved the dangers of alliance with the Social Democrats.[51] His entire argument followed the main lines of the Comintern's propaganda of the previous year.

Lefebvre and Guilbeaux were only two in a long string of delegates who took the rostrum to express alarm about the Comintern's new direction. Bordiga felt that Cachin's remarks constituted an unsatisfactory acceptance of the Conditions, and he wanted explicit assurances that Renaudel and his allies would be driven from the party. A young French delegate named Goldenberg pointed out the inconsistency of the Comintern's new line.[52] Serrati spoke again, skillfully elaborating the point already made by Guilbeaux that the Right wing of the Italian party had been more faithful to revolutionary principles and more consistent in revolutionary conduct than the French party.[53]

Serrati eventually voted for the Conditions, having expressed the hope that they would be applied with care to those countries where special conditions existed. His vote, however, was less notable than his argument. He explained that he would agree to the expulsion of the Right wing of his party eventually, but only when the right-wing members had given proof of their anti-revolutionary intentions. For the present, he said, a split was not justified.

Lenin then took the Italian leader to task for his attitude, comparing him with the centrists in the USPD and with the Mensheviks.[54] The branding of Serrati was now complete; he had been identified with the evils of the Center and Right. Shortly before, Cachin—who actually did belong to the Center and who had collaborated with the Right during and since the war—had been welcomed and praised, even though he refrained from promising an expulsion of the Right in his own party. There was no more striking inconsistency in the Comintern's first year and a half than its attitude toward these two men. Serrati and Cachin symbolize what happened to the Third International between March 1919 and August 1920. By the second summer, the Comintern leaders had become interested more in a man's willingness to follow their lead and to do their organizational chores than in his revolutionary record or his doctrinal consistency.

Cachin and Frossard seem to have left Moscow before the Conditions debate had been completed. The discussion was held on July 29 and 30, and the two Frenchmen apparently left on July 29. They did not know of the ultimate disposition of the Conditions at the time of their departure, although it was certainly obvious they would be approved in substance. A few hours after their departure, the Nineteen Conditions became the Twenty-One Conditions by the addition of two provisions that would certainly have bothered the Frenchmen if they had been present.

The new Point 20 had been under consideration before the French Socialists left. It proposed that all member parties of the Third International must reorganize so that two-thirds of each party's central committee would be composed of persons who had unconditionally endorsed the Third International prior to the Second Congress. Lenin had proposed this measure early in the Congress, but there had been much opposition to it, including that of Frossard. When Zinoviev opened the discussion on July 29, he indicated that a decision had been made not to impose this requirement but "to express it only as a wish and not as a condition or instruction."[55] On the following day, when the Frenchmen had gone, it was adopted as a condition.

Point 21 provided that all who voted against accepting the Conditions at future congresses of the Communist parties in the various countries should be expelled from the party.[56] This provision was one of the shortest and most rigid of all the requirements. Proposed by Bordiga and supported by Humbert-Droz, it was later described by Zinoviev as being of non-Russian origin.[57] If the Russian delegation had not approved it, however, it never would have been added. If the first twenty conditions had been allowed to stand without the twenty-first, some small area of doubt might have been possible on the question of expulsions; Frossard, and possibly Cachin, carried away some hope that expulsions could be avoided even after affiliation. When they returned to France to defend their endorsement of the Comintern, they found that their action meant a certain end to the party unity they had both tried for so long to preserve.

The German Impasse

The Comintern had placated left-wing Communists like Bordiga by demanding the expulsion of all who opposed the conditions for membership, and it had given some satisfaction to the Center Socialists from France by hinting that it was less interested in expelling members than in eradicating treasonous and incorrect ideas. It had to perform a similar balancing operation among the Germans.

The three-way feud between the USPD, the KPD, and the KAPD had not abated when the representatives of these parties reached the Kremlin. As we have seen, the KPD delegates were able to keep the KAPD members from obtaining voting rights at the Congress, and Levi had been cool toward the Independents. The ECCI wanted to capture the Left wing of the powerful USPD without losing either of the two small parties, but this proved to be impossible. The KAPD delegates, Rühle and Merges, remained in Moscow only briefly. After reading the ECCI's preliminary theses and observing the accommodations made for other, less radical parties, they declared the Comintern too opportunistic and departed.[58] The Comintern, however, in an effort to keep some kind of tie with the revolutionary elements in the KAPD, recognized it as a sympathizing member party. This is another instance of the Bolsheviks' duplicity. If the twenty-first condition had been applied objectively, the leaders and most of the members of the KAPD should have been denied the right of affiliation; they openly objected to the conditions requiring parliamentary activity and complete subservience to the policies of the Congresses. But the Bolsheviks decided to wink at this rebellion.

Meyer, Levi, Crispien, Dittmann, and Stöcker all made long speeches in plenary sessions of the Congress on the conditions of affiliation, and they engaged in extended quarrels about recent revolutionary events in Germany. Levi's desire to reach an understanding with the leftists in the USPD motivated much of his conduct and served the ends of the Bolsheviks, whose main objective was to split the party. Levi's colleague, Meyer, took a different position. He felt that the leftist faction, represented by Stöcker and Däumig, could not be trusted because it too often made concessions to the Right wing. He did not want any portion of the USPD admitted to the Comintern in its existing form.[59] Stöcker wanted to affiliate the Independents with the Third International, but did not want to create a split in the party. According to him, the Spartacists had committed a "disastrous blunder" when they broke away from the USPD to form the KPD, and a further split could repeat that blunder.[60]

Since the Germans had reached an impasse, the Comintern leaders had the deciding voice. The quarrels among the Germans were a justification for establishing Lenin's "democratic centralism." The Bolsheviks had already decided that a split of the USPD was essential, and they used the presence of Crispien and Dittmann to prove their point.

Early in the discussion of the Conditions, Crispien and Dittmann became the targets of bitter criticism. The Hungarian Rákosi compared them to the Social Democrats who betrayed the Hungarian Soviet Republic. Meyer went so far as to say that they preferred bourgeois dictatorship to proletarian dictatorship.[61] They were accused of collaborating with Social Democrats in the 1918 Ebert government, of violating revolutionary solidarity when they declined an offer of Russian grain in 1918, and of a number of other actions that had annoyed the Bolsheviks a year or so earlier. Once the charges had been made, Crispien and Dittmann were given an opportunity to speak. The Bolsheviks believed that the proceedings would be read by millions of workers, and they were obviously confident of their ability to humiliate the two Germans.

Both Crispien and Dittmann made well-organized, intelligent statements. They were basically defensive in tone, and they pleaded the revolutionary integrity of the USPD. Like Serrati, they were subjected to heckling. The schedule was so arranged that the two men spoke at a late evening session, about midnight or later, and Dittmann's speech followed Crispien's immediately.[62] This meant that they had no chance to rebut the criticism that was later heaped upon them. And certainly midnight was a poor time to put their case. It is impossible to prove that the Russian delegation conspired to arrange the Independents' speeches in the most awkward manner; one can only speculate. It is clear, at any rate, that Crispien and Dittmann had small opportunity to convince the Congress of either their sincerity or their correctness.

Among those who spoke on the following day against Crispien and Dittmann was Lenin. He labeled Crispien's attitude as "Kautskian," thus putting him in the class of the worst "social traitor." He systematically answered all the key points, and made the most of his talent for ridicule. He acknowledged none of the revolutionary qualities that the two Germans, with accuracy, had claimed, and he linked his censure of them with his sharpest criticisms of Serrati, implying they were birds of a feather.[63]

The Bolsheviks' purpose in inviting the USPD delegates to Moscow for the Second Congress had been fulfilled. They had heckled and insulted two of them, and they had dealt more gently with the other two, Däumig and Stöcker, although both had shared many of the so-called crimes for which Crispien and Dittmann were indicted. The political opinions of the delegates had again proved less important than their willingness to serve unconditionally the organizational requirements of the Comintern.

The Americans and the Trade Union Question

An example of the Bolsheviks' readiness to adjust their principles to establish their authority can be seen in the handling of the trade union question. According to Bolshevik theory, as expressed in Lenin's *"Left-Wing" Communism* and other pre-Congress documents, Communists were to be required to join the existing unions and to transform their memberships and their bureaucracies into revolutionary units. The trade union question was handled in a special commission, as were the other important questions, and there the Leninist position was challenged by John Reed. He and his colleagues in the Communist Labor Party were convinced that no revolutionary purpose could be achieved by trying to convert the AFL. Reed preferred to have no association with the Federation, but he finally conceded that Communists could operate within it for the sake of destroying it so that industrial unions could be built in its place. His position was different from that of the British Shop Stewards, who wanted to remain outside the reformist unions, but in the debate, Reed and Gallacher were allied in their oppostion to the majority statement. They felt there was no more point in trying to change the nature of the old unions than in trying to change the nature of the capitalist state.[64]

Radek and Zinoviev shared the responsibility of presenting the majority case. Zinoviev accused the dissenters of wanting to run away from the trade unions and thus to abandon the workers to the reformist leaders. He chided the British and American delegates for suggesting that they could destroy capitalism but not the trade union bureaucracy.[65] Ironically, even as Radek and Zinoviev insisted on their position as a matter of principle and discipline, the Bolsheviks were establishing a separate Red International of Trade Unions to compete with the older International Federation of Trade Unions (IFTU).

Simultaneously with the Second Congress, the Bolsheviks assembled the first meeting of the Red International of Trade Unions, the Profintern. Although this had no formal connection with the Comintern, some of the Comintern delegates participated in the founding congress, and one of the Comintern statutes mentioned the creation of trade union sections of the Third International.[66] No direct steps were taken at the Second Congress to recognize the Profintern, but after the Congress ended, the Comintern in effect had a new appendage not of its own creation.

For some time now, the Bolshevik leaders had been eager to create the Profintern to oppose the IFTU, which was established in Amsterdam in July 1919. They regarded the IFTU—sometimes called the Amsterdam International—as a greater threat than the Second International, since the Western trade unionists were having more success in organizing than the Western Socialists. The decision to form the Profintern seems to have been taken on impulse, and little regard was given to the possible effect on the Comintern program.[67]

In effect, the Bolsheviks adopted a program of running away from the IFTU at the same time that they were reprimanding the British and American delegates for running away from its branches. Zinoviev and his colleagues ridiculed Reed and Gallacher for wanting to keep Communists outside the reformist trade unions, but demanded that Communist trade union members avoid the Amsterdam International. It is doubtful whether the Russian leaders saw the extent of their ambivalence in the summer of 1920. In the confusing last days of the Second Congress, they seem to have been so preoccupied with the mechanics of getting their program approved that they lost some of their perspective.

A subplot of the trade union story involved Louis Fraina. Near the end of the Congress, just as the trade union question was about to come up, a delegate arrived from America and reported that the Communist Labor Party and the Communist Party had merged into a United Communist Party. However, a small group of the Communist Party, with which Fraina was associated, had rejected the merger, according to the report. It was suggested that Fraina's voting right be rescinded. Radek, as head of the credentials committee, recommended that Fraina should not be denied his voting right on the basis of such inconclusive evidence. Fraina defended himself before the Congress, and Reed sought to initiate a debate on the whole question of the relationship betwen the two parties. Radek's motion carried, and Reed's attempt to initiate a debate was quashed.[68] Shortly afterward, Fraina partially supported the Bolsheviks' position on trade unions, noting that his party had always wanted to work in the trade unions whereas the other American Communist faction had opposed such cooperation.[69]

The Results of the Congress

The Second Congress came to an end on August 7 with the usual flurry of optimistic speeches and predictions of swift victory. The leaders of the Comintern had won approval for all the important measures they had advocated, and—perhaps more important—they had selected those persons on whom they could rely, and had identified the "errors" of those whom they intended to eliminate.

The separation of the desirables from the undesirables was one of the chief tasks the Bolsheviks had assigned themselves; the business of choosing and indoctrinating future subordinates of the Comintern occupied much of their time between July 19 and August 7. But the process of selection did not always tally with the principles that the Congress itself was adopting. The Comintern leaders overlooked or minimized the fact that Cachin, Stöcker, the KAPD delegates, and Reed had all registered objections to some aspects of their program, but they would not overlook the deviations of such persons as Serrati and Crispien.

The selection of future Comintern agents and the elimination of those who could not be controlled was an unofficial part of the Congress's work. Structural changes in the Comintern and formal pronouncements were the official functions of the delegates. The Congress established the size of the ECCI more precisely, providing that there should be five members from the country in which the Committee was based, and one member from ten to thirteen other major Communist parties.[70] In other words, there should be five Bolsheviks, and only one person from each other country or party deemed worthy of a seat. The ECCI was empowered to manage Comintern affairs in the intervals between Congresses. Thus, the Russian control of the organization was more firmly established. In later years, the centralization increased, and Russian leadership became more and more evident, until the Comintern and all its members had become merely instruments of the foreign policy of the Soviet government. This process had begun in 1919 and 1920, but at that time it was still ill-defined. At the First Congress and in the months following it, the Comintern cast its nets widely and attracted many species of Socialists and idealists. At the Second Congress, it began the process of disciplining, converting, or eliminating them. The Second Congress marked the end of the Comintern's most idealistic and optimistic era.

Chapter eleven Conclusion

The adjustment that occurred in the policies and procedures of the Comintern was not unprecedented in Bolshevik history. Robert Daniels has convincingly demonstrated that in the fall of 1917 Lenin "put aside his usual obsession with organizational rigor and conspiratorial discipline, and he penned bold visions of the party's success and the new order which it would bring to Russia and the whole civilized world."[1] Revolutionary zeal and optimism typified Lenin's thinking just before the October *coup,* and, as Daniels sees it, this was a departure from his usual caution and concern for organizational firmness. In his essay *State and Revolution,* written in the late summer of 1917, Lenin identified himself ideologically with the "Left Communists" and with a kind of "utopian anarchism." His adherence to "Left Communism," however, was brief; after the October Revolution, when consolidation became the most urgent need, he shifted his position and became identified with the Right Bolsheviks. When the peace negotiations with Germany went badly, he demanded capitulation to save the Bolshevik regime, and this involved suspension of the international revolutionary war that the Left Communists advocated.[2]

The Communist International went through the same kind of transition in its first fifteen months of activity. The position of the Comintern leaders during most of 1919 was that of "Left Communism," with its emphasis on immediate and violent action, its courting of anarchists and other Left extremists, and its de-emphasis of parliamentary activity. By early 1920, the Comintern leadership had moved toward the Bolshevik Right—to a position roughly corresponding with Lenin's attitude at the time of the Brest-Litovsk peace. The Polish war in the middle of 1920, and the revolutionary fervor that it momentarily produced, camouflaged this adjustment at the time of the Second Congress, but the adjustment was under way nonetheless.

The leaders of the Comintern, who claimed special powers of prediction for themselves, had proved to be very bad prophets in the year and a half that followed the 1918 armistice. They had forecast the immediate violent transition of industrialized society under the banner of the international proletariat. After eighteen months of disappointments, they were still predicting and proclaiming success, but with different emphasis. Now they measured their victories according to the degree of institutional growth rather than in terms of revolutionary action by the working class.

The greatest disappointment to the Comintern leaders in the period between the First and Second Congresses occurred in Hungary. Because they had endorsed the Hungarian Soviet Republic almost without qualification, they were especially disturbed when it collapsed. There was evidence that the workers in Hungary had failed to support the Communist cause, and that the Soviet regime had been created prematurely; but the Comintern headquarters could not accept such evidence. It was an article of the Bolshevik faith that the proletariat would support Communism, and that the situation throughout Europe was revolutionary; therefore, the Bolsheviks sought the cause of the Hungarian failure elsewhere. They attributed the defeat to the treason of the Social Democrats who had shared power with the Communists in Budapest. From this, the Bolsheviks deduced that in the future the Communist movement must apply a rigid organizational formula. They also decided to avoid contacts with the Social Democrats, but they found reason to amend this decision in certain cases.

The defeat in Hungary was softened by organizational achievements in other European countries. The successful creation of Communist or Left Socialist parties in the Netherlands, Austria, France, Sweden, Poland, Greece, and Yugoslavia helped to sustain the Comintern's belief in a world-wide revolutionary movement. The endorsement of the Third International by most of the Socialists of Norway, Bulgaria, and Italy seemed especially encouraging. No Communist-type revolution occurred in any of these countries, but as long as a party existed in a state, the Bolsheviks could entertain dreams of revolution and claim progress.

The three key countries in the International's planning were Germany, Britain, and France. In all three, the Comintern and its agents became preoccupied with organization and operational tactics when the anticipated uprisings did not materialize. They placed most of their early hopes on Germany and the KPD. Contrary to expectations, the German Communists adopted a virtually non-revolutionary policy early in 1919 and alienated many potential Communists. The Comintern's sympathizers were divided among the USPD, the KPD, and the KAPD, and the Bolsheviks decided that they must exercise a measure of parental control to unify the movement. Here, as in Hungary, they tended to attribute the lack of a revolution to organizational weakness. A similar situation existed in Britain, where four small parties warmly endorsed the International and the principles of violent revolution. These parties could not agree upon a basis for unification, and as a result no single Communist movement existed in Britain prior to 1921. Once more, Moscow could point to organizational weakness. In France, the controversy among the Comintern's admirers was less damaging than in Germany or Britain, but the work of the Committee for Adhesion to the Third International seemed to be progressing too slowly.

The episodes involving the West European Bureau also increased the Russians' desire for firmer control of the so-called revolutionary parties. At the First Congress, the Comintern had accused both the Center and the Right Socialists of betraying the working class, and it had appealed specifically to the Socialists of the extreme Left. The West European Bureau, functioning a year after the First Congress, retained much of the original spirit and orientation of the parent organization. By 1920, however, the attitude of Comintern headquarters had changed. The Bolsheviks had decided that they must relax their harsh attitude toward the Center Socialists in order to convert some of them to Bolshevism, even though this practice at times ran counter to their propaganda about the Hungarian error. They abolished the West European Bureau because it was too "leftist," thus tacitly rejecting the original "left-wing" orientation of the Comintern.

This process of shifting toward the Center and modifying original objectives reached a climax in the late spring and summer of 1920, when the Bolsheviks brought representatives of the major Center Socialist parties to Moscow. At the Second Congress and in the weeks preceding it, the ECCI concentrated on wooing the Center Socialists. It began to select its allies and agents on the basis not of their revolutionary conduct, as it had done in 1919, but of their willingness to repeat certain theoretical arguments and to perform certain organizational tasks for the Third International.

Other manifestations of the Comintern's new direction came soon after the Second Congress. The failure of the revolution in the West, tacitly recognized by now, helped to turn the Bolsheviks' attention to the East. The Baku Congress in September represented the first substantial effort to sell Bolshevism to the peoples of the Middle East and Asia. Hundreds of so-called delegates from thirty-two Middle Eastern and Asian regions met to discuss the revolution against imperialism. A delegation that included Zinoviev, Kun, Radek, Rosmer, Reed, and Quelch acted on behalf of the Comintern.

Soon afterward, Zinoviev made his famous visit to Halle in order to hasten the split in the USPD, and before the end of the year he and his allies had interfered from a distance in the Congress of Tours of the French Socialist Party. In each case, Zinoviev was more interested in creating schism than in agitating for street action.

During the remainder of 1920 and into 1921, the cause of the world revolution continued to sustain defeats. The failure of War Communism in Russia, and the clumsy, humiliating effort at revolution in Germany in March 1921, served to drive the Comintern and Bolshevism generally into a policy of retrenchment. By the time of the Third Congress in June–July 1921, the Bolsheviks were openly acknowledging that it might take several years to achieve the revolution, and they continued the process of subordinating the non-Russian parties to their program. This was a logical and natural extension of their work in the Second Congress. As time passed, non-Russian members of the Comintern became more and more reconciled to the delay of the revolution and to the fact of Russian domination. This process was accelerated because the Bolsheviks rewarded those who were most responsive to their wishes, and also because many of the "left-wing" Communists—people like Sylvia Pankhurst, members of the KAPD, members of the IWW, and many of the Dutch Communists—left the movement either voluntarily or by expulsion. They would not fall in with the Comintern's new requirements.

In brief, the direction the Comintern took in the 1920's had been foreshadowed in the months leading up to the Second Congress. The Comintern was no longer regarded by its founders as a great league of working men, moving with predetermined certainty into the era of proletarian revolution. It was becoming a rigid, disciplinarian institution, led by a few Russians who planned to create revolutionary situations by manipulating small, well-controlled groups.

Notes

Notes

In general, complete authors' names, titles, and publication data are given in the Bibliography, pp. 251–64. The relevant information for newspaper articles, which are not included in the Bibliography, is given in the Notes.

Chapter One

1. The invitation appeared in *Pravda* (Moscow), Jan. 24, 1919, 1: 6–7, 2: 1–2.

2. The most satisfactory treatment of Comintern affairs up to 1926 is Carr, *A History of Soviet Russia*. Another important work is Degras, *The Communist International*; the two volumes published to date cover the years 1919–28. This is a collection of documents, but it also contains many editorial notes giving the background to the documents; the notes, however, are too brief and general to constitute a history of the Third International. For an excellent summary of Soviet Russian writing on the Comintern, see Degras's article "Revisiting the Comintern," which includes an examination of recent Russian scholarship on the subject. The best work dealing with the entire period of the Comintern's operation (and also carrying the story into the post-war years and the Cominform era) is Nollau, *Die Internationale,* recently translated into English as *International Communism and World Revolution*. Nollau gives special attention to the organizational structure of the Third International. Before these works appeared, the only histories of the Comintern available in English were Borkenau, *The Communist International,* and James, *World Revolution,* both of which were published before the organization was abolished and have been outdated for several years. Borkenau's study is still useful for its evaluations of Comintern leaders and the incidents with which the author was personally familiar; the book by James is basically a vehicle for the author's Trotskyite bias rather than a historical examination of the evidence.

3. Helpful works on this period are Gankin and Fisher; Gankin; and Trofimov (the most valuable of recent Soviet writing on the subject).

4. Gankin and Fisher, pp. 338–42.

5. *Ibid.,* pp. 450–51.

6. For Zinoviev's preoccupation with the idea of a Third International, see his *Sochineniia,* Vols. VII and VIII.

7. Keynes, p. 4.

8. Lenin, *Sochineniia,* XXIII, 241.

9. *Ibid.,* p. 264.

10. Trofimov, pp. 39–40.

11. Zinoviev, *Sochineniia*, VIII, 217.

12. Com. Int., *Sowjet-Russland*, p. 11.

13. As quoted in Cumming and Pettit, p. 268.

14. *Ibid.*, pp. 271-72.   16. Ransome, p. 224.

15. *Ibid.*, p. 274.   17. Cumming and Pettit, pp. 297-98.

18. *Pravda*, Jan. 25, 1919, 1: 1. According to Louis Fischer, I, 167, the Soviet radio received a news broadcast about the proposal on January 23, and it is conceivable that it did not come to the attention of the Bolshevik leaders before the Chicherin invitation was broadcasted. Although it has been commonly accepted that the invitation was issued on January 24, *L'Humanité* (Paris), Mar. 17, 1919, 1: 3, reported it had received a garbled radio-telegram version of the message dated January 23.

19. Cumming and Pettit, pp. 298-99.

20. For a discussion of the differences between Luxemburg and Lenin, see Ruth Fischer, pp. 16-27, 47-51.

21. Eberlein, pp. 676-77.

22. *Pravda*, Jan. 24, 1919, 1: 1-2. Lenin, *Sochineniia*, XXIII, 494-95. According to Carr, *History*, III, 108, this letter was written on January 12. I have decided that the correct date was January 21, relying on the editor's note in *Sochineniia*, XXIII, 642. See also Lenin's report to the All-Russian Congress of Trade Unions on January 20, in which he deplored the deaths of Luxemburg and Liebknecht but used them to strengthen his arguments against Luxemburg's philosophy about democracy in the working class movement; *Sochineniia*, XXIII, 478-93.

23. Zinoviev's remarks to the Eighth Congress of the Russian Communist Party in March demonstrated an early application of this argument. He said, "The Third International was born when, under the banner of internationalism, the working class in Russia gained its brilliant victory. This was the first stone of the Third International." He added that one party does not constitute an International, and it remained only for a second party—the KPD—to come into existence to make the organization a reality. *Pravda*, Mar. 26, 1919, 4: 2.

24. *Le Temps* (Paris), Jan. 3, 1919, 1: 2-3, had a report on the Bolsheviks' objections to the proposed meeting at Lausanne.

25. Renaudel, p. 34. De Kay has a slightly different version, but the tone is essentially the same. For the official record of the Berne conference, see Second International, *Bulletin*.

26. Renaudel, pp. 133-34. De Kay provides the texts of the resolutions in English.

27. Renaudel, pp. 136-37.

28. *Ibid.*, pp. 88-90.

29. *Ibid.*, pp. 80-82.

30. *Ibid.*, pp. 35-57, has a summary of the debate. The resolution is at pp. 57-58.

31. *Ibid.*, pp. 111-17. This resolution was also adopted by the International Syndicalist Conference, which was meeting simultaneously at Berne.

32. *Pravda*, Feb. 6, 1919, 1: 1-2.   35. *Ibid.*, pp. 156-57.

33. *Ibid.*, Feb. 15, 1919, 2: 6.   36. *Ibid.*, pp. 157-60.

34. Ransome, p. 156.   37. Fineberg, pp. 443-45.

38. Trofimov, p. 41. Among those who have relied upon the questionable Fineberg account are Carr, *History,* III, 118, and Lazitch, p. 91.

39. *Pravda,* Jan. 24, 1919, 1: 6–7, 2: 1–2. An English translation is available in Degras, *Communist International,* I, 1–5.

Chapter Two

1. The best secondary summaries of the First Congress are Gankin; Carr, *History, III,* 119–26; Lazitch, pp. 96–121; Fainsod, pp. 201–11; and Page, pp. 125–33. Although Borkenau has generally been regarded as an important work on the Comintern, it is weak and inaccurate in its treatment of the First Congress (pp. 161–64). For a sample of the current Soviet interpretation on this subject, which emphasizes Lenin's role and excludes reference to nearly all other participants, see Akademiia Nauk SSSR, pp. 442–46.

2. The list of delegates appears in Com. Int., *Der I. Kongress,* pp. 4–5. There is doubt about whether Stalin actually participated; Guilbeaux (p. 135) does not mention him, and he does not seem to be in the photograph of the delegates that appeared in *Kommunisticheskii Internatsional* (Petrograd), No. 2 (June 1, 1919), opposite cols. 193–94.

3. A summary of Grimlund's report appears in *Die Kommunistische Internationale* (Berlin?), No. 3 (July, 1919), pp. 92–93, the West European Secretariat's reprint of the Petrograd edition. This is probably not an exact transcript, since none was taken at the First Congress.

4. See his remarks as reported in Com. Int., *Der I. Kongress,* p. 52. This refutes statements, such as that in Degras, I, 6, that he had come especially to serve as a delegate to the Congress.

5. Kommunistische Partei Deutschösterreichs, *Der Erste Parteitag.* The invitation appeared in *Die Soziale Revolution* (Vienna), Jan. 29, 1919, p. 1.

6. Guilbeaux later wrote that he had arrived in Moscow on March 5, after the conference had begun. *La Vie Ouvrière* (Paris), July 30, 1919, 2: 4–5. He was officially designated as the representative of the French Left Zimmerwaldians, but he voted as though he were spokesman for the entire French Socialist Party. His participation in the Moscow Congress caused a controversy at the French Socialist Party Congress in Paris in April, when it was established that he had had no mandate from the party. He did hold a "limited mandate" from the Committee for the Resumption of International Relations, the small group within the party that later supported the Third International, but it had nothing to do with the First Congress. *L'Humanité* (Paris), Apr. 24, 1919, 2: 2–5.

7. Platten apologized to the Congress because he could not give a detailed report. His remarks are summarized in Com. Int., *Der I. Kongress,* pp. 27–33.

8. *Ibid.,* p. 52.

9. Balabanoff, *My Life,* pp. 213–16.

10. Fineberg (p. 444), for example, acknowledged that he had no mandate, although he acted as a "deliberative" delegate for the British Socialist Party and endorsed the actions of the Congress in its name.

11. Com. Int., *Der I. Kongress,* pp. 8–9.

12. Vorovsky, III, 370. Eberlein's arguments appear in Com. Int., *Der I. Kongress*, pp. 115–29, 168–72, 202–6. The summary of Steinhardt's argument, which is said to have been decisive against Eberlein's view, is at pp. 152–60, 218–20. This text, however, hardly suggests the emotional impact that unofficial commentaries have attributed to his statements. See also Balabanoff, *My Life*, pp. 215–16; Reinstein, pp. 433–34; and Ransome, p. 219.

13. Com. Int., *Der I. Kongress*, pp. 309–10.

14. *Pravda*, Mar. 2, 1919, 2: 1–7, 3: 1–3.

15. The Manifesto and other documents are printed in various editions of the *Kommunisticheskii Internatsional* and can be found also in Com. Int., *Der I. Kongress*, in their original form. They are available in Russian in manageable form in Kun, *Kommunisticheskii Internatsional v Dokumentakh* (pp. 52–88), which is a Comintern publication.

16. Com. Int., *Der I. Kongress*, p. 264.

17. Ransome, pp. 220–21; Balabanoff, *My Life*, pp. 218–19.

18. *Izvestiia*, Mar. 11, 1919, 3: 3–4. Also see Trotsky, *First Five Years*, p. 35.

19. For samples of these reports, see *Pravda*, Mar. 9, 1919, 1: 6–7; 2: 1–2; and Mar. 15, 3: 6–7; 4: 1–2.

20. *Ibid.*, Mar. 20, 1919, 3: 2–3, has Lenin's opening remarks. For Zinoviev's report, see *ibid.*, Mar. 26, 3: 1–7; 4: 1–2; Mar. 27, 3: 1–3.

21. Balabanoff, *My Life*, p. 222.

22. *Ibid.*, pp. 219–20. Many of Balabanoff's assertions are substantiated by other evidence.

23. *Ibid.*, pp. 222–23 (quoted by courtesy of Harper and Row). See also Serge, *Le Tournant Obscur*, pp. 38–39.

24. Piiashev, p. 297.

25. *Ibid.*, p. 236. *La Vie Ouvrière*, June 25, 1919, 2: 1.

26. Serge, *Mémoires*, p. 87. See also his "La IIIe Internationale," pp. 23–24.

27. *L'Internationale Communiste* (Stockholm reprint), No. 7/8 (November/ December 1919), cols. 1165–70. Serge, *Mémoires*, pp. 88, 100–101.

28. Serge, "La IIIe Internationale," p. 23. See also Tivel', p. 14. Tivel' indicates that such persons as Ernst Meyer of the KPD, G. K. Klinger of the German Volga colonies, and Rudniansky were active in Comintern affairs between the First and Second Congresses. Bukharin also had considerable responsibility during this period.

29. *Die Kommunistische Internationale* (Petrograd), No. 1 (May 1, 1919), cols. 59–60.

30. Almond, pp. 68–69.

31. This listing is an adaptation of the Table of Contents for the first seven numbers of *Kommunisticheskii Internatsional*, which appeared in the issue of November/December 1919, cols. 1187–94.

32. *L'Humanité*, Mar. 31, 1919, 3: 4. Among those monitoring such broadcasts was the French government. The Hoover Institution has a collection of mimeographed reports prepared by the Ministère de la Guerre, *Radiotélégrammes Étrangères*, and a similar group, prepared by the Ministère des Affaires Étrangères, *Radiotélégrammes de Propagande des Puissances Ennemies*, for 1919, and they contain a few references to messages broadcasted from Russia and Hungary.

33. *De Tribune* (Amsterdam), Mar. 4, 1919; 1: 1–4. Most other left-wing newspapers in the West failed to note and reproduce this document quickly.

34. Rutgers, p. 90.

35. *Kommunisticheskii Internatsional,* No. 1 (May 1, 1919), col. 138; No. 2 (June 1, 1919), col. 240.

36. *L'Humanité,* Sept. 21, 1919, 3: 5; *Berner Tagwacht* (Berne), June 2, 1920, 1: 3; June 3, 2: 4; June 4, 2: 2.

37. Serge, *Le Tournant Obscur,* p. 38.

38. Carr, *History,* III, 18.

39. See Chapter 3.

40. Four issues of this newspaper are available in the collection of the Hoover Institution: for November 9 and November 20, 1918, and for January 19 and February 17, 1919. These numbers do not specifically appeal for the creation of a Third International, but it is possible that the project received favorable attention in other issues.

41. Churchill, pp. 138–39.

42. *L'Humanité,* May 20, 1919, 3: 2–3, printed the two documents together.

43. Chicherin, cols. 817–28. For detailed discussions of the relationship between the International and the Soviet government, see Carr, *History,* III, 128–31, and Korey, pp. 117–27.

44. Vorovsky, III, 375.

45. *Kommunisticheskii Internatsional,* No. 1 (May 1, 1919), cols. 31–38; also in Lenin, *Sochineniia,* XXIV, 246–52.

46. Trotsky, "Mysli," p. 28. For Zinoviev's remark, see *Pravda,* Mar. 27, 1919, 3: 2.

47. Zinoviev, *Die Weltrevolution,* pp. 52–53. This is a copy of a speech delivered at Halle, Germany, on October 14, 1920.

48. *Ibid.*

Chapter Three

1. Coolidge, in Deák, pp. 365–67. On the fall of Károlyi and the rise of the Communist-Social Democratic regime, see Kaas and Lazarovics; Karolyi, pp. 142–57; Jászi; Böhm; and Szántó. None of these works is free of bias, but taken together, they provide a fair account of the era. Also helpful is the collection of documents edited by Geiger.

2. Quoted in Kaas and Lazarovics, pp. 46–47.

3. Szamuely, p. 79.   5. *Ibid.,* pp. 36–39. Jászi, p. 87.

4. Szántó, p. 16.   6. Kaas and Lazarovics, p. 54.

7. *Vörös Ujság,* Mar. 13, 1919, 2: 1.

8. Translations of the agreement can be found in *Kommunisticheskii Internatsional,* No. 2 (June 1, 1919), cols. 237–38; in Kaas and Lazarovics, p. 260; or in Szántó, pp. 53–54.

9. *Vörös Ujság,* Mar. 23, 1919, 3: 2–3.

10. Lenin, *Sochineniia,* XXIV, 183.

11. *Ibid.,* pp. 195–96.

12. *Kommunisticheskii Internatsional*, No. 1 (May 1, 1919), cols. 83–84.

13. Szamuely, pp. 218–25, 228–29; Böhm, pp. 485–88; *Vörös Ujság,* June 13, 1919, pp. 5–6; June 14, 1919, p. 1.

14. Rudniansky, col. 642.

15. *Vörös Ujság,* May 1, 1919, 1: 2–4.

16. *Ibid.,* June 5, 1919, 1: 2.

17. See *The Times* (London), Apr. 5, 1919, 12: 4; Apr. 7, 1919, 12: 4; Apr. 8, 1919, 12: 3; Apr. 17, 1919, 12: 2. Böhm, pp. 375, 384, was basically correct when he said Kun's foreign policy consisted exclusively of propagandizing for the Bolsheviks.

18. Kommunistische Partei Deutschösterreichs, *Der Erste Parteitag,* pp. 8–9.

19. *Ibid.,* pp. 22–27.

20. *Ibid.,* p. 25.

21. An excellent description of Adler's handling of the Bolshevik threat can be found in Gulick, pp. 70–83.

22. *Ibid.,* p. 76.

23. Kaas and Lazarovics, pp. 210–16.

24. *Ibid.;* Gulick, pp. 80–81. See also Benedikt, pp. 49–59; and Radek's article in *Kommunisticheskii Internatsional,* No. 9 (Mar. 22, 1920), cols. 1261–66.

25. *La Troisième Internationale* (Budapest), May 30, June 13, June 27, and July 25, 1919.

26. A series of pamphlets issued by the People's Commissariat for Public Instruction dealt with many of the usual Bolshevik themes (the historical mission of the proletariat, the unity of the Communists and the Social Democrats, etc.), as well as publishing the text of the Manifesto of the Comintern.

27. Kun told a correspondent for *The Times* of London (probably C. A. Macartney) on about April 12 that "foreign propaganda was no part of the State functions, and that the complex propaganda department now under Szamuely is only intended for Hungary itself." The correspondent expressed skepticism in his dispatch to London, and described the propaganda system as "ubiquitous." Apr. 24, 1919, 10: 1–2.

28. The best description of the Smuts mission is in Nicolson, pp. 292–305. He shared with Smuts the belief that Kun was in contact with Moscow at all important junctures, and most subsequent writers have left this unchallenged. However, the coverage in *Pravda* of the Smuts mission raises questions on this point. The first mention of the mission appeared on April 9, 1919, 3: 3, and this was only a brief announcement (although it was regarded as important enough to receive front-page mention in the news summary). On April 11, 2: 5, there was another brief article, datelined from Nauen, reporting that an exchange of notes had occurred between Smuts and the Hungarians. This belated and indirect reporting suggests that the Bolsheviks had no direct contact with Kun while the negotiations were under way; otherwise they would surely have commented on this prospect for peace with the Allies.

29. For a recent restatement of this position, see Rákosi, pp. 54, 60.

30. *Kommunisticheskii Internatsional,* No. 2 (June 1, 1919), cols. 155–58.

31. *Ibid.,* No. 3 (July 1, 1919), cols. 373–74.

32. *Ibid.,* No. 2 (June 1, 1919), cols. 199–202.

33. Kaas and Lazarovics, p. 242.

34. *Pravda,* Aug. 6, 1919, 1: 1-8.

35. For the Bolsheviks' use of the Hungarian developments as a lesson for the International, see Cattell, pp. 27-38.

36. *Pravda,* Aug. 6, 1919, 1: 4-5, and *Kommunisticheskii Internatsional,* No. 4 (August 1919), cols. 541-42.

37. Rudniansky, cols. 637-42.

38. Koloszváry (pseudonym for Kun), pp. 13, 51-55. This essay was written in November 1919, but a final chapter was composed about two and a half months later. The language against the Social Democrats was more pointed in this later addition (pp. 50-55).

39. On the controversies among the Hungarian exiles, see Mályusz, pp. 24-31, 355-57. This book has a valuable selection of translated documents.

40. Szántó, pp. 59, 67-68.

41. *Workers' Dreadnought,* Nov. 22, 1919, 1546: 1-3.

42. *Ibid.,* May 29, 1920, 2: 3. A series of articles by Kun appeared in the issues of May 22, 1: 1-2; May 29, 2: 2-3; and June 5, 3: 1-2.

43. *The Call* (London), Jan. 29, 1920, 3: 1-3.

44. Gabor, cols. 1159-68.   46. *Ibid.,* pp. 244.

45. Lenin, *Sochineniia,* XXV, 32-33.   47. *Ibid.,* pp. 312-13.

48. The Twenty-One Conditions can be found in Com. Int., *Vtoroi Kongress Kominterna,* pp. 499-505. An English translation is available in Degras, *The Communist International,* I, 168-72.

49. Com. Int., *Rapports,* pp. 39-59.

50. *L'Humanité,* Apr. 3, 1920, 3: 1. *Kommunisticheskii Internatsional,* No. 12 (July 20, 1920), cols. 2213-14.

51. Mályusz, pp. 33-35.

Chapter Four

1. Korey, pp. 19-20, 36-37.

2. *Ibid.,* p. 51.

3. This figure is cited by Bonomi, p. 36, for autumn 1920.

4. *L'Humanité,* Mar. 23, 1919, 3: 1-2, gives a French translation of the committee's document. I have not had access to *Avanti!* or other Italian Socialist newspapers or documents for the middle of March.

5. For an excellent discussion of the Italian Socialist Party and its relations with the Comintern during this period, see Urquidi, which demonstrates that the Italian revolutionary movement was not produced by Lenin or the Bolsheviks, but was largely an indigenous movement. It also shows that Moscow had very little influence on the Italian Socialist Party prior to spring 1920. See also Balabanoff, *My Life,* pp. 114-29.

6. Balabanoff, "Greetings," col. 55.

7. Quoted in Young, pp. 28-29.

8. *Ibid.,* pp. 101-2.

9. A detailed summary of Bordiga's position was printed in *Workers' Dread-*

nought, Nov. 8, 1919, 1526: 2–3, and 1527: 1–3. Pankhurst, the *Dreadnought*'s editor, attended the Bologna Congress and gave considerable attention to Bordiga's attitude.

10. Young, p. 100.

11. The letter originally appeared in *Avanti!* in two parts. The first part was printed on December 6, 1919, 1: 3–4, and the second on December 7, 6: 1. This second section was apparently delayed by censorship. The second edition of Lenin's *Sochineniia,* XXIV, 504, offers only the first part.

12. *Workers' Dreadnought,* Nov. 1, 1919, 1523: 2.

13. Young, p. 103.

14. Borkenau, p. 169.

15. For a detailed examination of the work of the Swiss Social Democrats and their relations with the Bolsheviks during the war, see Gankin and Fisher.

16. Egger, pp. 197–98. For a contemporary report, see *Berner Tagwacht,* July 17, 1919, 1: 1–2, and 2: 2–3; July 18, 1919, 1: 1–2; July 19, 1919, 1: 1–2; and Aug. 18, 1919, 1: 1–2.

17. Sozialdemokratische Partei der Schweiz, pp. 3–8.

18. *Ibid.,* p. 153.

19. *Ibid.*

20. Egger, p. 199. *Berner Tagwacht,* Sept. 19, 1919, 2: 2.

21. *L'Humanité,* July 13, 1919, 3: 4; July 17, 1919, 3: 2.

22. For Humbert-Droz's remarks, see Sozialdemokratische Partei der Schweiz, pp. 57–69; for Welti's, see *ibid.,* pp. 30–43.

23. Quoted in Egger, pp. 199–200.

24. Humbert-Droz and Bringolf, in Com. Int., *Rapports,* pp. 86–97.

25. The motions are reprinted in *Le Phare* (May–June 1920), pp. 402–4.

26. *Ibid.* (May–June 1920), pp. 404–7; *ibid.* (July–August 1920), pp. 590–91.

27. Com. Int., *Rapports,* p. 99.

28. The best study of the Bulgarian Communist Party is that of Rothschild.

29. For the crucial parts of the Tesniaks' statements against the wars and in favor of Socialist federation, see Kabakchiev, Boshkovich, and Vatis, pp. 73–74, 76. See also Blagoev, p. 682, which reproduces an article written February 15, 1915.

30. Rothschild, pp. 80–81, 95. For other summaries of this period, see Asteriou, pp. 26–32, 88–93, and also the official Bulgarian Communist Party version, Bulg. KP, *Materiali,* pp. 116–50.

31. There has been extensive discussion of this so-called error of the Tesniaks. For recent commentary, see Dimitrov, *Political Report,* pp. 11–13; and Bulg. KP, *Istoriia,* pp. 158, 174 (in places, this work is a translation of Bulg. KP, *Materiali,* cited in n. 30 above). See also Rothschild, pp. 81–84.

32. Com. Int., *Sowjet-Russland,* pp. 50–54.

33. Rakovsky, "Doklad," cols. 555–56.

34. Bulg. KP, *Materiali,* p. 156.

35. For Dimitrov's speeches to the trade union and party conferences in May 1919, see his *Suchineniia,* V, 205–39 (esp. pp. 224, 239).

36. Bulg. KP, "Programnaia Deklaratsiia," cols. 503–12. See also Dechev, cols. 499–502.

37. *Ibid.,* col. 510. See also Bulg. KP, "Rezoliutsiia," cols. 689–95.

38. Bulg. KP, *Materiali*, pp. 158–60, or *Istoriia*, pp. 162–63.

39. Bulg. KP, *Materiali*, pp. 161–62; Rothschild, pp. 96–97.

40. For example, see *L'Humanité*, Aug. 25, 1919, 1: 3.

41. Zinoviev himself stressed this point; see Zinoviev, "K Proletariatu," cols. 1405–10.

42. Rothschild, pp. 97–99.

43. B., cols. 1827–28.

44. *Ibid.*, cols. 1829–30; Rothschild, p. 102.

45. Rothschild, p. 106.

46. *L'Humanité*, July 31, 1920; 3: 3, has a report based on information from *Rabotnicheski Vestnik*. See also Blagoyeva, pp. 34–35.

47. Stavrianos, p. 202. Bulgaria did not enter the war until 1915, so the Tesniaks are not included in this generalization.

48. Serb. SDRP, cols. 77–78.

49. Milkich had represented Serbia at the Eighth International Socialist Congress in Copenhagen in 1910, and had played an insignificant role.

50. Milkich, "Doklad," cols. 555–58.

51. For a later contribution by Milkich to the cause of the Comintern, see his article "Sotsializm v Serbii." For a document issued by the Yugoslav Communist faction in Russia on March 27, 1919, which received attention in Central Europe, see *Die Rote Fahne* (Mannheim), July 24, 1919, 3: 2–3. Here the Yugoslav group, including Milkich, urged the creation of a Balkan Communist federation, an idea which, as will be seen below, the Comintern supported.

52. The invitation appeared in the party's newspaper *Radničke Novine*.

53. Asteriou, pp. 110, 115. The name "Communist" had been frequently applied to the party after the Belgrade Congress.

54. *Kommunisticheskii Internatsional*, No. 7/8 (November/December 1919), col. 1110, has a message from the Yugoslav party to the Comintern dated October 11, 1919, in which it was asserted that the party had joined the Third International at the time of the Belgrade Congress.

55. Stavrianos, p. 213, n. 41.

56. *Kommunisticheskii Internatsional*, No. 7/8 (November/December 1919), col. 1110, editor's note.

57. Stavrianos, p. 213; Asteriou, p. 112; Markovic, pp. 8–11.

58. See the report given by Milkich to the Second Congress of the Comintern in July, in Com. Int., *Rapports*, pp. 143–64.

59. Asteriou, p. 114.

60. See Com. Int., *Rapports*, pp. 143–64.

61. Asteriou, p. 100.

62. Com. Int., *Rapports*, pp. 165–74. See also the account in *L'Humanité*, June 30, 1919, 3: 2, which appears to have been written by Demetrios Pournaras, later a historian of the Greek Communist movement. A quotation from the resolution of the meeting is cited in *Workers' Dreadnought*, Aug. 9, 1919, 1422: 1–3.

63. Com. Int., *Rapports*, p. 173; Asteriou, pp. 123–24.

64. Zinoviev, "K Proletariatu," cols. 1405–10.

65. Asteriou, p. 129.

66. *Ibid.*, p. 125.

67. Rakovsky, "Kommunisticheskoe Dvizhenie," cols. 2563–66.

68. *Ibid.* See also "A Letter from Rumania" and "Pis'mo iz Rumynii."

69. Stavrianos, pp. 186–95.

70. *Ibid.,* pp. 198–99.

71. *Ibid.,* p. 205, gives a good summary of the information available, but little detailed information on the conference.

72. Balkan Com. Fed., "Rezoliutsii." Also printed in Stavrianos, pp. 303–6.

73. B., cols. 1820–21. *The Call,* Apr. 29, 1920, 5: 3.

74. *Le Phare* (Apr. 1, 1920), p. 391.

75. Balkan Com. Fed., "Rezoliutsii."

76. Zinoviev, "K Proletariatu," col. 1408. Parts of this document are translated in Degras, *The Communist International,* I, 85–87, but she has made some errors in dating in the editorial note on p. 85.

77. Zinoviev, "K Proletariatu," col. 1408 (emphasis in the original).

78. Balkan Com. Fed., "Manifest."

79. Comment on this appeal appeared in *The Communist* (London), Sept. 23, 1920, 3: 1.

80. Borkenau, pp. 67–68, 167.

81. Quoted in Nordskog, pp. 52–53.

82. This portion of the party's statement is quoted in Tollefson, p. 155.

83. *Ibid.*

84. The Norwegian Labor Party's affiliation was mentioned briefly in *Kommunisticheskii Internatsional,* No. 3 (July 1, 1919), col. 365; and in No. 5 (September 1919), cols. 695–96.

85. Zinoviev, "Skandinavskim rabochim."

86. *L'Humanité,* Feb. 29, 1920, 2: 3; *De Tribune,* June 14, 1920, 1: 5.

87. *Le Phare* (July–August 1920), pp. 587–88.

88. The program was reprinted in Com. Int., *Rapports,* pp. 248–52.

89. *Ibid.,* pp. 276–79.

90. *Le Phare* (Sept. 1, 1919), pp. 46–48. *The Communist International* (Paris reprint), No. 3 (July 1, 1919), p. 369.

91. Com. Int., *Rapports,* p. 284. *Kommunisticheskii Internatsional,* No. 5 (September 1919), cols. 695–96.

92. *L'Humanité,* Aug. 27, 1919, 3: 5.

93. *Le Phare* (Oct. 1, 1919), pp. 110–11.

94. Com. Int., *Rapports,* p. 279. *Le Phare* (January–February 1920), pp. 301–4.

95. Com. Int., *Rapports,* pp. 279–82.

96. *Kommunisticheskii Internatsional,* No. 7/8 (November/December 1919) col. 1122.

Chapter Five

1. Much scholarly work has been devoted to the German revolution and the efforts of the Comintern to control it. Particularly useful are Waldman; Lowenthal, pp. 23–71; Carr, *History,* III, 132–40, 170–76; Flechtheim, pp. 37–99; and Borkenau, pp. 134–60. For a survey of the founding of the KPD, see Copping, pp. 137–63.

2. Radek, *Der Zusammenbruch,* p. 48.

3. Radek, *Die Russische und Deutsche Revolution,* p. 31.

4. KPD, *Bericht über den Gründungsparteitag,* p. 55.

5. For the January uprising and its effects, in addition to the works cited in n. 1 of this chapter, see Ruth Fischer, pp. 82–87; and Rotter, pp. 63–69.

6. Radek, "Noiabr'," pp. 155–58.

7. *Die Rote Fahne* (Berlin), Feb. 3, 1919, 1: 1. The journal suspended publication again from March 3 until April 11, when it reappeared in Leipzig. It stopped publishing again on May 9 and apparently did not resume until December 12. The December issues do not specify where they were being published. The paper was brought out daily in this edition during its periods of publication.

8. *Spartakus* (Frankfurt), Mar. 18, 1919, 1: 4.

9. *Die Rote Fahne* (Munich), Mar. 21, 1919, 1: 1; Apr. 1, 1: 1–2; 2: 3; 3: 1; and April 9, 2: 1–3; 3: 1.

10. *Die Rote Fahne* (Leipzig), Apr. 20, 1919, 3: 1.

11. *Ibid.,* Apr. 27, 1919, 1: 1–3; 2: 1–2.

12. *Die Rote Fahne* (Mannheim), May 6, 1919, 2: 1–3; 3: 1–3; May 8, 1919, 2: 1–3; May 10, 1919, 2: 1–3; 3: 1; and May 13, 2: 1–3; 3: 1. For a discussion of the early activities of both the Mannheim and the Munich editions of this newspaper, see Stolzenburg, pp. 525–41.

13. *Die Rote Fahne* (Leipzig), Apr. 17, 1919; 3: 2–3. One of these messages originated in Petrograd and carried Zinoviev's signature. The other came from Moscow, and it had no signature; it may have been the work of Balabanoff.

14. Lowenthal, p. 30.

15. The best study of the relationship between the Bolshevik government in Russia and the various Bavarian governments in the period from November 1918 to May 1919 is Neubauer. See also Ruth Fischer, pp. 100–108; and Beyer.

16. Neubauer, pp. 38–41; Ruth Fischer, pp. 100–102.

17. Neubauer, p. 46. *Die Rote Fahne* (Munich), Apr. 1, 1919, 1: 1–2.

18. A good collection of documents on the first Bavarian Soviet Republic (Zentralrat) is available in Werner, pp. 131–51. This includes contemporary Communist comment on the government of April 7–13. A recent example of the effort to discredit this regime is Beyer, pp. 68–92, which includes references to many contemporary documents. See also Borkenau, pp. 149–50, and Ruth Fischer, pp. 102–4, bearing in mind that the authors are ex-Communists. For a more sympathetic view by a participant in the experiment, see Mühsam.

19. *Die Rote Fahne* (Munich), Apr. 7, 1919; 1: 1–3. Quoted in Werner, pp. 145–49, and in Beyer, pp. 152–54.

20. Neubauer's presentation on this point is excellent (pp. 53–59).

21. *Pravda,* Apr. 9, 1919, 1: 1–2; 3: 3.

22. Neubauer, p. 57.

23. *Die Rote Fahne* (Munich), Apr. 11, 1919, as quoted in Institut für Marxismus-Leninismus beim ZK der SED, p. 48.

24. Ruth Fischer, p. 105.

25. *Ibid.,* pp. 105–6.

26. *Pravda,* Apr. 17, 1919, 2: 1.

27. *Ibid.,* Apr. 18, 1919, 3: 3.

28. *Mitteilungen des Vollzugsrats der Betriebs- und Soldatenräte* (Munich), Apr. 15, 1919, 1: 3. Quoted in Werner, pp. 156–57, and in Neubauer, p. 70.

29. Lenin, *Sochineniia,* XXIV, 264. Neubauer, pp. 74–75.

30. Ruth Fischer, p. 107.

31. *Kommunisticheskii Internatsional,* No. 1 (May 1, 1919), col. 84. Neubauer, p. 56, cites another reference by Zinoviev to the Bavarian Soviets, but this came earlier and refers to remarks at the First Congress about action taken shortly after the assassination of Eisner. See also the greetings to the Bavarian Soviet Republic from the Congress of Social Democrats in Moscow, in *Die Rote Fahne* (Munich), Apr. 28, 1919, 3: 2, and the messages from the Latvian and Estonian Soviet governments, quoted in Beyer, pp. 160–61.

32. Several scholars have taken note of Zinoviev's statement in the first number of *Kommunisticheskii Internatsional* (May 1, 1919), col. 38, that the Third International now had as its foundation three Soviet republics—in Russia, Hungary, and Bavaria. "But no one will be surprised," he added, "if by the time these lines appear in print, we will have not only three, but six or a greater number of Soviet republics."

33. *Pravda,* May 4, 1919, 3: 3; May 5, 3: 2.

34. "Evgenii Levine," cols. 543–48.

35. Borkenau, p. 151.

36. Ruth Fischer, pp. 77–78. See also Carr, *History,* III, 103–4.

37. Borkenau, p. 143.

38. KPD, *Bericht über den Gründungsparteitag,* pp. 13–18. Radek may have converted Levi to this position; see Ruth Fischer, pp. 118–19.

39. Radek's activities in Germany in 1919 have received considerable attention. His own account is "Noiabr'," part of which is translated in Carr, "Radek's 'Political Salon,'" pp. 411–30. This has been used extensively by Rotter, pp. 70–81, in his close study of the period. Also see Carr, *History,* III, 132–40; and Lowenthal, pp. 32–37.

40. Struthan (pseudonym for Radek), *Die Entwicklung,* p. 50. Writing in later years, Radek said he had favored the plan for the KPD to steer a course toward unification with the USPD Left; see Radek, "Noiabr'," p. 167, or Carr, "Radek's 'Political Salon,'" pp. 422–23. But an examination of *Die Entwicklung* suggests that he was not so definite at the time.

41. Struthan, *Die Entwicklung,* pp. 51–53.

42. *Ibid.,* p. 56.

43. See below, p. 118.

44. KPD, *Bericht über den 2. Parteitag,* pp. 4, 61–62. The final statement of principles adopted at the conference appears on pp. 60–67.

45. Radek, *Zur Taktik des Kommunismus.*

46. For the vote and its effects, see KPD, *Bericht über den 2. Parteitag,* pp. 42–45.

47. See below, pp. 152–62.

48. I have not examined this movement in detail because it had little direct connection with the Comintern except to the extent that it shared some of its membership and tendencies with the KAPD. Summaries are available in Carr, *History,* III, 310–12, 321–22, and Ruth Fischer, pp. 92–96.

49. Carr, *History,* III, 138, mentions the presence of this person at the conference, but attributes only one statement to him. KPD, *Bericht über den 2. Partei-*

tag, indicates two remarks, at pp. 35 and 48–49. The quotation here is from pp. 48–49.

50. Struthan (Radek), "Die Unabhängigen," pp. 290–99.

51. Scholars are not in agreement on these figures. Compare Flechtheim, pp. 60–61; Ruth Fischer, p. 119; Carr, *History,* III, 138.

52. Lenin, "Geroi," cols. 176–77.

53. Zinoviev, "Sotsial-demokratiia," col. 186.

54. Renaudel, p. 140.

55. For Däumig's position at the conference, see *Freiheit,* Supplement to the issue of Mar. 9, 1919, 1: 3 and 2: 1. For Kautsky's report, see the same supplement at 2: 2–3. Zetkin's response is at 3: 1–2.

56. For Haase's position, see *ibid.* (Supplement), 1: 1–2.

57. Second International, *The International at Lucerne,* pp. 3–7.

58. *Vorwärts* (Berlin), Aug. 3, 1919, 3: 2–3.

59. *Freiheit,* Aug. 20, 1919 (morning edition), 1: 3, 2: 1.

60. Prager, pp. 204–5.

61. *Ibid.,* p. 207.

62. USPD, *Protokoll Leipzig,* pp. 62–66; *Freiheit,* Dec. 1, 1919 (morning edition), 1: 3.

63. USPD, *Protokoll Leipzig,* pp. 38–41, 306–95. The resolutions can also be found in Crispien, pp. 40–43, or in *Freiheit,* Dec. 5, 1919 (morning edition), 3: 1–2.

64. USPD, *Protokoll Leipzig,* pp. 326–42.

65. *Ibid.,* p. 369; Crispien, p. 49.

66. USPD, *Protokoll Leipzig,* p. 388; Crispien, p. 50.

67. Carr, *History,* III, 135–36; Ruth Fischer, pp. 134–35n. Fischer incorrectly applies the term "Bureau" to the Secretariat on this occasion.

68. Com. Int., West European Secretariat, cols. 1153–56.

69. The earliest editions of *Spartakus* are not dated, but internal evidence suggests that the first three numbers were published in about November and December. The fourth and fifth numbers appeared in January.

70. *Workers' Dreadnought,* Jan. 31, 1920 (Supplement), 1: 1. See also the supplement of Feb. 7, 1920, and the issue of Mar. 13, 1920, 3: 3.

71. I have not discovered a copy of Crispien's letter, but its contents can be inferred from the responses to it. The Secretariat's initial response can be found in *Spartakus,* No. 5–6 (January 1920), 1: 1–3. See n. 69 above.

72. The Berlin Secretariat's answer was not published in *Kommunisticheskii Internatsional* until May. See No. 10, cols. 1605–10.

73. Zinoviev, "Ko vsem rabochim Germanii," cols. 1381–92. This was later printed by the West European Secretariat as Zinoviev, *Der Leipziger Kongress.*

74. Zinoviev, *Der Leipziger Kongress,* pp. 18–19.

75. For examples of Zinoviev's vitriolic attacks on the German Social Democrats, see *Kommunisticheskii Internatsional,* No. 2 (June 1, 1919), cols. 181–86; No. 3 (July 1, 1919), cols. 375–76; No. 6 (October 1919), cols. 781–92.

76. Zinoviev, *Der Leipziger Kongress,* p. 12.

77. Lenin, *Sochineniia,* XXIV, 502–3.

78. Carr, *History,* III, 136.

79. This edition, identified as *Die Rote Fahne (Bezirk Gross-Berlin)*, should not be confused with the paper issued for a time in Berlin by the national central committee of the KPD (see n. 7 of this chapter). The newspaper published by the local Berlin organization originally appeared as *Kampf-Flugblatt* on April 29, 1919. Several numbers that appeared between April and July carried the name *Der Kämpfer*. In about July, with No. 22-23 (all issues are numbered, but some are not dated), the paper assumed the name of *Die Rote Fahne*. It later became *Kommunistische Arbeiter-Zeitung*.

80. *Die Rote Fahne (Bezirk Gross-Berlin)*, No. 51-52, 1: 1-3; No. 53-54, 1: 1-3; No. 55-56, 1: 1-2.

81. *Ibid.*, No. 65-66, pp. 1-4, describes the Left Opposition's reaction to the Heidelberg conference.

82. *Workers' Dreadnought* (Nov. 8, 1919), 1531: 1-3. *La Vie Ouvrière*, Oct. 29, 1919, 1: 2-4.

83. *The Call*, Mar. 11, 1920, 7: 1-3.

84. For helpful summaries of the Kapp Putsch and the reactions of the Comintern, see Carr, *History*, III, 171-76; and Borkenau, pp. 153-60. Some of the original documents of this period are quoted in Braun. See also Ruth Fischer, pp. 117-34.

85. Levi, cols. 2077-80.

86. *Die Rote Fahne (Bezirk Gross-Berlin)*, No. 86, 1: 1-3. The article is dated Mar. 27, 1920.

87. For an official report of the conference, see *Kommunistische Arbeiter-Zeitung* (formerly *Die Rote Fahne, Bezirk Gross-Berlin*) No. 90 (Apr. 23, 1920).

88. *Ibid.*, 2: 1.

89. *Die Rote Fahne* (Berlin), Apr. 22, 1920, 1: 1.

90. KAPD, pp. 7-12. (The KAPD printed all its correspondence with the ECCI in this pamphlet.) The ECCI reply is also in *Kommunisticheskii Internatsional*, No. 11 (June 14, 1920), cols. 1866-84.

91. *Ibid.*

92. Radek, "K tsentral'nomu komitetu," cols. 1885-86. Radek and Zinoviev, cols. 2257-60.

93. For the USPD response to Moscow's taunting, see *Freiheit*, June 16, 1920 (morning edition), 3: 1-2; (evening edition), 3: 1-3; June 17 (morning edition), 5: 1-3; (evening edition), 3: 1-2; June 18 (morning edition), 5: 1-3; June 25 (morning edition), 5: 1-3, 6: 1; June 26 (morning edition), 5: 1-3, 6: 1; and June 27 (Sunday, one edition), 5: 2-3, 6: 1-2.

94. KAPD, pp. 13-15.

Chapter Six

1. According to Bell, *Pioneering Days*, p. 260, the British "have never had a really revolutionary movement after the example of some of the continental countries." Pelling, p. 182, reached the same conclusion: "All the absurdities of the history of the party spring from this one fact, that it has been a revolutionary party in a non-revolutionary situation." Similarly, Brand, pp. 199-286, felt that

a strong Labour Party dedicated to evolutionary change represented the will of the British Left more than a revolutionary party did.

2. Lenin, *Lenin on Britain*, pp. 178–79.

3. British Bolshevik sympathizers apparently learned of the Moscow Congress from Paris newspapers. So far as I can find, the earliest English newspaper account of the First Congress is in *Workers' Dreadnought*, Mar. 29, 1919, 1: 1–3.

4. Brand, p. 208.

5. Bell, *Pioneering Days*, pp. 194–95. See also Wood, p. 23, and Pelling, p. 7.

6. According to Brand, p. 74, the BSP had the "only considerable body of Marxians in Great Britain."

7. *Ibid.*, pp. 74–75.

8. See especially the editions for July 11, 1918, 2: 2–3; and July 25, 1918, 2: 2–3. The arguments appear on p. 2 in most issues.

9. *The Call*, Dec. 12, 1918, pp. 4–5.

10. *Ibid.*; see the editions of June 5, 12, 19, 26; July 31; August 7, 28; and September 11.

11. Murphy, p. 66.

12. Bell, *Pioneering Days*, p. 45.

13. *Ibid.*, pp. 156–57.

14. Pankhurst, *Life*, pp. 151–52.

15. *Workers' Dreadnought*, Sept. 15, 1917, 850: 1.

16. *Ibid.*, Jan. 26, 1918, 932: 1–3, 933: 3.

17. *Ibid.*, Mar. 29, 1919, 1: 1–3.

18. *The Call*, Apr. 17, 1919, 3: 1–2.

19. For summaries of the unity efforts, see Bell, *The British Communist Party*, pp. 47–58; and Brand, pp. 234–35.

20. Bell, *The British Communist Party*, pp. 50–51. See also the article "Socialist Unity" in *The Call*, Nov. 20, 1919, 6: 1–3.

21. *Workers' Dreadnought*, June 14, 1919, 1364: 1–2.

22. Wood, p. 26.

23. *Forward* (Glasgow), Mar. 29, 1919, 1: 4.

24. For Pankhurst's first three articles in the Comintern journal, see *The Communist International* (Petrograd edition), No. 2 (June 1, 1919), cols. 171–76; No. 3 (July 1, 1919), cols. 291–98; and No. 4 (Aug. 1, 1919), cols. 31–38.

25. Pankhurst, "Progress." I have used a London reprint of the Petrograd English edition in this instance; the reprint was apparently made several months after the original September edition.

26. *The Communist International* (London reprint of Petrograd edition), No. 5, pp. 51–53. There is also a translation of Lenin's letter in Lenin, *Lenin on Britain*, pp. 243–48. I have followed the latter (p. 246) because it is more faithful to the Russian original.

27. *The Call*, Feb. 12, 1920, 2: 3; 3: 1.

28. *Ibid.*, Jan. 22, 1920, 2: 1–3; 3: 1–2.

29. *Ibid.*, Feb. 19, 1920, 2: 1–3.

30. *Ibid.*, Apr. 22, 1920, 7: 1–3. Copies of the letters are at pp. 7–9.

31. *Ibid.*, Feb. 19, 1920, 2: 1–3.

32. *Ibid.*, Apr. 8, 1920, 4: 1–2.

33. *Workers' Dreadnought*, Apr. 10, 1920, 3: 1–2; Apr. 24, 8: 3; *The Call*, Apr. 15, 6: 1–3; Apr. 22, 10: 3.

34. *The Call,* May 6, 1920, 10: 3.

35. For a discussion of the international aspects of the parliamentary controversy, see Chapter 8 below.

36. Lenin, *Left-Wing Communism,* pp. 76–77, 81–82. Inkpin, Quelch, and MacLaine were contributors to the *Communist International* in June and July 1920. Their account of the British scene was quite different from Pankhurst's. Gallacher gives an interesting explanation of how he came to be identified with the "left-wing" group in his *Rolling of Thunder,* pp. 8–12.

37. *Workers' Dreadnought,* June 26, 1919, 1: 1.

38. Lenin, as quoted in Bell, *The British Communist Party,* p. 52. An almost identical translation appears in *The Call,* July 22, 1920; 1: 1.

39. *Workers' Dreadnought,* July 24, 1920, 4: 1.

40. For Pankhurst's role in the Second Congress, see Chapter 10.

41. Bell, *The British Communist Party,* pp. 56–57. There is a slight error in Bell's figures: he reports 115 votes for affiliation rather than 100. See *The Communist* (London), Aug. 5, 1920, p. 1. This is the newspaper formerly known as *The Call,* which changed its name simultaneously with the creation of the new party. In his *Pioneering Days,* pp. 184–94, Bell has a good account of the unity efforts of 1920, and here (p. 192) he reports the vote on affiliation correctly.

42. Brand, pp. 242–86.

43. *L'Humanité,* Apr. 14, 1919, 1: 1–2.

44. *Forward,* Apr. 26, 1919, 1: 1–2.

45. *Labour Leader,* Apr. 24, 1919, pp. 2–7, 10; and May 1, 1919, pp. 2, 8–10.

46. *Avanti!* (Milan), June 2, 1919, 1: 1–3; June 3, 1: 1–4; *Berner Tagwacht,* June 5, 1919, 1: 3. See also *Workers' Dreadnought,* June 21, 1919, 1: 2.

47. *Forward,* June 14, 1919, 1: 1–2.

48. *Berner Tagwacht,* June 7, 1919, 1: 2–3.

49. Lenin, "O zadachakh III-go Internatsionala," cols. 447–62. Also printed in Lenin, *Lenin on Britain,* pp. 227–42.

50. MacDonald, *Parliament and Revolution,* pp. 87–88.

51. Brand, p. 210.

52. Brockway, pp. 137–38.

53. *Labour Leader,* Jan. 8, 1920, 3: 1–4.

54. Philip Snowden, II, 536.

55. *Daily Herald* (London), Mar. 27, 1920, 4: 3–5.

56. ILP, *Report of the 28th Annual Conference,* pp. 66–76, 79–86; Philip Snowden, pp. 536–37.

57. MacDonald, editorial in *The Socialist Review,* pp. 110–11.

Chapter Seven

1. Zinoviev, "Vozzvanie," col. 82.

2. Prélot, pp. 204ff.

3. *Ibid.,* pp. 211–18.

4. For brief surveys of French Socialism during the war, in addition to Prélot, see Brogan, pp. 530–34; Louis, pp. 321–55; and Ligou, pp. 238–301.

5. Louis, pp. 347–48.

6. *Pravda,* Jan. 24, 1919, 2: 1–2.

7. Gankin and Fisher, pp. 561–65, summarizes the activity of the Zimmerwald Left in France during the war. See also Walter, pp. 21–23, and Ferrat, pp. 47–64, for secondary accounts. The most extensive primary account is Rosmer, *Le Mouvement Ouvrier.*

8. News of Loriot's letter arrived in Moscow at approximately the same time as Guilbeaux reached there, which suggests that he may have carried a report of it from Switzerland. Guilbeaux was still in Switzerland at the time of the Berne conference, although not at Berne; see *La Feuille* (Geneva), Feb. 8, 1919, 1: 2–3; 2: 1. According to an account he wrote later, he was expelled from Switzerland on February 18 and went to Moscow via Germany. He carried a large number of papers, books, and manuscripts. See *La Vie Ouvrière* (Paris), July 30, 1919, 2: 4–5, for this account. See also Guilbeaux's article on Loriot in *Pravda,* Apr. 5, 1919, 1: 3–4.

9. *Le Populaire* (Paris), Feb. 22, 1919, 1: 2. After the Tours Congress, Dunois became a Communist and a supporter of the Third International. See his article in *L'Humanité,* July 23, 1922, 1: 6, 2: 1.

10. *L'Humanité,* Mar. 23, 1919, 3: 1.

11. *Ibid.,* Apr. 14, 1919, 1: 1–2.

12. *Ibid.,* 3: 6. *Le Temps* (Paris), Apr. 15, 1919, 1: 2, gave a different vote total, but the basic result was the same.

13. *L'Humanité,* Apr. 22, 1919, 1: 3–5; Apr. 23, 2: 2; Apr. 24, 2: 2–5.

14. *Ibid.,* Apr. 24, 1919, 2: 5. See also Zévaès, pp. 188–89, and Louis, pp. 357–59.

15. *La Vie Ouvrière* (Paris), Apr. 30, 1919, 1: 1; 3: 4.

16. *L'Humanité,* Sept. 20, 1919, 3: 1. See also nn. 30 and 31, below.

17. *La Vie Ouvrière,* Oct. 1, 1919, 4: 4–5; Oct. 8, 4: 4.

18. *Ibid.,* July 30, 1919, 2: 4.

19. *Ibid.,* June 25, 1919, 1: 5.

20. *Ibid.,* Oct. 8, 1919, 2: 4–5, and Oct. 22, 3: 1–2.

21. *L'Internationale Communiste,* No. 6 (October 1919), pp. 929–32.

22. Loriot, *Les Problèmes.*

23. *L'Internationale* (Paris), Feb. 15, 1919, as cited in *The Communist International,* No. 3 (July 1, 1919), cols. 371–74. See also Guilbeaux's article on the founding of *L'Internationale* in *Pravda,* Apr. 4, 1919, 1: 5. I have not had access to the files of this newspaper.

24. *La Vie Ouvrière,* July 23, 1919, 1: 5 and 2: 1; July 30, 1919, 4: 3.

25. *L'Avenir Internationale* (Paris), August–September 1919, pp. 2, 22.

26. *Le Libertaire,* Aug. 3, 1919, 3: 5–6; 4: 1, has the culmination of the debate on this question.

27. Ferrat, pp. 72–73. See also Serge, "Frame of Mind," cols. 141–42; Cartini, cols. 409–11; and Fabrice, pp. 46–49.

28. *L'Humanité,* Aug. 4, 1919, 1: 3–4; Aug. 10, 1: 2–3; Aug. 11, 1: 3–6. Aug. 12, 1: 4.

29. *Le Populaire,* Sept. 15, 1919, 1: 3–4; Sept. 17, 1: 1–2. *L'Humanité,* Sept. 13, 1: 5–6; 2: 1–3; Sept. 14, 1: 2–4; Sept. 15, 3–4.

30. *L'Humanité,* Sept. 17, 1919; 1: 3-4; Sept. 18, 1: 3-4; 3: 4-5; Sept. 19, 1: 5-6; 3: 3-5; Sept. 20, 1: 5-6; 2: 1; 3: 1-2. *La Vie Ouvrière,* Sept. 24, 1919, 1: 5; 2: 1-5. Monatte, p. 151.

31. The text of the minority is in CGT, pp. 181-83. A brief summary is available in Jouhaux, pp. 44-45.

32. For a collection of Sadoul's letters to France, see his *Notes.*

33. See above, Chapter 2, n. 40.

34. *L'Humanité,* Oct. 22, 1919, 1: 5; Oct. 24, 1: 1-2. For an example of the opposing arguments, see *Le Petit Parisien* (Paris), Oct. 23, 1: 6, and Oct. 24, 1: 6.

35. Prélot, p. 218.

36. *L'Humanité,* Nov. 6, 1919, 1: 1; Nov. 7, 1: 1-2; Nov. 8, 1: 1, and 2: 1. *Le Populaire,* Nov. 7, 1: 3-4; Nov. 8, 1: 3-6 (with photograph); Nov. 10, 1: 3-4.

37. *Le Temps* (Paris), Oct. 26, 1919, 2: 4. *Le Petit Parisien,* Nov. 7, 1919, 1: 5-6; 2: 1.

38. *Le Populaire,* Nov. 1, 1919, 1: 3.

39. Prélot, p. 220. The election returns are summarized in *L'Humanité,* Nov. 19, 1919, 1: 1-6.

40. Sadoul's articles in *Kommunisticheskii Internatsional* in 1919 are in No. 1 (May 1), cols. 62-64; No. 3 (July 1), cols. 381-86; No. 4 (August), cols. 473-80; No. 6 (October), cols. 793-96; and No. 7/8 (November/December), cols. 989-94.

41. Guilbeaux's articles in *Kommunisticheskii Internatsional* in 1919 are in No. 1 (May 1), cols. 65-68; No. 3 (July 1), cols. 341-44; No. 4 (August), cols. 479-84; and No. 6 (October), cols. 795-98.

42. Serge, "La IIIe Internationale," p. 24.

43. Blonina, cols. 333-38.

44. [Serge], "Chronique," cols. 1211-14.

45. Com. Int., *Der I. Kongress,* pp. 100-101.

46. Sadoul, "L'Esprit," cols. 829-32.

47. Sadoul, "Appel," pp. 1017-22.

48. *Pravda,* Mar. 20, 1919, 3: 5-6.

49. Zinoviev, "K piatiletiiu," cols. 537-40.

50. Zinoviev, "Parlamentarizm," col. 703.

51. Trotsky, "Pis'mo," cols. 611-14.

52. Lenin, "Privet," col. 907.

53. Lenin, *Sochineniia,* XXIV, 501.

54. *L'Humanité,* Feb. 23, 1920, 1: 2-4.

55. *Ibid.,* Feb. 4, 1920, 2: 2-3.

56. *Ibid.,* Feb. 11, 1920, 1: 1-2.

57. PSF, pp. 282-478.

58. *Ibid.,* pp. 403, 419.

59. *Ibid.,* pp. 406-9.

60. *Ibid.,* pp. 405, 420.

61. *Ibid.,* pp. 414-15.

62. *Ibid.,* p. 476.

63. For an excellent discussion of the revolutionary career of Raymond Lefebvre, see Wohl, pp. 177-202.

64. PSF, p. 559.

65. *Ibid.*

66. *Ibid.,* pp. 564-67.

Chapter Eight

1. In his essay "The State and Revolution," written shortly before the October Revolution, Lenin had said Marxists must make use of the modern state during the period of preparing the workers for revolution, and he had criticized the anarchists who wanted to destroy existing bourgeois institutions without first making use of them for the sake of seizing power. See his *Sochineniia,* XXI, 400, 449. The essay is at pp. 365–454.

2. Lenin, "Tezisy tov. Lenina," col. 95–104; also in his *Sochineniia,* XXIV, 7–15.

3. Com. Int., First Congress, cols. 13–14.

4. Lenin, "O zadachakh," col. 455, and *Sochineniia,* XXIV, 393.

5. Zinoviev, "Parlamentarizm," cols. 703–8.

6. Relatively little has been written about this experiment. The best accounts are Draper, pp. 232–36; Carr, *History,* III, 169–70; and Rutgers, pp. 90–92.

7. *De Tribune* (Amsterdam), Mar. 20, 1920 (Supplement), 1: 3; *Workers' Dreadnought,* Mar. 20, 1920, 5: 1.

8. Rutgers, p. 90.

9. Borkenau, pp. 66–67.

10. Com. Int., *Der I. Kongress,* p. 77.

11. See above, Chapter 2, n. 33.

12. *De Tribune,* Apr. 10, 1919, 1: 1. Petrograd learned of this decision with more speed than usual because it was reported on the Berlin radio. See *Kommunisticheskii Internatsional,* No. 1 (May 1, 1919), col. 80, and France, Ministère des Affaires Etrangères, p. 8.

13. *L'Humanité,* Aug. 7, 1919, 3: 5–6.

14. See Pannekoek, cols. 165–70; Horter, cols. 297–300; and Roland-Holst, pp. 22–26.

15. Rutgers, p. 91.

16. The best information on the conference can be derived from contemporary newspapers. See *De Tribune,* Mar. 20, 1920, Supplement; and *Workers' Dreadnought,* Mar. 20, 1920, 5: 1–3. Another account appears in Murphy, pp. 86–89.

17. *Workers' Dreadnought,* Mar. 20, 1920, 5: 1.

18. *Ibid.,* 5: 2.

19. Her account appears in KPD, *Bericht über den 3. Parteitag,* pp. 78–84.

20. *Workers' Dreadnought,* Mar. 20, 1920, 5: 2. Murphy, pp. 88–89.

21. KPD, *Bericht über den 3. Parteitag,* pp. 81–82.

22. *Workers' Dreadnought,* Mar. 20, 1920, 5: 2–3; see also the conference resolution on the Secretariat, 6: 1.

23. *Ibid.*

24. *Ibid.,* 6: 1–2.   26. *Ibid.,* 7: 1, 3.

25. *Ibid.,* 6: 2–3, 7: 1.   27. *Ibid.,* 7: 2.

28. *De Tribune,* Mar. 20, 1920 (Supplement), 1: 1–3. Murphy, p. 88.

29. *De Tribune,* Mar. 27, 1919, 1: 1–3.

30. *De Tribune,* Mar. 20, 1919 (Supplement), 1: 2–3.

31. See Chapter 5 above.

32. *Die Rote Fahne* (Berlin), Apr. 22, 1920, 1: 1. *De Tribune,* Apr. 30, 1920, 2: 1.

33. *Workers' Dreadnought,* May 8, 1920, 7: 1.

34. *The Call,* May 13, 1920, 4: 1–3.

35. PSF, p. 132.

36. *Ibid.,* pp. 376–77.

37. Frossard, p. 261.

38. *Workers' Dreadnought,* Apr. 17, 1920, 6: 1–3.

39. Reports of the broadcast were carried in *Le Phare* (May–June 1920), pp. 484–85; and in *The Call,* May 20, 1920, 11: 1.

40. *De Tribune,* June 14, 1920, 1: 5.

41. Lenin, "Zapis'," p. 183.

42. Lenin, "Detskaia Bolezn'," p. 227.

43. *Ibid.,* pp. 185–206, 216–25.   45. *Ibid.,* p. 193.

44. *Ibid.,* p. 174.   46. *Ibid.,* p. 201.

47. See Chapter 6 above.

48. Lenin, "Detskaia Bolezn'," pp. 225, 232–34.

49. *Ibid.,* p. 206n.   52. [Lukács], pp. 161–72.

50. *Ibid.,* p. 188.   53. *Ibid.,* pp. 164, 172.

51. *Ibid.,* pp. 198, 249–50.   54. *Ibid.,* pp. 166–69.

55. [Kun], "Die Durchführung," pp. 549–55.

56. *Ibid.,* p. 555.

57. *Workers' Dreadnought,* June 12, 1920, 3: 1–3.

58. *Kommunismus,* I (Mar. 27, 1920), 338; *ibid.* (Apr. 3, 1920), pp. 384–90.

59. *Kommunisticheskii Internatsional,* No. 11 (June 14, 1920), cols. 1917–18. See also Lenin, "Tezisy," col. 1981.

60. *Socialisme* (Brussels), No. 2 (August 1919), pp. 14–15, 18.

61. *Ibid.,* No. 5 (November 1919), p. 57.

62. *L'Ouvrier Communiste* (Brussels), May 1, 1920, 3: 2–3, 4. *Le Phare* (Mar. 1, 1920), pp. 334–35. Com. Int., *Rapports,* p. 226.

63. *L'Ouvrier Communiste,* May 15, 1920, 3: 1–2; July 1, 1920, 3: 1–4.

64. *Le Phare* (January–February 1920), p. 286.

65. Com. Int., *Rapports,* p. 227.

66. The program of the Communist Federation of Wallonia appeared in *L'Ouvrier Communiste,* June 1, 1920, 2: 1–4; 3: 1–2.

Chapter Nine

1. Guilbeaux, p. 137.   3. Goldman, pp. 9, 154.

2. Balabanoff, *My Life,* p. 241.   4. *Ibid.,* pp. 22–23, 31.

5. ILP, *Report of the 29th Annual Conference,* pp. 51–52.

6. *Ibid.,* pp. 57–58; cf. Balabanoff, *My Life,* p. 258, who said Allen was "definitely sympathetic to the Soviets." His report did leave open the possibility of some kind of affiliation with the Comintern.

7. Balabanoff, *My Life,* pp. 236–37.

8. Zinoviev, "Chem byl Kommunisticheskii Internatsional do sikh por," cols. 1993–2008.

9. *Ibid.*, col. 1993 (emphasis in the original).

10. Lenin, "Tezisy," col. 1979.

11. Zinoviev, "Nabolevshie Voprosy," col. 1730.

12. Com. Int., Executive Committee, "Tezisy," cols. 1937–38.

13. Com. Int., First Congress, cols. 19–20.

14. Lenin, "Tezisy tov. Lenina," col. 104.

15. Zinoviev, "Kogda i pri Kakikh Usloviiakh," cols. 1965–68.

16. [Lukács], pp. 161–72.

17. For primary accounts of the reception of the British delegation in Russia, see Balabanoff, *My Life*, pp. 257–60; ILP, *Report of the 29th Annual Conference*, pp. 49–61; Ethel A. Snowden, pp. 53–55; and Goldman, pp. 91–93.

18. ILP, *Report of the 29th Annual Conference*, p. 52.

19. See n. 10 above, and also Zinoviev's speech to the opening session of the Second Congress, in Com. Int., *Der zweite Kongress*, p. 12. His remarks refer to the ILP in a non-specific but obvious way.

20. For the Comintern's response, see Com. Int., Executive Committee, "A Clear Reply." It also appeared separately as a pamphlet entitled *The I.L.P. and the Third International*.

21. Com. Int., *Der zweite Kongress*, p. 88.

22. Ethel A. Snowden, p. 121.

23. Balabanoff, *My Life*, pp. 258–59.

24. *Izvestiia*, June 15, 1920, 1: 1–2. Balabanoff, *My Life*, pp. 260–62; Goldman, pp. 121–23.

25. Bombacci, col. 2107. Also see Balabanoff, *My Life*, pp. 262–66.

26. Balabanoff, *My Life*, pp. 263, 267.

27. Lenin, *Sochineniia*, XXV, 206n.

28. Frossard, pp. 52–54.

29. *Ibid.*, p. 49.

30. Zinoviev, "To the French Proletariat," col. 2449. According to Frossard, p. 264n., the Committee for Adhesion to the Third International later denied that Deslinières had a mandate to represent it. The point is, however, that the Comintern headquarters was willing to accept anyone who claimed to be a legitimate representative.

31. Rosmer described his impressions in *Moscou Sous Lénine*.

32. Cachin's report is printed in Frossard, pp. 246–55. This is apparently not the original French version but a re-translation of the Russian version; the original French version of the remarks of both Cachin and Frossard was apparently lost (see p. 246n). The Russian-language version appears in *Kommunisticheskii Internatsional*, No. 12 (July 20, 1920), cols. 2065–70.

33. Frossard, pp. 255–63. *Kommunisticheskii Internatsional*, No. 12 (July 20, 1920), cols. 2069–74.

34. Frossard, pp. 62–65, 264–69. Rosmer, *Moscou Sous Lénine*, pp. 60–61.

35. Sokolov, p. 12.

36. *Pravda*, June 17, 1920, 2: 1–2; June 18, 1920, 2: 1–2. *Izvestiia*, June 17, 1920, 1: 5–8.

246 NOTES TO PAGES 182–96

37. Frossard, p. 77.
38. *Ibid.*, pp. 109–10.
39. *Ibid.*
40. *L'Humanité*, July 21, 1920, 1: 4.
41. *L'Humanité*, July 28, 1920, 1: 1–2.
42. Cachin and Frossard, col. 2076.
43. *L'Humanité*, May 4, 1920, 1: 2; May 6, 1: 1; May 7, 1: 3.
44. USPD, *Protokoll der Reichskonferenz*, pp. 5–10. This description of the meeting was given by Artur Crispien after his return to Germany.
45. *Ibid*, p. 7.
46. *Ibid.*, pp. 7–10; Frossard, pp. 97–101.
47. KPD, *Bericht über den 5. Parteitag*, pp. 27–29.
48. For a study of the birth of the Communist parties in the United States and the situation in Chicago in 1919, see Draper, pp. 164–84.
49. *Ibid.*, pp. 229–32.
50. *Ibid.*, pp. 252–53.
51. *Ibid.*, p. 254.
52. *Ibid.*, p. 186.
53. Carr, *History*, III, 209–10.
54. Lenin, "Tezisy," col. 1973.
55. Com. Int., Second Congress, col. 2449.
56. Dziewanowski, pp. 75–79.
57. *Ibid.*, pp. 81, 83.
58. *Ibid.*, pp. 81.
59. Com. Int., *Der zweite Kongress*, pp. 49–50.
60. *Ibid.*, p. 53.
61. Dziewanowski, p. 94. Ruth Fischer, pp. 136–37.

Chapter Ten

1. For descriptions of the festivities, see Harrison, pp. 180–82; Hicks, p. 391; Murphy, pp. 138–39; Rosmer, *Moscou Sous Lénine*, pp. 98–100; and Frossard, pp. 113–16.
2. It is impossible to determine the exact number of participants in the Congress, since the lists of delegates in the official protocols do not contain the names of all persons who spoke and presumably voted. The protocol report was published in German, Russian, and English, under the titles *Der zweite Kongress, Vtoroi Kongress,* and *The Second Congress,* respectively (see Bibliography, Communist International, for full titles and publication data). The basic edition is the German one. The three editions do not always agree; most of the differences are minor, but in a few cases some material has been omitted from one or all of the protocols.
3. Com. Int., *Der zweite Kongress*, pp. 780–88.
4. *Ibid.*
5. *Ibid.*, pp. 15–16.
6. *Ibid.*, pp. 58–59; Murphy, p. 148.
7. Com. Int., *Der zweite Kongress*, pp. 403–4.
8. *The Worker* (Glasgow), Sept. 18, 1920, 2: 1–2.
9. Com. Int., *Der zweite Kongress*, pp. 59–75.
10. *Ibid.*, pp. 63–69.
11. Murphy, p. 148.

12. The names of Pankhurst and Gallacher do not appear in the list of delegates in Com. Int., *Der zweite Kongress*, p. 781, because of their late arrival. Murphy, p. 143.

13. Com. Int., *The Second Congress*, pp. 61–62; Com. Int., *Der zweite Kongress*, pp. 75–77.

14. Com. Int., *The Second Congress*, p. 65; Com. Int., *Der zweite Kongress*, pp. 78–79, deletes some portions of Tanner's remarks.

15. Com. Int., *Der zweite Kongress*, pp. 79–81.

16. *Ibid.*, pp. 81–83.

17. *Ibid.*, pp. 87–91.

18. *Ibid.*, p. 89. The English version, Com. Int., *The Second Congress*, p. 70, has Lenin attributing the warning against being too dogmatic to Ramsay instead of Tanner. This must be a translator's error, since Ramsay did not make any such remarks, according to the protocols.

19. Com. Int., *Der zweite Kongress*, p. 91.

20. *Ibid.*, pp. 91–95.

21. It is difficult to establish the exact membership of the special committee on the British question, since its numbers apparently increased during the course of the deliberations. The initial appointments are in Com. Int., *Der zweite Kongress*, p. 99. See also Murphy, p. 149; and the article by MacLaine in *The Communist* (London), Sept. 23, 1920, 1: 1.

22. Com. Int., *The Second Congress*, pp. 286–87; Com. Int., *Der zweite Kongress*, pp. 434–36.

23. Com. Int., *The Second Congress*, p. 295; Com. Int., *Der zweite Kongress*, p. 447.

24. *The Worker*, Sept. 18, 1920, 2: 2.

25. *Ibid.* Also Com. Int., *The Second Congress*, pp. 304–5; Com. Int., *Der zweite Kongress*, p. 462.

26. See n. 21, above.

27. Com. Int., *The Second Congress*, pp. 404–13; Com. Int., *Der zweite Kongress*, pp. 641–54.

28. Com. Int., *The Second Congress*, p. 413. According to Com. Int., *Der zweite Kongress*, p. 654, and Com. Int., *Vtoroi Kongress*, p. 447, the vote was 58 to 24. However, MacLaine later reported it as 48 to 24, so this result is probably the correct one; *The Communist*, Sept. 23, 1920, 1: 1.

29. Gallacher, *Revolt*, p. 251.

30. Pankhurst, *Soviet Russia*, pp. 44–46. *Workers' Dreadnought*, Sept. 25, 1920, 4: 1–2.

31. For a list of the Italian delegates, see Com. Int., *Der zweite Kongress*, p. 783.

32. Lenin, "Pervonachal'nyi Nabrosok," cols. 1719–24.

33. An excellent discussion of this debate and the compromise that followed is Whiting, pp. 42–58. See also Carr, *History*, III, 252–57.

34. Com. Int., *Der zweite Kongress*, pp. 137–232.

35. *Ibid.*, p. 139.

36. *Ibid.*, p. 216.

37. *Ibid.*, pp. 216–17.

38. Korey, pp. 19–20, 36–37.

39. Com. Int., *Der zweite Kongress,* pp. 218–19.

40. *Ibid.,* pp. 223–24.

41. *Ibid.,* p. 407. Bordiga's speech and theses are at pp. 421–34.

42. *Ibid.,* pp. 464–65.

43. *Ibid.,* pp. 341–44.

44. Balabanoff, *My Life,* pp. 274–75.

45. The original version of the Nineteen Conditions (later Twenty-One Conditions) is in the *Kommunisticheskii Internatsional,* No. 12 (July 20, 1920), cols. 1937–42.

46. Frossard, pp. 131–34.

47. Com. Int., *Der zweite Kongress,* p. 233.

48. *Ibid.,* p. 243.   51. *Ibid.,* pp. 272–74.

49. *Ibid.,* pp. 261–64.   52. *Ibid.,* pp. 277–86.

50. *Ibid.,* pp. 264–70.   53. *Ibid.,* pp. 338–46.

54. *Ibid.,* p. 352.

55. *Ibid.,* pp. 235–36; Com. Int., *The Second Congress,* p. 189.

56. The Twenty-One Conditions in their final form are in Com. Int., *Der zweite Kongress,* pp. 387–95, and Com. Int., *The Second Congress,* pp. 531–37.

57. For an excellent discussion of this point, see Carr, *History,* III, 194–95.

58. Com. Int., *Der zweite Kongress,* pp. 382–83.

59. *Ibid.,* pp. 293–98.   63. *Ibid.,* pp. 346–53.

60. *Ibid.,* p. 374.   64. *Ibid.,* pp. 625–29.

61. *Ibid.,* pp. 290–98.   65. *Ibid.,* pp. 629–33.

62. *Ibid.,* pp. 310–29.   66. *Ibid.,* p. 605.

67. For a fuller discussion, see Carr, *History,* III, 201–8.

68. Com. Int., *Der zweite Kongress,* pp. 607–10.

69. *Ibid.,* pp. 633–35.

70. *Ibid.,* pp. 603–4.

Chapter Eleven

1. Daniels, p. 51.   2. *Ibid.,* pp. 70ff.

Bibliography

Bibliography

Akademiia Nauk SSSR. Institut Istorii. (Academy of Sciences of the USSR. Institute of History.) Sovetskaia Rossiia i Kapitalisticheskii Mir v 1917–1923 gg. (Soviet Russia and the Capitalist World in 1917–1923.) Moscow, 1957.

Almond, Gabriel A. The Appeals of Communism. Princeton, N.J., 1954.

Asteriou, Socrates J. "The Third International and the Balkans, 1919–1945." Unpublished doctoral dissertation, University of California, Berkeley, 1959.

"B." "Kommunisticheskoe Dvizhenie v Bolgarii." (The Communist Movement in Bulgaria.) Kommunisticheskii Internatsional, No. 11 (June 14, 1920), cols. 1817–30.

Balabanoff, Angelica. "Greetings to Our Italian Comrades." The Communist International, No. 1 (May 1, 1919), cols. 55–62.

———. My Life as a Rebel. New York and London, 1938.

Balkan Communist Federation. "Manifest Balkano-Dunaiskoi Kommunisticheskoi Federatsii." (Manifesto of the Balkan-Danubian Communist Federation.) Kommunisticheskii Internatsional, No. 14 (Nov. 6, 1920), cols. 2893–2900.

———. "Rezoliutsii Balkanskoi Sotsialisticheskoi Konferentsii." (Resolutions of the Balkan Socialist Conference.) Kommunisticheskii Internatsional, No. 12 (July 20, 1920), cols. 2215–18.

Bell, Thomas. The British Communist Party: A Short History. London, 1937.

———. Pioneering Days. London, 1941.

Benedikt, Heinrich, ed. Geschichte der Republik Osterreich. Munich, 1954.

Beyer, Hans. Von der Novemberrevolution zur Räterepublik in München. Berlin, 1957.

"B.K." See Kun, Béla.

Blagoev, Dimitur. Izbrani Proizvedeniia. (Selected Works.) Vol. II. Sofia, 1951.

Blagoyeva, Stella D. Dimitrov: A Biography. New York, 1934.
Blonina, E. "Perspektivy revoliutsii vo Frantsii." (Perspectives of the Revolution in France.) *Kommunisticheskii Internatsional*, No. 3 (July 1, 1919), cols. 333–38.
Böhm, Wilhelm. Im Kreuzfeuer Zweier Revolutionen. Munich, 1924.
Bombacci, Nicolo. "Oppozitsiia Reformistov Kommunisticheskoi Revoliutsii v Italii." (Reformist Opposition to the Communist Revolution in Italy.) *Kommunisticheskii Internatsional*, No. 12 (July 20, 1920), cols. 2103–8.
Bonomi, Ivanoe. From Socialism to Fascism: A Study of Contemporary Italy. London, 1924.
Borkenau, Franz. The Communist International. London, 1938.
Brand, Carl F. British Labour's Rise to Power. Stanford, Calif., 1941.
Braun, M. J. Die Lehren des Kapp-Putsches. Leipzig, 1920.
Brockway, Fenner. Inside the Left: Thirty Years of Platform, Press, Prison and Parliament. London, 1942.
Brogan, D. W. The Development of Modern France (1870–1939). London, 1940.
Bulgarskata Komunisticheska Partiia. Istoriia Bolgarskoi Kommunisticheskoi Partii. (History of the Bulgarian Communist Party.) Moscow, 1960.
———. Materiali po Istoriia na Bulgarskata Komunisticheska Partiia. (Materials on the History of the Bulgarian Communist Party.) Sofia, 1955.
———. "Programnaia Deklaratsiia Bolgarskoi Kommunisticheskoi Partii. Sotsialistov 'Tesniakov' sektsii Kommunisticheskogo Internatsionala." (Program Declaration of the Bulgarian Communist Party. Socialist "Tesniak" Section of the Communist International.) *Kommunisticheskii Internatsional*, No. 4 (August 1919), cols. 503–14.
———. "Rezoliutsiia s'ezda Bolgarskoi Kommunisticheskoi Partii o Polozhenii Bolgarii." (Resolution of the Congress of the Bulgarian Communist Party on the Bulgarian Situation.) *Kommunisticheskii Internatsional*, No. 5 (September 1919), cols. 689–95.
Cachin, Marcel, and Frossard, L. O. "Zaiavlenie Kashena i Frossara Ispolnitel'nomu Komitetu Kommunisticheskogo Internatsionala." (The Declaration of Cachin and Frossard to the Executive Committee of the Communist International.) *Kommunisticheskii Internatsional*, No. 12 (July 20, 1920), cols. 2073–76.
Carr, E. H. A History of Soviet Russia. 6 vols. London and New York, 1951–59.
———. "Radek's 'Political Salon' in Berlin 1919." *Soviet Studies*, III (April 1952), 411–30.

Cartini, André. "France." *The Communist International*, No. 3 (July 1, 1919), cols. 409–11. Paris reprint.

Cattell, David T. "The Hungarian Revolution of 1919 and the Reorganization of the Comintern in 1920." *Journal of Central European Affairs*, XI (January/April 1951), 27–38.

[CGT]. Confédération Générale du Travail. La Confédération Générale du Travail et le Mouvement Syndical. Historique des Fédérations Nationales, des Unions Départmentales. Paris, 1925.

Chicherin, Georgii. "Mezhdunarodnaia Politika Dvukh Internatsionalov." (The International Politics of Two Internationals.) *Kommunisticheskii Internatsional*, No. 6 (October 1919), cols. 817–28.

Churchill, Winston S. "The Aftermath." Vol. IV of The World Crisis. New York, 1929.

Communist International. Der I. Kongress der Kommunistischen Internationale: Protokoll der Verhandlungen in Moskau vom 2. bis zum 19. März 1919. Petrograd, 1920.

———. Pervyi kongress Kommunisticheskogo Internatsionala: protokoly Zasedanii v Moskve s 2 po 19 marta 1919 goda. (First Congress of the Communist International: Records of the proceedings in Moscow from March 2 to 19, 1919.) Petrograd, 1921.

———. Rapports sur le Mouvement Communiste International, Présentés au Deuxième Congrès de l'Internationale Communiste, Moscou, 1920. Petrograd, 1921.

———. The Second Congress of the Communist International: Report of the Proceedings of the Petrograd Session of July 17th, and of the Moscow Sessions of July 23rd–August 7th, 1920. Moscow, 1920.

———. Sowjet-Russland und die Völker der Welt: Reden auf der Internationalen Versammlung in Petrograd am 19. Dezember, 1918. Petrograd, 1920.

———. Vtoroi Kongress Kominterna: Iiul'–Avgust 1920 g. (Second Congress of the Comintern, July–August, 1920.) Edited by O. Piatnitsky, D. Manuilsky, V. Knorin, B. Kun, and M. Zorky. Moscow, 1934.

———. Der zweite Kongress der Kommunist. Internationale: Protokoll der Verhandlungen vom 19. Juli in Petrograd und vom 23. Juli bis 7. August 1920 in Moskau. Hamburg, 1921.

———. Executive Committee. "A Clear Reply from the Executive Committee of the Communist International to the Questions of the British Independent Labour Party." *The Communist International*, No. 11/12 (June/July 1920), cols. 2473–94. Petrograd edition.

———. ———. "Tezisy Ispolnitel'nogo Komiteta Kommunisticheskogo Internatsionala ko Vtoromu Kongressu Kommunisticheskogo Internatsionala." (Theses of the Executive Committee of the Communist International to the Second Congress of the Communist International.) *Kommunisticheskii Internatsional,* No. 12 (July 20, 1920), cols. 1937–42.

——. First Congress. "Manifest Kommunisticheskogo Internatsionala k Proletariiam Vsego Mira." (Manifesto of the Communist International to the Proletariat of the Whole World.) *Kommunisticheskii Internatsional,* No. 1 (May 1, 1919), cols. 5–20.

——. Second Congress. "Tezisy ob Osnovnykh Zadachakh Kommunisticheskogo Internatsionala." (Theses on the Fundamental Tasks of the Communist International.) *Kommunisticheskii Internatsional,* No. 13 (Sept. 28, 1920), cols. 2445–58.

——. West European Secretariat. "Aufruf der Westeuropäischen Sekretariats der Kommunistischen Internationale." *Die Kommunistische Internationale,* No. 7/8 (November/December 1919), cols. 1153–56. Petrograd edition.

Coolidge, Archibald Cary. "Report (Number 26) of Professor Archibald Cary Coolidge on His Mission to Hungary, January 19, 1919," in Francis Deák, Hungary at the Peace Conference: The Diplomatic History of the Treaty of Trianon. New York, 1942.

Copping, David Gordon. "German Socialists and the Revolution of 1918–1919." Unpublished doctoral dissertation, Stanford University, Calif., 1952.

Crispien, Artur. Die Internationale: Vom Bund der Kommunisten bis zur Internationale der Weltrevolution. Second enlarged printing. Berlin, 1920.

Cumming, C. K., and Pettit, Walter W., eds. Russian-American Relations, March 1917–March 1920: Documents and Papers. New York, 1920.

Daniels, Robert Vincent. The Conscience of the Revolution: Communist Opposition in Soviet Russia. Cambridge, Mass., 1960.

Deák, Francis. Hungary at the Peace Conference: The Diplomatic History of the Treaty of Trianon. New York, 1942.

Dechev, N. N. "Tesniaki—Bolgarskaia Kommunisticheskaia Partiia." (The *Tesniaks*—The Bulgarian Communist Party.) *Kommunisticheskii Internatsional,* No. 4 (August 1919), cols. 499–502.

Degras, Jane. The Communist International, 1919–1943: Documents. London, New York, Toronto, 1956–60. 2 vols.

——. "Revisiting the Comintern." *Soviet Survey,* No. 33 (July–September 1960), pp. 38–47.

De Kay, John. The Spirit of the International at Berne. N.p., n.d.

Dimitrov, Georgi. Political Report Delivered to the V Congress of the Bulgarian Communist Party. Sofia, 1949.

——. Suchineniia. (Works.) Vol. V. Sofia, 1952.

Draper, Theodore. The Roots of American Communism. New York, 1957.

Dziewanowski, M. K. The Communist Party of Poland: An Outline of History. Cambridge, Mass., 1959.

Eberlein, Hugo [Max Albert]. "Die Gründung der Komintern und der Spartakusbund." Die Kommunistische Internationale, X (Mar. 13, 1929), 675–84. Hamburg-Berlin edition.

Egger, Heinz. Die Entstehung der Kommunistischen Partei und des Kommunistischen Jungendverbandes der Schweiz. Zurich, 1952.

"Evgenii Levine" [Eugen Leviné]. Obituary article in Kommunisticheskii Internatsional, No. 4 (Aug. 1, 1919), cols. 543–48.

Fabrice, Jean. "A Letter from France," The Communist International, No. 5, pp. 46–49. London reprint. Date of original, September 1919; reprint undated.

Fainsod, Merle. International Socialism and the World War. Cambridge, Mass., 1935.

Ferrat, A. Histoire du Parti Communiste Français. Paris, 1931.

Fineberg, J. "The Formation of the Communist International," The Communist International, VI (1929), 443–45. New York edition.

Fischer, Louis. The Soviets in World Affairs: A History of the Relations Between the Soviet Union and the Rest of the World. London, 1930. 2 vols.

Fischer, Ruth. Stalin and German Communism: A Study in the Origins of the State Party. Cambridge, Mass., 1948.

Flechtheim, Ossip K. Die Kommunistische Partei Deutschlands in Der Weimarer Republik. Offenbach, 1948.

France. Ministère de la Guerre. Radiotélégrammes Etrangères, 1919. Mimeographed collection in the Hoover Institution, Stanford, Calif.

———. Ministère des Affaires Etrangères. Radiotélégrammes de Propagande des Puissances Ennemies, 1919. Mimeographed collection in the Hoover Institution, Stanford, Calif.

Frossard, L. O. De Jaurès a Lénine: Notes et Souvenirs d'un Militant. Paris, 1930.

Gabor, M. "Doklad o padenii sovetskoi vlasti v Vengrii." (Report on the Fall of Soviet Power in Hungary.) Kommunisticheskii Internatsional, No. 7/8 (November/December 1919), cols. 1159–68. Stockholm reprint.

Gallacher, William. Revolt on the Clyde: An Autobigraphy. London, 1936.

———. The Rolling of Thunder. London, 1947.

Gankin, Olga Hess. "The Bolsheviks and the Founding of the Third International," *Slavonic and East European Review*, XX (1941), 88–101.

——, and Fisher, H. H. The Bolsheviks and the World War: The Origins of the Third International. Stanford, Calif., 1940.

Geiger, B., ed. 1919 god v Vengrii: Sbornik Materialov k 40-Letiiu Vengerskoi Sovetskoi Respubliki. (The Year 1919 in Hungary: A Collection of Materials on the 40th Anniversary of the Hungarian Soviet Republic.) Moscow, 1959.

"G.L." *See* Lukács, Georg.

Goldman, Emma. My Disillusionment in Russia. Garden City, N.Y., 1923.

Guilbeaux, Henri. La Fin des Soviets. Paris, 1937.

Gulick, Charles A. "Labor's Workshop of Democracy." Vol. I of Austria from Habsburg to Hitler. Berkeley and Los Angeles, 1948.

Harrison, Marguerite E. Marooned in Moscow: The Story of an American Woman Imprisoned in Russia. London, 1921.

Hicks, Granville. John Reed: The Making of a Revolutionary. New York, 1936.

Horter, Herman [Herman Gorter]. "World Revolution (Chapters from a New Book)." *The Communist International*, No. 3 (July 1, 1919), cols. 297–300. Paris reprint.

[ILP]. Independent Labour Party. The I.L.P. and the Third International. Manchester, 1920.

——. Report of the Twenty-Eighth Annual Conference, Held at Glasgow, April 1920. London, 1920.

——. Report of the 29th Annual Conference, Southport, March 27, 28, & 29, 1921. London, 1921.

Institut für Marxismus-Leninismus beim ZK der SED. Die Ungarische Räterepublik im Jahre 1919 und ihr Widerhall in Deutschland: Eine Sammlung von Aufsätzen und Dokumenten. Berlin, 1959.

James, C. L. R. World Revolution, 1917–1936: The Rise and Fall of the Communist International. London, 1937.

Jászi, Oscar. Revolution and Counter-Revolution in Hungary. London, 1924.

Jouhaux, Léon. Le Mouvement Syndical en France. Berlin, 1931.

Kaas, Albert von, and Lazarovics, Fedor von. Der Bolschewismus in Ungarn. Munich, 1930.

Kabakchiev, Khr., Boshkovich, B., and Vatis, Kh. D. Kommunisticheskie Partii Balkanskikh Stran. (Communist Parties of the Balkan Countries.) Moscow, 1930.

[KAPD]. Kommunistische Arbeiter-Partei Deutschlands. Das Exekutivkomitee der 3. Internationale und die Kommunistische Arbeiter-Partei Deutschlands. Berlin [1920?].

Karolyi, Michael. Memoirs of Michael Karolyi: Faith Without Illusion. Translated from the Hungarian by Catherine Karolyi. New York, 1957.

Keynes, John Maynard. The Economic Consequences of the Peace. New York, 1920.

Koloszváry, Blasius [Béla Kun]. Von Revolution zu Revolution. Vienna, 1920.

Kommunistische Partei Deutschösterreichs. Der Erste Parteitag der Kommunistischen Partei Deutschösterreichs. Vienna, 1919.

Korey, William. "Zinoviev on the Problem of World Revolution, 1919–1927." Unpublished doctoral dissertation, Columbia University, New York, 1960.

[KPD]. Kommunistiche Partei Deutschlands. Bericht über den Gründungsparteitag der Kommunistischen Partei Deutschlands (Spartakusbund) vom 30. Dezember bis 1. Januar 1919. Berlin, [1919?].

———. Bericht über den 2. Parteitag der Kommunistischen Partei Deutschlands (Spartakusbund) vom 20. bis 24. Oktober 1919. Berlin, [1919?].

———. Bericht über den 3. Parteitag der Kommunistischen Partei Deutschlands (Spartakusbund) am 25. und 26. Februar 1920. Berlin, [1920?].

———. Bericht über den 5. Parteitag der Kommunistischen Partei Deutschlands (Sektion der Kommunistischen Internationale) vom 1. bis 3. November 1920 in Berlin. Berlin, 1921.

[Kun, Béla]. "B.K." "Die Durchführung des Parlamentsboykotts." Kommunismus, I (May 8, 1920), 549–55.

Kun, Béla, ed. Kommunisticheskii Internatsional v Dokumentakh: Resheniia, Tezisy i Vozzvaniia Kongressov Kominterna i Plenumov IKKI, 1919–1932. (The Communist International in Documents: Decisions, Theses, and Appeals of the Congresses of the Comintern and the Plenums of the ECCI, 1919–1932.) Moscow, 1933.

———. See also Koloszváry.

Lazitch, Branko. Lénine et la IIIe Internationale. Neuchâtel, 1951.

Lenin, N. "Detskaia Bolezn' 'Levizny' v Kommunizme." ("Left-Wing" Communism: An Infantile Disorder.) Sochineniia, XXV (1932), 165–250. Second edition.

———. "Geroi Bernskogo 'Internatsionala.'" (Heroes of the Berne "International.") Kommunisticheskii Internatsional, No. 2 (June 1, 1919), cols. 175–80.

———. "Left-Wing" Communism: An Infantile Disorder. Detroit, 1921.

———. Lenin on Britain. A compilation, with an Introduction by Harry Pollitt. London, 1934.

————. "O zadachakh III-go Internatsionala." (On the Problems of the Third International.) *Kommunisticheskii Internatsional,* No. 4 (Aug. 1, 1919), cols. 447–62.

————. "Pervonachal'nyi Nabrosok Tezisov po Natsional'nomu i Kolonial'nomu Voprosam." (Preliminary Draft of Theses on the National and Colonial Questions.) *Kommunisticheskii Internatsional,* No. 11 (June 14, 1920), cols. 1719–24.

————. "Privet Ital'ianskim, Frantsuzskim i Nemetskim Kommunistam." (Greetings to the Italian, French, and German Communists.) *Kommunisticheskii Internatsional,* No. 6 (October 1919), cols. 907–14.

————. "Progress of the International Communist Movement: Socialism in Great Britain. Lenin's Reply." *The Communist International,* No. 5 [1920?], pp. 51–53. London reprint of the Petrograd edition.

————. Sochineniia. (Works.) Second edition, edited by N. I. Bukharin, V. M. Molotov, and M. A. Savel'ev. Institut Lenina pri TS.K.V.K.P. (b.) (The Lenin Institute of the Central Committee of the All-Union Communist Party (Bolshevik).) XXI, XXIII, XXIV, XXV. Moscow and Leningrad, 1928–32.

————. "Tezisy ob Osnovnykh Zadachakh Vtorogo Kongressa Kommunisticheskogo Internatsionala." (Theses on the Fundamental Tasks of the Second Congress of the Communist International.) *Kommunisticheskii Internatsional,* No. 12 (July 20, 1920), cols. 1969–82.

————. "Tezisy tov. Lenina o burzhuaznoi demokratii i proletarskoi diktature." (Theses of Comrade Lenin on Bourgeois Democracy and Proletarian Dictatorship.) *Kommunisticheskii Internatsional,* No. 1 (May 1, 1919), cols. 95–104.

————. "Tretii Internatsional: ego mesto v istorii." (The Third International: Its Place in History.) *Kommunisticheskii Internatsional,* No. 1 (May 1, 1919), cols. 31–38.

————. "Zapis' radio-telegrammy Bela Kunu 23 Marta 1919 g." (Radio-telegram Message to Béla Kun, March 23, 1919.) Sochineniia, XXIV, 183. Second edition.

"A Letter from Rumania." *The Communist International,* No. 11/12 (June/July 1920), cols. 2431–34. Petrograd edition.

Levi, P. "Pis'mo k tsentral'nomu komitetu kommunisticheskoi partii Germanii." (A Letter to the Central Committee of the German Communist Party.) *Kommunisticheskii Internatsional,* No. 12 (July 20, 1920), cols. 2077–80.

Ligou, Daniel. Histoire du Socialisme en France, 1871–1961. Paris, 1962.

Loriot, Fernand. Les Problèmes de la Révolution Prolétarienne. Paris, 1928.

Louis, Paul. Histoire du Socialisme en France. Fifth edition. Paris, 1950.

Lowenthal, Richard. "The Bolshevisation of the Spartacus League." *International Communism,* edited by David Footman. St. Antony's Papers No. 9. London, 1960.

[Lukács, Georg]. "G. L." "Zur Frage des Parlamentarismus." *Kommunismus,* I (March 1, 1920), 161–72.

MacDonald, J. Ramsay. Editorial in *The Socialist Review,* XVII (April–June 1920), 97–115.

——. Parliament and Revolution. Manchester, 1919.

Mályusz, Elemér. The Fugitive Bolsheviks. London, 1931.

Markovic, S. Der Kommunismus in Jugoslavien. Hamburg, 1922.

Milkich, Il'ia. "Doklad tov. I. Milkicha." (Report of Comrade I. Milkich.) *Kommunisticheskii Internatsional,* No. 4 (Aug. 1, 1919), cols. 555–58.

——. "Sotsializm v Servii." (Socialism in Serbia.) *Kommunisticheskii Internatsional,* No. 3 (July 1, 1919), cols. 319–26.

Monatte, Pierre. Trois Scissions Syndicales. Paris, 1958.

Mühsam, Erich. Von Eisner bis Leviné: Die Entstehung der Bayerischen Raeterepublik. Berlin, 1929.

Murphy, J. T. New Horizons. London, 1941.

Neubauer, Helmut. München und Moskau 1918/1919: Zur Geschichte der Rätebewegung in Bayern. Munich, 1958.

Nicolson, Harold. Peacemaking, 1919. London, 1933.

Nollau, Günther. Die Internationale: Wurzeln und Erscheinungsformen des proletarischen Internationalismus. Cologne, 1959. Translated into English as International Communism and World Revolution: History and Methods. New York, 1961.

Nordskog, John Eric. Social Reform in Norway: A Study of Nationalism and Social Democracy. Los Angeles, 1935.

Page, Stanley W. Lenin and World Revolution. New York, 1959.

Pankhurst, E. Sylvia. The Life of Emmeline Pankhurst: The Suffragette Struggle for Women's Citizenship. London, 1935.

——. "Progress of the International Communist Movement: Socialism in Great Britain." *The Communist International,* No. 5 [1920?], pp. 50–51. London reprint of the Petrograd edition.

——. Soviet Russia as I Saw It. London, 1921.

Pannekoek, Anton. "The New World." *The Communist International,* No. 2 (June 1, 1919), cols. 165–70. Paris reprint.

Pelling, Henry. The British Communist Party: A Historical Profile. New York, 1958.

Piiashev, N. F. Vorovskii. Moscow, 1959.

"Pis'mo iz Rumynii." (A Letter from Rumania.) *Kommunisticheskii Internatsional,* No. 14 (Nov. 6, 1920), cols. 2881–84.

Prager, Eugen. Geschichte der U.S.P.D.: Entstehung und Entwicklung der Unabhängigen Sozialdemokratischen Partei Deutschlands. Berlin, 1922.

Prélot, Marcel. L'Evolution Politique du Socialisme Français, 1789–1934. Paris, 1939.

[PSF]. Parti Socialiste Français. 17e Congrès National tenu à Strasbourg les 25, 26, 27, 28, et 29 Février 1920. Compte Rendu Sténographique. Paris, 1920.

Radek, Karl. "Istoriia Odnoi Neudavsheisia Buntarskoi Popytki." (The History of One Unsuccessful Rebellious Effort.) Kommunisticheskii Internatsional, No. 9 (Mar. 22, 1920), cols. 1257–66.

——. "K tsentral'nomu Komitetu Germanskoi Nezavisimoi Sotsial-Demokraticheskoi Partii." (To the Central Committee of the German Independent Social-Democratic Party.) Kommunisticheskii Internatsional, No. 11 (June 14, 1920), cols. 1885–86.

——. "Noiabr'." Krasnaia Nov' (October 1926), pp. 139–75.

——. Die Russische und Deutsche Revolution und die Weltlage. Berlin, 1919.

——. Zur Taktik des Kommunismus: Ein Screiben an den Oktober-Parteitag der KPD. Hamburg, 1919.

——. Der Zusammenbruck des Imperialismus und die Aufgaben der Internationalen Arbeiterklasse: Rede, gehalten am 7. Oktober 1918 in Moskauer Sowjet-Theater. Munich, [1919?].

——, and Zinoviev, G. "Ko vsem chlenam Nezavisimoi Partii Germanii." (To all Members of the Independent Party of Germany.) Kommunisticheskii Internatsional, No. 12 (July 20, 1920), cols. 2257–60.

——. See also Struthan, Arnold.

Rákosi, Mátyás. "Sozdanie kommunisticheskoi partii Vengrii. Venger-skaia sovetskaia respublika, 1917–1919 gg." (The Creation of the Hungarian Communist Party. The Hungarian Soviet Republic, 1917–1919.) Voprosy Istorii (November 1955), pp. 41–64.

Rakovsky, K. "Doklad tov. Kh. Rakovskogo." (Report of Comrade K. Rakovsky.) Kommunisticheskii Internatsional, No. 4 (Aug. 1, 1919), 555–56.

——. "Kommunisticheskoe Dvizhenie v Rumynii." (The Communist Movement in Rumania.) Kommunisticheskii Internatsional, No. 13 (Sept. 28, 1920), cols. 2563–66.

Ransome, Arthur. Russia in 1919. New York, 1919.

Reinstein, Boris. "On the Road to the First Congress." The Communist International, VI (1929), 428–35. New York edition.

Renaudel, Pierre. L'Internationale à Berne. Paris, 1919.

Roland-Holst, Henriette. "The Bolsheviks and Their Doings." The Com-

munist International, No. 5, pp. 22–26. London reprint. N.d.; original version presumably published in September 1919.

Rosmer, Alfred. Le Mouvement Ouvrier Pendant la Guerre. Paris, 1936. 2 vols.

———. Moscou Sous Lénine: Les Origines du Communisme. Paris, 1953.

Rothschild, Joseph. The Communist Party of Bulgaria: Origins and Development, 1883–1936. New York, 1959.

Rotter, Seymour. "Soviet and Comintern Policy Toward Germany, 1919–1923: A Case Study in Strategy and Tactics." Unpublished doctoral dissertation, Columbia University, 1954.

Rudniansky, A. "Professional'nye soiuzy i kontr-revoliutsiia v Vengrii." (Trade Unions and the Counter-revolution in Hungary.) *Kommunisticheskii Internatsional*, No. 5 (September 1919), cols. 637–42.

Rutgers, S. "Vstrechi s Leninym." (Meetings with Lenin.) *Istorik Marksist*. No. 2–3 (42–43), pp. 85–98. Moscow, 1935.

Sadoul, Jacques. "Appel aux ouvriers et aux paysans de France." *L'Internationale Communiste*, No. 7/8 (November/December 1919), cols. 1017–22. Stockholm reprint.

———. "L'Esprit de Révolution." *L'Internationale Communiste*, No. 6 (October 1919), cols. 829–32. Stockholm reprint.

———. Notes sur la Révolution Bolchevique. Sixteenth edition. Paris, 1920.

[Second International]. Labor and Socialist International. Bulletin Officiel de la Conférence Internationale Ouvrière et Socialiste: Publié par le Comité de Presse de la Conférence. Vol. I (Feb. 4–12, 1919). Berne, 1919.

———. The International at Lucerne, 1919. The Resolutions. The Provisional Constitution. London, 1919.

Serbskaia Sotsial-demokraticheskaia Rabochaia Partiia. (The Serbian Social Democratic Workers' Party.) "Prisoedineniia k Kommunisticheskomu Internatsionalu. I. Obrashchenie Serbskoi s.-d. rabochei partii k biuro Tret'ego, Kommunisticheskogo Internatsionala." (Additions to the Communist International. I. Address of the Serbian Social Democratic Workers' Party to the Bureau of the Third, or Communist, International.) *Kommunisticheskii Internatsional*, No. 1 (May 1, 1919), cols. 77–78.

[Serge, Victor]. "V.S." "Chronique: France," *L'Internationale Communiste*, No. 7/8 (November/December 1919), cols. 1211–14. Stockholm reprint.

Serge, Victor. "Frame of Mind of the French Proletariat." *The Communist International*, No. 1 (May 1, 1919), cols. 141–42.

———. Mémoires d'un Révolutionnaire: 1901–1941. Paris, 1951.

————. Le Tournant Obscur. Paris, 1951.

————. "La IIIe Internationale." *Crapouillot,* Numéro Spécial, "De Lénine à Staline." Paris, January 1937.

Snowden, Ethel A. Through Bolshevik Russia. London, 1920.

Snowden, Philip Viscount. An Autobiography. London, 1934. 2 vols.

Sokolov, Boris. Le Voyage de Cachin et de Frossard dans la Russie des Soviets: (Faits et Documents). Paris, 1920.

Sozialdemokratische Partei der Schweiz. Protokoll über die Verhandlungen des ausserordentlichen Parteitag der Sozialdemokratischen Partei der Schweiz vom 16. und 17. August 1919 in der Burgvogteihalle in Basel. Basel, 1919.

Stavrianos, L. S. Balkan Federation: A History of the Movement Toward Balkan Unity in Modern Times. Northampton, Mass., 1944.

Stolzenburg, Albert. "Im Feuer der Revolution wurde die Ortsgruppe der Kommunistischen Partei in Mannheim gegründet." Chapter in Vorwärts und Nicht Vergessen. Berlin, 1958.

Struthan, Arnold [Karl Radek]. Die Entwicklung der Deutschen Revolution und die Aufgaben der Kommunistischen Partei. Stuttgart, 1919.

————. "Die Unabhängigen und die Internationale." *Die Internationale,* I (Nov. 1, 1919), 290–99.

Szamuely, Tibor. Alarm: Ausgewählte Reden und Aufsätze. Berlin, 1959.

Szántó, Béla. Klassenkämpfe und Diktatur des Proletariats in Ungarn. Berlin, 1920.

Third International. *See* Communist International.

Tivel', A., ed. 5 Let Kominterna v Resheniiakh i Tsifrakh. (Five Years of the Comintern in Decisions and Statistics.) Moscow, 1924.

Tollefson, Roy M. "Political Thought Inside the Norwegian Labor Party: 1917–1928." Unpublished doctoral dissertation, University of Chicago, 1957.

Toma, Peter A. "The Slovak Soviet Republic of 1919." *The American Slavic and East European Review,* XVII (April 1958), 203–15.

Trofimov, K. S. "Lenin i osnovanie Kommunisticheskogo Internatsionala." (Lenin and the Founding of the Communist International.) *Voprosy Istorii* KPSS, No. 4 (1957), pp. 28–48.

Trotsky, Leon. The First Five Years of the Communist International. Vol. I. New York, 1945.

————. "Mysli o khode proletarskoi revoliutsii." (Thoughts on the Movement of the Proletarian Revolution.) Sochineniia (Works), Vol. XIII. Moscow and Leningrad, 1926.

————. "Pis'mo k Frantsuzskim tovarishcham." (A Letter to the French Comrades.) *Kommunisticheskii Internatsional,* No. 5 (September 1919), cols. 611–14.

Urquidi, Donald William. "The Origins of the Italian Communist Party, 1918–1921." Unpublished doctoral dissertation, Columbia University, New York, 1962.

[USPD]. Unabhängige Sozialdemokratische Partei Deutschlands. Protokoll der Reichskonferenz vom 1. bis 3. September 1920 zu Berlin. Berlin, n.d.

———. Protokoll über die Verhandlungen des ausserordentlichen Parteitages in Leipzig vom 30. November bis 6. Dezember 1919. Berlin, n.d.

"V.S." See Serge, Victor.

Vorovsky, V. V. "Rozhdenie Tret'ego Internatsionala." (The Birth of the Third International.) Sochineniia (Works), Vol. III. Edited by Ia. S. Ganetsky, N. L. Meshcheriakov, and M. A. Savelev. Moscow, 1933.

Waldman, Eric. The Spartacist Uprising of 1919 and the Crisis of the German Social Movement: A Study of the Relation of Political Theory and Party Practice. Milwaukee, 1958.

Walter, Gérard. Histoire du Parti Communiste Français. Paris, 1948.

Werner, P. Die Bayrische Räterepublik: Tatsachen und Kritik. Petrograd, 1920.

Whiting, Allen S. Soviet Policies in China: 1917–1924. New York, 1954.

Wohl, Robert. "La Révolution ou la Mort: Raymond Lefebvre and the Formation of the French Communist Party." International Review of Social History, VII (1962), 177–202.

Wood, Neal. Communism and British Intellectuals. New York, 1959.

Young, W. Hilton. The Italian Left: A Short History of Political Socialism in Italy. London, 1949.

Zévaès, Alexander. Le Parti Socialiste de 1904 à 1923. Paris, 1923.

Zinoviev, G. "Chem byl Kommunisticheskii Internatsional do sikh por i chem on dolzhen stat' teper'." (What the Communist International Has Been Until Now and What It Must Now Become.) Kommunisticheskii Internatsional, No. 12 (July 20, 1920), cols. 1993–2008.

———. "K piatiletiiu so dnia ubiistva Zhoresa." (In Commemoration of the Fifth Anniversary of the Murder of Jaurès.) Kommunisticheskii Internatsional, No. 4 (Aug. 1, 1919), cols. 537–40.

———. "K Proletariatu Balkano-Dunaiskikh Stran, k Kommunisticheskim Partiiam Bolgarii, Rumynii, Serbii i Turtsii. Ot Kommunisticheskogo Internatsionala." (To the Proletariat of the Balkan-Danubian Countries, to the Communist Parties of Bulgaria, Rumania, Serbia, and Turkey. From the Communist International.) Kommunisticheskii Internatsional, No. 9 (Mar. 22, 1920), cols. 1405–10.

———. "Ko vsem rabochim Germanii, tsentral'nomu komitetu Germanskoi kommunisticheskoi partii i tsentral'nomu komitetu nezavisimoi sotsial-demokraticheskoi partii." (To All the Workers of Germany, to the Central Committee of the German Communist Party and to the Central Committee of the Independent Social Democratic Party.) *Kommunisticheskii Internatsional*, No. 9 (Mar. 22, 1920), cols. 1381–92.

———. "Kogda i pri Kakikh Usloviiakh Mozhno Sozdavat' Sovety Rabochikh Deputatov." (When and Under What Conditions Soviets of Workers' Deputies Should Be Formed.) *Kommunisticheskii Internatsional*, No. 12 (July 20, 1920), cols. 1965–68.

———. Der Leipziger Kongress der USP und die Kommunistische Internationale. [Berlin?], 1920.

———. "Nabolevshie Voprosy Mezhdunarodnogo Rabochego Dvizheniia. Vtoroi Kongress Kommunisticheskogo Internatsionala i Ego Zadachi." (Urgent Questions of the International Labor Movement. The Second Congress of the Communist International and Its Tasks.) *Kommunisticheskii Internatsional*, No. 11 (June 14, 1920), cols. 1725–50.

———. "Parlamentarizm i bor'ba za Sovety." (Parliamentarianism and the Struggle for the Soviets.) *Kommunisticheskii Internatsional*, No. 5 (Sept. 1919), cols. 703–8.

———. "Perspektivy proletarskoi revoliutsii." (Perspectives of the Proletarian Revolution.) *Kommunisticheskii Internatsional*, No. 1 (May 1, 1919), cols. 37–44.

———. "Skandinavskim rabochim, rabochemu klassu Norvegii, Norvezhskoi Rabochei Partii. Ot Kommunisticheskogo Internatsionala." (To the Scandinavian Workers, to the Working Class of Norway, to the Norwegian Labor Party. From the Communist International.) *Kommunisticheskii Internatsional*, No. 9 (Mar. 22, 1920), cols. 1403–4.

———. Sochineniia. (Works.) Vols. VII (Part One), VII (Part Two), and VIII. Leningrad, 1925–26.

———. "Sotsial-demokratiia kak orudie reaktsii." (Social Democracy as an Instrument of Reaction.) *Kommunisticheskii Internatsional*, No. 2 (June 1, 1919), cols. 181–86.

———. "To the French Proletariat From the Petrograd Soviet of Workers' and Red Army Deputies." *The Communist International*, No. 11/12 (June/July 1920), cols. 2449–52. Petrograd edition.

———. "Vozzvanie k rabochim i soldatam vsekh stran ot Kommunisticheskogo Internatsionala." (An Appeal to the Workers and Soldiers of All Countries from the Communist International.) *Kommunisticheskii Internatsional*, No. 1 (May 1, 1919), cols. 81–83.

———. Die Weltrevolution und die III. Kommunistische Internationale: Rede auf dem Parteitag der USPD in Halle am 14. Oktober 1920. Berlin, 1920.

Index

tacks on, 21f; Italy leaves, 54f, 57; Swiss withdraw, 58f; and Balkan countries, 62, 67ff; in Scandinavia, 76f; Leipzig Congress repudiates, 97ff; and British parties, 110f, 114, 123ff; French attitude toward, 131ff, 138f; Strasbourg Congress and, 147ff; Belgians, 167; *see also* Berne Congress; Lucerne conference
Section Française du Parti Communiste (Bolshevik) Russe, 32
Seine Confederation, 133, 145, 147
Serbia, 10, 31, 66, 70ff
Serbian Social Democratic Party, 66–67
Serge, Victor (Victor Lvovich Kibalchich), 25–26, 29, 144f, 172
Serrati, Giacinto, 55–56, 163, 178–80; attacked, 181, 201–4, 210, 216; at Second Congress, 194f, 197–98, 209–10
Shop stewards: German, 81; Clydeside, 114; British, 186f, 196–97, 214
Slovak Soviet Republic, 78n
Slovenia, 66f
SLP, *see* British Socialist Labour Party
Smuts, Jan Christian, 44, 230
Snowden, Ethel A., 126, 177
Snowden, Philip, 123, 125ff
Social Democracy of the Kingdoms of Poland and Lithuania, 189
Social Democrats: and lesson of Hungary, 45, 47, 50; Comintern's stand in other countries, 59, 79, 89, 219; Radek warns of, 91; Leipzig affects Comintern position on, 97; Serrati on, 203; Guilbeaux on, 209
Socialisme, 167
The Socialist, 114
Socialist Labour Party, *see* British Socialist Labour Party
Socialists: violate anti-war pledge, 1; Zimmerwald conferences, 2; Lenin on, 15: First Congress and, 17, 21f; seek unity, 57, 61, 124, 139; in Balkans, 70; Versailles hurts, 95; Comintern exclusion of, 98; Comintern woos Centerists, 169, 221; *see also*

Berne Congress; Second International; Social Democrats
Sofia conference (Jan. 1920), 70–71
South Wales Socialist Society, 111, 113, 116f, 119, 121
Souvarine, Boris, 133, 138, 184
Soviets: Serrati on creation of, 55; Workers' and Soldiers', German congress of, 90; and Pankhurst's party, 116; Comintern modifies stand on, 173–75
Spain, 78
Spartakusbund, 7, 79, 81f; shuns Berne Congress, 10; Stöcker on Spartacist-USPD split, 212
Spartakus, 82, 100
SPD, *see* German Social Democratic Party
Spengler, Oswald, 3
Stalin, Joseph, 17
Stambuliski, Alexander, 63, 65
Stefanovich, L., 72
Steinhardt, Karl (Gruber): at First Congress, 17, 19; at Second Congress, 193, 199
Stöcker, Walter, 95; at Leipzig Congress, 98f; at Second Congress, 184, 212f, 216
Stockholm Congress (Dec. 1919), 76–77
Stockholm Congress of Swedish Socialists (June 1919), 75
Strange, Emil, 17
Strasbourg Congress (Feb. 1920), 126, 147–50, 159
Strikes: and Hungarian Republic, 51; in Bulgaria, 65; against Kapp regime, 104, 158
Sudetenland, 42
Suffrage movement (England), 114–15
Sweden, 75–77
Swedish Left Social Democratic Party, 17, 75–77
Swedish Social Democratic Party, 75, 101
Swiss Communist Party, 60–61